Hardcore JFC

Advances in Object Technology Series
Dr. Richard S. Wiener, Series Editor
and Editor-in-Chief of
Journal of Object-Oriented Programming
SIGS Publications, Inc.
New York, New York

and

Department of Computer Science
University of Colorado
Colorado Springs, Colorado

Additional Volumes in Preparation

Hardcore JFC
Conquering the Swing Architecture

Mitch Goldstein

PUBLISHED BY THE PRESS SYNDICATE OF THE UNIVERSITY OF CAMBRIDGE
The Pitt Building, Trumpington Street, Cambridge, United Kingdom

CAMBRIDGE UNIVERSITY PRESS
The Edinburgh Building, Cambridge CB2 2RU, UK
40 West 20th Street, New York, NY 10011-4211, USA
10 Stamford Road, Oakleigh, VIC 3166, Australia
Ruiz de Alarcón 13, 28014 Madrid, Spain
Dock House, The Waterfront, Cape Town 8001, South Africa

http://www.cambridge.org

Published in association with SIGS Books

© 2001 Cambridge University Press

First published in 2001

Design and composition by Andrea Cammarata
Cover design by Andrea Cammarata

Printed in the United States of America

A catalog record for this book is available from the British Library.

Library of Congress Cataloging in Publication Data available

ISBN 0 521 66489 6 paperback

DEDICATION

For Julie and Zak,
the water in the well of my soul.

This book is also dedicated
to the memory of two special people:

To my Aunt Esther Goldstein,
one of the cleverest people I have ever met,
who taught me how to think for myself and how
to read between the lines.

To my Aunt Arlene Schumer,
my Godmother, the other face over my crib,
for her unconditional love, for her joy and pride;
the second person I always called
when I got any good news.

Contents

Acknowledgments

See here how everything
led up to this day
and it's just like any other day
that's ever been
Sun goin' up and then the
sun it goin' down
Shine through my window and
my friends they come around

"Black Peter"
Robert Hunter

This book was particularly inspired by two of my favorite authors. My heartfelt thanks to Dr. Michio Kaku for his stimulating book *Hyperspace* and his weekly radio program on WBAI in New York. Dr. Kaku's legacy begins with his refusal to use his skills in physics to build weapons of mass destruction, focusing instead on the relationship of science and peace. The other person I would like to thank is Douglas R. Hofstadter, author of *Gödel, Escher, Bach: An Eternal Golden Braid*, the comprehension of which was the fan that kindled my spark of curiosity about the essence of programming and how logic and nature relate to the way we think and behave. Thanks also to E. A. Crowley for his works of poetic majesty and his assistance in discovering the unseen.

My thanks to Ethan Henry and Tom Crawley for their masterful technical editing and other invaluable assistance. A very special thank you to the staff of SIGS and Cambridge University Press, but especially to Lothlórien Homet, a good friend and the best editor in the world. Without her perseverance, you would be staring at a blank page, or, even more unthinkably, someone else's book.

To Jay Goldberg, Jim Incollingo and Beth Fand, Rob and Janet Sala, Erez and Amy Levav, Dan and Lena Smart, Rob and Karen Loomis: my gratitude for your friendship and support throughout the years is immeasurably beyond words.

To my in-laws Jan and Pat Collins for their sustenance and love during these past months. To my parents Ira and Judy, whom I would not trade for any two people on Earth, for a lifetime of love and inspiration. To my sister Bonnie, my sister-in-law Susan, and my sister-in-law Juli for their support and affection, and special thanks to my brother Barry for his wisdom, guidance, ideas, encouragement, and uncanny ability to make me feel hopeful and energized.

Last, to the two most important and special people in my life: my son Zachary, who is my good friend and fellow adventurer and the absolute delight of my life. And, to the person who is most responsible for my achievements, my wife Julie. My love and admiration for her is enough for a thousand lifetimes. She is more than the ultimate wife; she is my best friend and my staunchest critic. Whatever I shall do, wherever I shall go, no matter what situation I shall find myself, I will always know that I am the luckiest man who has ever lived.

Hardcore JFC

Creativity is a fickle muse. Just when we get it, we don't know how to keep it. It maddens us with its quirky rhythms. It comes in fits and starts, bursts and flashes. First you had it, then you lost it, now what do you do? Or it can be slow, methodical, tedious: the working out of possibilities, the ruling out of options.

—Peter Engel, *Origami from Angelfish to Zen*, Dover 1989

Chapter 1

Introduction

The Java Foundation Classes are a new way of looking at programming applets and applications. More than two years in the making, the effort to give reality to the Swing component architecture is challenging many of the conventional notions of how user interfaces are constructed. The Java Foundation Classes are an extension to the Java Developer's Kit (JDK), which is freely available on practically every computing platform currently in use.

Like most revolutionary ideas, JFC is an amalgam of past successes and radical thinking. Building on the sound object-oriented foundation of the Java language, it gives application designers power and flexibility that previously could have been achieved only through tedious and difficult custom coding. JFC not only erases the boundaries between different graphical interface platforms, it provides a new capability for integration and reuse of business-oriented entities.

1

The Java Language

Java, too, is a synthesis of experience and innovation. Its history is a sequence of efforts to distill the best features of several languages to provide a solid foundation for object-oriented programming. Unlike many of its predecessors, Java was designed from its inception to be a platform-neutral language. This, coupled with its object-oriented capabilities, makes it an ideal language for deploying on the widest range of hardware platforms, from personal data assistants to super-parallel multiprocessors.

The secret of this capability is that Java was not originally intended to directly generate code that operates on a target platform. Instead, Java compilers generate *byte code*, a form of platform-neutral intermediate object code. This code is then executed by a platform-specific operating arena called a *virtual machine*. The Java Virtual Machine specification dictates the rules by which byte code must be interpreted. Thus, any operating platform that has an available JVM can execute Java programs. There are not too many commonly used operating systems without a JVM implementation. Although originally targeted for the consumer electronics market, the main thrust of Java was redirected at the World Wide Web. With the capability for distribution of class code, Java-enabled web browsing soon became ubiquitous.

Java is most like the C++ language in all respects, although some important differences exist. These differences are for both aesthetic and practical purposes. For example, C++ supports multiple class inheritance whereas Java does not. The developers of Java determined that the awkwardness introduced by multiple inheritance did not justify its retention, and that interfaces were a better approach. Other characteristics that were not carried over into Java were features such as preprocessor directives, which were awkward to implement in the Java architecture and were contrary to its intended spirit.

Java Graphical Interfaces

Java soon provided a mechanism known as the Abstract Window Toolkit or AWT. In the same vein as the virtual machine concept, AWT provided a set of classes that enabled construction of graphical user interfaces. AWT introduced the idea of *peer classes*, which encapsulate platform-specific interface components. It enabled Java programs to have two faces: graphical interfaces could be written that could appear inside a web browser as well as in a stand-alone application.

The peer classes have one very important drawback: because they are expected to operate in a platform-neutral environment, AWT peer classes implement a least common denominator approach. The implication of this is that it becomes difficult to customize graphical components and impossible to get applications to take on a consistent look-and-feel across platforms.

As a result, a conundrum developed: two apparently contradictory requirements are desirable. First, the ability to control the overall look-and-feel of an application by effectively bypassing the platform-specific characteristics and second, the ability to simulate platform-specific looks without sacrificing customizability. This is the fundamental quandary that the Swing architecture and Java Foundation Classes are intended to solve.

JFC Features

JFC contains four major APIs that represent extensions to the Java Abstract Window Toolkit. Of these, this book will be focusing only on one, the Swing component set. Swing components are similar to those implemented in AWT, but have a set of powerful and innovative features that make them significantly more flexible and customizable. Unlike AWT or heavyweight components, which map to native interface elements, JFC provides a set of lightweight components that are implemented without the associated overhead and restrictions.

Although beyond the scope of this book, the other APIs provided with JFC are:

- **Java 2D**—A set of extensions to AWT classes that provide advanced rendering and painting of shapes and text, along with powerful methods such as scaling and rotation transformations.

- **Drag and drop**—A set of classes to provide graphical data transfers within and among applications.

- **Accessibility**—An interface to provide more efficient manipulation of interface components by users who may require assistive technology, such as visual or hearing-impaired persons.

The Swing Architecture Design Goals

The Java Foundation Classes provide a wide array of graphical components and support classes that comprise the Swing architecture. A set of ambitious and clear goals were used as the driving principles behind the design:

- **100% Java implementation**—Taking advantage of the Java language's object-oriented features and platform-neutrality is a fundamental principle of the JFC design. Java is an ideal language for a litany of reasons, but its excellent support for encapsulation and inheritance makes it especially suitable for graphical and business programming.

- **Support of multiple Look-and-Feels**—A look-and-feel is defined as the overall way in which visual components are rendered or painted. JFC is designed to facilitate changes to the way an application appears by associating different sets of objects that support drawing of screen components. The ability to change look-and-feel without affecting underlying interface code is known as pluggability. JFC provides several of these pluggable look-and-feels, or PLAFs, that provide both platform-neutral and native emulation classes, including Microsoft Windows, Macintosh, and X/Motif schemes. The default PLAF is known as the Java Look-and-Feel or, more closely, the Metal Look-and-Feel. PLAFs and related issues are covered in depth in the chapters on UI delegation.

- **Enabling of model-driven programming**—This is an arrangement whereby the data that components represent are externalized in objects. JFC components introduce model-based programming by adopting the Model/View/Controller (MVC) architecture. This provides for extremely powerful and flexible components and tight integration with application objects. Another benefit of MVC is the delegation of component painting to external classes; this allows for implementation of pluggable look-and-feels.

- **Leveraging of JavaBeans design principles**—JavaBeans are a design pattern that was originally intended to support component manipulation in interactive development environments

(IDEs). All JFC components follow these patterns, which makes all visual components available for design-time screen construction. Additionally, the spirit of the patterns that JavaBeans specify is used throughout the design. This contributes to the consistency of the JFC architecture and positively affects the understandability and maintainability of JFC applications.

- **AWT compatibility**—Wherever possible, compatibility was preserved between the JFC components and their counterparts in the Abstract Window Toolkit. Many of the important elements of JFC directly inherit from AWT classes.

Lightweight Component Architecture

Swing components are implemented as lightweight. Lightweight components are defined as application controls that are implemented completely in Java without a corresponding native peer. Unlike native heavyweight components, lightweight controls do not have a peer entity in the operating system to manage the data, state, and appearance of a control.

Lightweight components are not a new phenomenon. AWT classes were designed to support these virtual custom components constructed within an AWT container. Lightweight components could be created by extending a generic container class, painting the desired appearance of the control, and setting up suitable event handling routines. The main difficulty in developing controls using this technique is it is difficult to enforce consistency of appearance and data management.

JFC provides an entire suite of lightweight components that support JavaBeans design patterns and the Model/View/Controller architecture. These components comprise the Swing component set. The underlying architecture defines a consistent way of dealing with the presentation aspects of all components by delegating the drawing of user interface components to external classes. In addition, the methods of managing the data and other aspects of component state are encapsulated in classes known as models.

Lightweight and heavyweight components can be treated much the same with regard to how the are used in an application. This is due to the design principle of retaining as much of the AWT capabilities as possible. Lightweight components do differ from their heavyweight counterparts in several essential points:

- Lightweight components have no peer components. They do not rely on a native analog to accept events and render its appearance. This eliminates the restriction of least-common-denominator features of graphical classes.

- Lightweight components cannot exist without being ultimately contained in a heavyweight component. JFC provides heavy-weight containers that are specifically designed to accommodate lightweight components.

- Swing components do not paint themselves. Instead, a user interface manager directs paint requests to a delegate object. This mechanism provides transparent control of the look-and-feel of JFC components.

- Unlike native platform components, Swing components are engineered to provide object-oriented access to the control's data and state. This separation is accomplished by the implementation of the Model/View/Controller paradigm.

- Because lightweight components are really only a figment of a JFC program, more sophisticated methods of organizing components can be achieved. JFC supports robust capabilities to layer and scroll components, as well as additional capabilities to interact with layout managers.

- Lightweight components are managed in a fundamentally different way than heavyweight components, and they cannot be easily mixed in applications. Although no technical reason exists why they cannot be combined, the peer components of heavyweight controls will always visually obscure all lightweight components within its bounds. The best advice is to avoid mixing components wherever possible.

The Model/View/Controller Paradigm

The heart of JFC is its adoption of the Model/View/Controller approach to component design. MVC provides for a separation of the features of graphical components and is the chief contributor to JFC's flexibility.

The Government Analogy

An excellent analogy to describe the MVC paradigm is that of the United States government. The U.S. Constitution provides for a three-way division of labor in the federal government, each with its own well-defined role. The legislative branch, consisting of the Congress, is responsible for creating laws. The executive branch, headed by the President, is responsible for enforcing laws. The judicial branch is comprised of the Supreme Court; it is responsible for ruling on interpretations of law. Although each of the branches is involved in some way with federal law, they each have their own specific role. See Figure 1-1.

Functional Separation

MVC provides for a separation, although not always a complete one, between the different features of a component. A component can also be

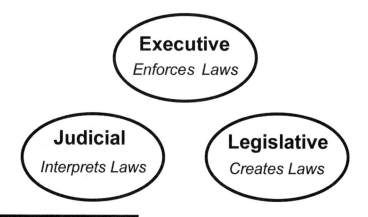

Figure 1-1: *Roles in government*

considered to have three divisions of labor. The model represents an abstraction of the data that a control contains, such as the list of items in a list box or the document in a text area. The view represents the visual appearance of the component. The controller portion accepts user input and interacts with the model and other interface components. This separation is only ideal because the view and controller portions of all JFC components are actually consolidated. Nonetheless, it is convenient to consider them separate for discussing their architectural foundation. See Figure 1-2.

Benefits of MVC Architecture

The facility of taking advantage of MVC is to understand how it can be used to create very tightly integrated application systems. In the heavyweight world, a strictly programmatic means must be used to manipulate the data contained in a component. The following example populates an AWT heavyweight list box with a list of strings:

```
import java.awt.*
. . .
// Add some strings to a heavyweight list
List heavyList = new List();
. . .
heavyList.add("Moe");
heavyList.add("Larry");
heavyList.add("Curley");
. . .
```

The lightweight version of the list control is called *JList*. Many of the JFC components that have analogs to AWT versions have the J prefix to distinguish them. Upon examining the interface to the *JList* component, it should become obvious that *JList* does not inherit from *java.awt.List*, and no *add()* method exists. So, how do strings get added into a lightweight list?

The model-oriented design of the *JList* control provides for an interface called *ListModel* that encapsulates an object-oriented view of the data contained in a list. The *ListModel* interface is the type associated with the data model for *JList*. Creating a model can be a relatively

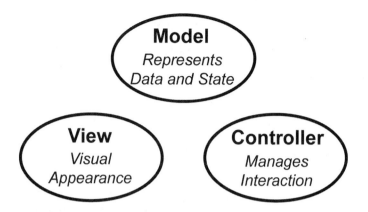

Figure 1-2. *Roles in the MVC architecture*

straightforward matter; the constructor for *JList* supports creation of a default model by specifying either an array of *Object* or a *Vector*. Alternatively, the *setModel()* method of *JList* allows the association of an object that implements *ListModel* with the list. The *getModel()* method returns the model object currently in use.

JFC supplies two canonical implementations of *ListModel*: *Abstract ListModel* and *DefaultListModel*. *AbstractListModel* is an abstract class that implements default event handling; *DefaultListModel* extends *AbstractList Model* and delegates storage of elements to an internally managed *Vector*.

```
// Add some strings to a lightweight list (version 1)
String[] stooges = { "Moe", "Larry", "Curley");
JList lightList1 = new JList(stooges);

// (version 2)
DefaultListModel model = new DefaultListModel();
model.addElement(stooges[0]);
model.addElement(stooges[1]);
model.addElement(stooges[2]);
JList lightList2 = new JList(model);
```

The advantages of model programming may not be obvious from these examples, but it is useful to point out the following observations:

- Whereas the heavyweight control uses *String* objects as its data, the lightweight version uses type *Object*. The consequence of this is that *JList* can display arbitrary data, even though its default behavior is to display the string version of its elements using the *toString()* method. As detailed in the chapter that focuses on this component, *JList* can be configured to render its contained objects based on their type and content.

- If there was a requirement to display two different lists of data, the lightweight control requires a call to the *removeAll()* method, followed by another series of calls to *add()*. The lightweight version would require two models to be constructed, and associated with the control through *setModel()* when appropriate.

- Another example could be given using a class that extends either *AbstractListModel* or *DefaultListModel*, or implements the *ListModel* interface. Use of these techniques and other aspects of the *JList* component are covered in detail in the chapter devoted to that component.

- Models can be used to manage certain aspects of a component's state as well as its data. This allows separate delegate objects to be used, for instance, to implement the data of a *JList* and to represent the set of selected data items. In many of the JFC components, data and state models are combined into a dual-purpose model. The best example of this is the implementation of Swing button components that use a single delegate—an implementation of the *ButtonModel* interface—to store a button's data and state. The *JComboBox* component, which is the Swing implementation of the drop-down list box, also uses a dual model for its data and state.

View Capabilities

Just as model delegates serve to encapsulate the data and state of a component, Swing components rely on external delegate objects to manage their appearance. This capability enables the implementation of the pluggable look-and-feel (PLAF) capabilities of the Swing architecture.

JFC components that support PLAF all derive from *JComponent*. Among its many duties, *JComponent* provides the mechanism by which view delegates are identified and associated with Swing controls. The *JComponent* class supports a bound property called *UI* that contains a reference to the view delegate object. The *UI* property is defined as supporting a type of *ComponentUI*, which is the ultimate base class for all UI delegate classes.

Unlike the AWT version of components that rely on peer components for rendering appearance, JFC components redirects paint requests to the specified view delegate. The *paint()* method of *JComponent* redirects its operations to its associated UI delegate classes when repainting is required. The pluggable look-and-feel mechanism of JFC is centered on this capability. The look-and-feel objects provide different versions of UI delegate classes for all supported JFC components. These UI delegate classes can be replaced dynamically at any time during the program's execution. Also, for specific implementation of graphical behavior, special UI classes can be created to replace the versions found in the standard LAF implementations.

Controller Support

The controller support is not consistently implemented in any particular place, and can be found in both the components itself, the data and state model, and the UI delegates for a control. This is because complete separation of controller support would cause significant inefficiency in managing events and other forms of communication among the various constituents of a component.

The controller functionality is primarily concerned with managing the interaction between user input and components. Although in many cases controller functionality is used to manage intercommunication between subcomponents or other tightly associated controls, such as is found in Swing's scrolling support.

Controversial Aspects of Swing

There are some issues that the Swing architecture engenders, mostly due to the lack of reliance on peer components to handle the bulk of user and component interaction, but some related strictly to design decisions made early in design of JFC.

- **Performance**—Swing components tend to perform noticeably slower than their peer counterparts primarily because they do not rely on the faster object code that exists in the native platform implementations. Since all of JFC's functionality is implemented in Java code, the inevitable performance degradation from native code comes into play.

- **Stability**—Early releases of the Swing architecture had a significant number of problems, some of which are still extant. To the credit of the JavaSoft developers, each successive release of Swing has had very obvious and notable improvements in the operation of components and the underlying infrastructure of the library.

- **Threading issues**—It is intended that developers understand that Swing components are not thread-safe. In an effort to conserve resources and boost performance, the additional code that would be needed to support full multi-threaded access to Swing component properties was foregone. Although this may seem like a severe impediment, it turns out to be little more than a slight inconvenience. The main reason that code must be structured this way is due to the asynchronous layout and painting mechanisms that Swing employs.

- **UI compatibility and extensibility**—Although attempts were made to make the various look-and-feel implementations consistent with each other and the platforms that they emulate, it seems to be a mammoth task to maintain this compatibility without afflicting performance. Thus, many of the look-and-feel implementations are tuned for speed rather than extensibility. The net effect of this is to make it somewhat difficult to implement a look-and-feel because it is difficult to borrow UI components from look-and-feel implementations.

In spite of these challenges, the Swing architecture is a viable and sound platform to develop Java applications. It appears that the ongoing releases of the component set will aggressively address performance and other issues.

Now everything's a little upside down
As a matter of fact the wheels have stopped
What's good is bad, what's bad is good
You'll find out when you reach the top
You're on the bottom.
            —Bob Dylan, *Idiot Wind*

Chapter 2

The JComponent
Class

JComponent is the fundamental class that supports Swing lightweight components. *JComponent* classes provide the following high-level features:

- Component painting is delegated to a set of classes specified by a pluggable look-and-feel also known as a PLAF or LAF. This enables the appearance of an application to be dynamically loaded and controlled. Look-and-feel classes and UI delegation are covered in depth in Chapter 9.

- Specification of keystroke combinations to produce action events. Many Swing components also support the management of an *ActionCommand* property. This property enables actions to be instantiated by multiple application components and provides effective re-use of event listener code.

- Rendering of *JComponent* elements can be buffered to a non-visible graphic context to improve painting efficiency and eliminate unnecessary flashing. A property called *DoubleBuffering* controls this property.

- Support of the *DebugGraphicsOptions* property. This development aid provides additional logging, slow motion drawing, and examination of off-screen buffers to provide diagnostic information during painting.

- Although Swing components do not inherently provide scrolling, scrollable components interact with scrolling containers to provide this capability. *JComponent* also provides Autoscrolling whereby dragging the mouse within a control causes it to scroll automatically.

- All *JComponent* classes support ToolTips, descriptive comments that appear over a component when the mouse pointer (cursor) is idled over it.

JComponent Inheritance Tree

In keeping with the fundamental design principles of the architecture, *JComponent* inherits from its equivalent class in the AWT package. Figure 2-1 shows the inheritance tree.

You may be surprised to see that *JComponent* inherits from *Container* as well as *Component*. This is an interesting design feature of the Swing architecture. The implication is that not only do Swing controls emulate the behavior of their heavyweight equivalents, they are also containers and implement many useful features of that class. This behavior would be impossible to provide with heavyweight controls because native components generally do not have container characteristics.

This architecture has some key benefits:

- All Swing components support nesting of child components. This implies that *JComponents* also support layout management as well as *Container* events (the default layout manager for Swing components is *null*, unless otherwise specified). Swing components also use some of the features such as *AlignmentX* and

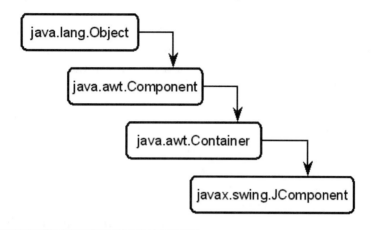

Figure 2-1. *The JComponent inheritance tree*

AlignmentY to support arrangement of children. Swing also manages the complexities of keystroke management that nesting components incurs.

- Preferred, maximum, and minimum size properties are supported for all Swing components.

- Swing components support a *Border* property that enables delegation of the painting of a component border. To account for the change in component area, the *Insets* property of *Container* is also supported. Borders are covered in detail in Chapter 9.

JComponent Features

JComponent is an extremely rich base class that provides a good deal of functionality to all JFC components. Many of the methods are value-added features that enrich the features of the *java.awt.Component* and *java.awt.Container* classes, but there is a lot of support for delegating user interface features to look-and-feel classes.

Because *JComponent* is a base class for all Swing component classes that have more flexibility than heavyweight components, *JComponent* contains quite a few more methods than *java.awt.Container*. Some implement functionality that is unique to JFC components and some are enhancements to methods provided by *java.awt.Container*.

The next sections describe all of the methods *JComponent* supports, organized by the type of functionality they provide.

Opacity

JFC components are not bound to the characteristics of peer counterparts, so there is a great deal more flexibility in how they can be displayed. One of the features that *JComponent* supports is the notion of opacity, which refers to whether a component paints its background. *JComponent* supports the *Opaque* property which is bound and *false* by default. The value of this property is stored as a bit value in a private flag word in *JComponent*.

If the value of the *Opaque* property is *true*, the default mechanism of *JComponent* causes the background color of the component to fill the component's bounds before any additional painting is done.

Size and Location Management

Most of these methods override methods that are provided by *java.awt.Component* and *java.awt.Container*. The override methods redirect to the bounds as represented by *JComponent* instead of heavyweight peers.

- *Rectangle getBounds(Rectangle rv)* [Overrides *java.awt.Component*]—Returns a rectangle representing the bounds of the component.

- *Dimension getSize(Dimension rv)* [Overrides *java.awt.Component*]—Returns the size of the component.

- *Point getLocation(Point rv)* [Overrides *java.awt.Component*]—Returns the position of the upper-left corner of the component, relative to its container.

- *int getHeight(), int getWidth(), int getX(), int getY()*—These methods, although intended for internal use, provide public access to the internal representation of the component's bounds. These methods are used by the *JComponent* implementation of *getBounds()*, *getSize()* and *getLocation()*.

- *void reshape(int x, int y, int w, int h)*—A JFC version of a deprecated method of *java.awt.Component*, provided for compatibility—use one of the versions of *setBounds()* instead.

- *Rectangle getVisibleRect()*—This method computes the visible rectangle of the component. This rectangle is calculated by intersecting the bounds of the component with that of each of its parents. A static method, *SwingUtilities. computeIntersection(...)* provides a rectangle intersection algorithm. If a component is clipped by any of its parent containers, this rectangle reflects that. This method is used to optimize painting methods to paint only areas that are exposed.

Preferred, Maximum, Minimum Sizes

JComponent ties together some important constructs by proving preferred, minimum, and maximum component sizes as full-fledged properties. Although *java.awt.Component* provides the accessor methods, it was assumed that the maximum and minimum sizes would be determined by characteristics of heavyweight peers, and that layout managers alone would assist in determining a component's preferred size. See Table 2-1.

In the lightweight world, no such restrictions exist because components are designed to behave according to a set of look-and-feel delegates and not peer components. Thus, these size characteristics have mutator methods that enable customization of these values.

JComponent provides a mechanism whereby the determination of preferred, maximum, and minimum sizes is delegated to the component UI, which is an extension of *javax.swing.plaf.ComponentUI*. This abstract

Table 2-1. *JComponent size properties*

Mutator Methods	Accessor Methods
public void setPreferredSize(Dimension preferredSize)	public Dimension getPreferredSize()
public void setMaximumSize(Dimension maximumSize)	public Dimension getMaximumSize()
public void setMinimumSize(Dimension minimumSize)	public Dimension getMinimumSize()

class provides default implementations of maximum and minimum sizes that delegate back to the component. In the case of preferred size, the default behavior is to return a *null*. This causes code in *JComponent* to attempt to get a preferred size from the component itself. In the event that too returns a *null*, the job of determining preferred size is left to the layout manager of the parent container.

All UI delegates inherit from *ComponentUI* in the same fashion that components inherit from *JComponent*. It is sensible to think of *ComponentUI* as an abstract base UI for *JComponent*, which serves as the abstract base component.

JFC Property Handling

One of the keys to the JavaBeans architecture is the notion of properties. JFC components—and the underlying infrastructure—take advantage of this capability and provide most of their functionality in the form of properties. The MVC characteristics of the architecture are achieved by designating certain properties as managing delegate objects.

The JavaBeans architecture specifies two methods for maintaining information on property value changes. A bound property is one that generates a *PropertyChangeEvent* object and distributes it to any listener objects that register their interest. Each property is identified by a string descriptor, which should be unique within each component. The descriptor for a property is usually contained in two places: It is often defined as a *public static String* on the component itself, and can be extracted from the property descriptors in the *BeanInfo* class as well.

Bound Property Handling

Whereas it is common for a component to contain a reference to a *java.beans.PropertyChangeSupport* object to provide the listener and event firing methods for bound properties, *JComponent* provides it own implementation directly in its API. The methods of *PropertyChangeSupport* are enhanced, providing specific methods for firing events for properties whose value is a primitive type, namely, *boolean, char, double, float, int, long,* and *short*. A *protected* method is provided for *Object* type; this is the implementation that ultimately gets invoked.

Constrained Property Handling

Although it is possible to use bound properties as a mechanism for detecting when properties change, it is not designed to prevent or restrict changes. Generally, a bound property change event is fired *after* the change has taken place. Although a property value can be restored after the fact, this is not as efficient as being able to prevent a change from occurring.

To provide this functionality, the JavaBeans architecture provides another type of property known as a constrained property. When a constrained property is modified, it sends a *java.beans.VetoableChangeSupport* object to any listener that registered interest. Each listener has the option of throwing a *java.beans.PropertyVetoException*, which causes the property change to be canceled. This mechanism also enables a listener to reject a change without necessarily having access to the mutator methods of a property.

The *JComponent* class contains a reference to a *java.beans.Vetoable ChangeSupport* that provides the vetoable listener and event methods.

It is conceivable that a property may be both constrained and bound; this causes both types of events to be generated. In this case, an interested listener would have the option of registering for one or both of these events.

None of the properties of *JComponent* are constrained by default.

Component Property Overrides

Some of the properties in JFC components have different characteristics depending on the JDK version. In the case of *java.awt.Component*, several properties are bound in the JDK 1.2 version that are not bound in previous versions. This can cause a problem with code that is designed to be ported across these environments. To reduce the impact, several of these methods were implemented in *JComponent*. The implementation determines the version level of the JDK and provides binding capability for pre-JDK 1.2 implementations. If this code did not exist, property changes would generate two property change events under code ported to JDK 1.2. The methods that are bound in JDK 1.2 but not in previous releases are listed in Table 2-2.

Table 2-2. *JComponent bound properties*

void setBackground(Color bg)	void setEnabled(boolean enabled)
void setFont(Font font)	void setForeground(Color fg)
void setVisible(boolean aFlag)	void setAlignmentX(float alignmentX)
float getAlignmentX()	void setAlignmentY(float alignmentY)
float getAlignmentY()	

Client Properties

Another version of property support was engineered into JFC. Client properties serve as a soft alternative to the JavaBeans property management architecture. Client properties leverage the property change event handling features of JFC but use an internal *Hashtable* dictionary to store values instead of depending on addition of accessor and mutator methods. It is a facility used by many different features of JFC classes to store per-component information. *JComponent* treats these properties as bound and causes a *PropertyChangeEvent* to be fired when a client property is created or modified.

Because client properties are stored in a *Hashtable*, they can be looked at as a key/value pair rather than a discrete property object. The key and values of a client property can be any extension of *java.lang.Object*, which only eliminates primitive types. Two *public final* methods are provided by *JComponent* to manage client properties:

- *Object getClientProperty(Object key)*—Retrieves the current value of the client property specified by the key parameter. If no such value exists, returns *null*.

- *void putClientProperty(Object key, Object value)*—Creates, updates, or deletes a client property. If the key is not in the client property set, a new key is created. If the key exists, the content of the property is updated with the supplied value. If the key exists and the value is *null*, the key is deleted.

In either case, specifying a *null* key causes a *NullPointerExcpetion* to be thrown.

Although it may be tempting to take advantage of client properties in application design, it must be done with great caution because so many elements of JFC rely on them for fundamental behavior. Table 2-3 lists the client properties used by *JComponent*.

A number of other instances of use of client properties are sprinkled through the Swing API. There is also a warning in the source code for *setClientProperty()* in *Jcomponent*:

> *The clientProperty dictionary is not intended to support large-scale extensions to JComponent nor should be it considered an alternative to subclassing when designing a new JComponent.*

Thus, if client properties are to be used, they should be used with the following concepts in mind:

- Do not store enormous amounts of data in a client property and try to keep the number of properties down to a minimum. Remember that they are all treated as bound, so extra code is invoked whenever values change. Also, creating very large property values or too many property entries can bloat a component with unnecessary storage.

- Do not use the reference to the component as a key because JFC internals use this method. Always create a distinctive key structure, preferably as a *static final String*, and document their intended behavior as well as possible.

- Do not attempt to modify any properties that JFC uses, although it is technically feasible to examine them.

Table 2-3. *Client property examples*

Key	Usage
NEXT_FOCUS	Used to store reference to next focusable component
KEYBOARD_BINDINGS_KEY	Contains *Hashtable* of key bindings
TOOL_TIP_TEXT_KEY	String for ToolTip display
JLabel.LABELED_BY_PROPERTY	Component to which a label refers, used for mnemonic processing

- Remember that access to client properties is not thread-safe. Because the methods are *final* they cannot be overridden to make them *synchronized* or change their behavior in any way. This appears to be a deliberate design decision to ensure the stability of client properties for JFC's internal functionality.

Deferred Layout

Another feature that *JComponent* provides the basic support for is deferred layout. In a traditional AWT application, the *validate()* method would have to be explicitly called when containers change shape in order to invoke their layout managers. The JFC architecture uses a *RepaintManager* object to enqueue asynchronous layout requests whenever *JComponent*-derived objects change shape. *JComponent* provides a method *revalidate()* that enqueues a layout request.

When *revalidate()* is called, it signals the *RepaintManager* that a layout change may have occurred. *RepaintManager* will call a method of *JComponent* called *isValidateRoot()*, which provides a mechanism to determine at what point in the component hierarchy a layout needs to be performed. The component tree is walked up until a component is found that returns *true* for *isValidateRoot()*. At that point, *invalidate()* is called, recalculating the layout for all descendant components. *JRootPane*, the encapsulation of window content, returns *true* for *isValidateRoot()* to catch all validation requests if no other container processes them.

Borders and Insets

JComponent-based controls all have the capability of being assigned a border. This border is painted around the perimeter of the component, and is controlled through a property interface. The value of this property will be a predefined border that the component provides, or one specified by the look-and-feel delegate.

When a JFC component is created, it will look to the look-and-feel classes to acquire a reference to the border to use for a particular class. This mechanism, as well as descriptions of the various border types available, is discussed in Chapter 9.

The border used for a particular class can be retrieved using the *getBorder()* method. The *setBorder()* methods is used to assign or replace a border for a component. The property can be set to *null,* which means that no border is to be used.

JComponent provides a protected method, *paintBorder(),* that can be used to change the way that borders are painted. By default, this method delegates the painting of the border to the object specified by the *Border* property. If this behavior needs alteration, subclasses of *JComponent* can override the *paintBorder()* method.

It is wise to be cautious about changing borders on common components because many of them use border delegates to paint important portions of their user interface.

To accommodate the difference in behavior, *JComponent* also overrides the *getInsets()* methods. Because the border changes the available space for painting the component, the insets are calculated by the border delegate instead of being stored in the control.

Keyboard Actions

JComponent provides a powerful capability that supports delivery of action commands by registering keystroke combinations. *JComponent* contains code that overrides the *processKeyEvent()* method of *java.awt.Component,* which allows it to filter all keystroke events that are dispatched to it. If a key event listener is added to a *Component,* or key events are enabled explicitly using *enableEvents(),* key events are generated and dispatched.

Keyboard actions are, in many cases, automatically created by components themselves, often at the direction of the *UIManager* object. This provision allows for general actions to be supported for components while also allowing for look-and-feel-specific actions to be automatically installed when components are created.

Registering a Keyboard Action

Keyboard actions are registered in a *java.util.Hashtable* object, which is stored in the client properties dictionary for the component. A keyboard action is comprised of the following information:

- An instance of a *KeyStroke* object. This object is an encapsulation of a virtual key and enables the specification of modifiers for the <Shift>, <Ctrl>, <Alt>, and <Meta> keys in any combination. Because the modifiers make the *KeyStroke* object unique, key combinations can have different actions assigned. The *KeyStroke* reference serves as the key to the *Hashtable* that contains the action information.

- A reference to an object that implements *ActionListener*. This is the listener that will get notified when the key combination is detected.

- Optionally, a command string. This capability allows menu or other command-oriented action listeners to be reused. If a command string is not specified, an empty string, not *null,* will be reported as the command for the event.

- Lastly, a condition that dictates when the binding is effective. Several valid options are available:

  - *WHEN_FOCUSED*—This means the binding is only active when the component currently owns the keyboard focus. If a component cannot receive focus because it is nontraversable or otherwise disabled, this condition will never be met.

  - *WHEN_ANCESTOR_OF_FOCUSED_COMPONENT*—Enables the binding to be activated when the target component is in the ancestor tree of the component with the focus. This condition is usually applied to containers.

  - *WHEN_IN_FOCUSED_WINDOW*—This condition code activates a binding so long as the component shares the same window as the target component.

  - *UNDEFINED_CONDITION*—This condition code is returned when an actual condition code cannot be evaluated. It is returned by the method *getConditionForKeyStroke()* when a keystroke that is not bound is passed as a parameter.

Querying for Keyboard Actions

JComponent provides methods to facilitate inquiries as to what keyboard bindings are set for a particular component:

- *ActionListener getActionForKeyStroke(KeyStroke keyStroke)*— Given a particular *KeyStroke* object, returns a reference to the action listener object associated with the binding. If there is no binding to the keystroke, this method returns *null*.

- *int getConditionForKeyStroke(KeyStroke keyStroke)*—By passing a reference to a registered *KeyStroke* object, this method returns the associated condition value. If there is no binding to the keystroke, this method returns the value *UNDEFINED_CONDITION*.

- *KeyStroke[] getRegisteredKeyStrokes()*—This method returns an array of *KeyStroke* objects that are registered with a particular *JComponent*. This method can be used in combination with the previous two methods to acquire a detailed account of what key bindings exist for a JFC component.

Unregistering a Keyboard Action

In the event that keyboard actions need to be removed, two options are available. To delete a single action on a component, call the method *unregisterKeyboardAction()* and pass a *KeyStroke* object as a parameter. All keyboard actions can be removed with the call *resetKeyboardActions()*. Bear in mind that all keyboard actions will be removed, even those that were bound by the look-and-feel delegates.

Key Event Processing

Lightweight components add a great deal of flexibility to keyboard event handling, which comes at a cost of somewhat significant complexity. The following flow diagram shows the process by which key events are processed by JFC components:

1. *JComponent* checks to see if a focus manager is active. If so, it lets the focus manager handle the keystroke. If the focus manager consumes the event, processing of that keystroke is complete. Components that do their own focus management, such as *JTable* and *JTextArea*, supersede this step with internal focus checking.

2. Listeners that register for key events are given the second opportunity to consume keystrokes. This enables events listeners to

intercept keystrokes that would ordinarily be passed through to the keyboard action handlers.

3. At this point, the dictionary that contains the keystroke bindings is checked to see if the keystroke has an entry that maps it to an action. The bindings are checked by firing events to the dispatchers added by the keystroke binding process. Whether a keystroke has been handled or not is a matter of checking the event object with the *isConsumed()* method. Bindings are checked in this order:

   • Key bindings that have the *WHEN_FOCUSED* condition are checked first.

   • Next, the focused component's ancestor tree is examined for any bindings with the modifier *WHEN_ANCESTOR_OF_FOCUSED_COMPONENT*.

   • Last, the component tree for the current window is checked for any bindings with the condition *WHEN_IN_FOCUSED_WINDOW*.

4. If no bindings are found, or no ancestor or peer consumes the event, it is passed to the menu bar of the root window.

5. If the menu does not want the event, a check is done to see if the root window is an internal frame. If so, the creator of the internal frame gets the keystroke. If there are no takers, the ancestors of the internal pane are iterated and the event is delivered to each ancestor until the root window is found and notified.

6. At this point, if the keystroke event is not consumed, it is discarded.

Event Handling

JFC provides some value-added support to the event mechanisms supported by AWT components:

   • *protected void processComponentKeyEvent(KeyEvent e)*—This method can be overridden by components that want to have an additional crack at consuming a key event after the focus manager and key listeners but before key bindings are resolved. Its only current use seems to be the explicit consumption of <Tab> characters by text components to prevent them from being interpreted and to allow for special keyboard mappings that are only available inside classes that extend *JTextComponent*. The default behavior for this method is a no-op.'

- *protected void processFocusEvent(FocusEvent e)*—Overriding this method allows stealing of focus events before the component passes it along. Use caution when overriding this method. Ensure the superclass version is called; otherwise, undesirable side-effects may occur. The default behavior for this method is to set a client property indicating the component has focus and calling the *java.awt.Component* implementation.

- *protected void processKeyEvent(KeyEvent e)*—An override of this method allows handling of key events before any other handler, including the focus manager and any key event listeners. Unless the superclass is called, the component will not process any key events.

- *protected void processMouseMotionEvent(MouseEvent e)*—This method provides autoscrolling support by interpreting mouse drags as scroll operations. If autoscrolling is not active, the default behavior is to call the *java.awt.Component* implementation.

Ancestor Events

JComponent has an additional notification mechanism that is lacking in its AWT counterpart. A new interface, *AncestorListener*, provides notification of *AncestorEvent* occurrences. *AncestorEvent* objects are delivered to JFC components when their ancestor components are made visible, hidden, or moved. This enables components to react to these eventualities without modifying their parent components or, for that matter, without the parent component's knowledge.

JComponent provides the *addAncestorListener()* and *removeAncestor Listener()* methods to manage ancestor listener lists. The default behavior of these methods is to delegate management of ancestor notification to a class *AncestorNotifier*. This class administers the ancestor component hierarchy, fires ancestor events to interested listeners and also manages the binding of the parent and ancestor properties.

JComponent also overrides the *addNotify()* and *removeNotify()* methods to enable ancestor and related property notification. Thus, it is extremely important to call the *JComponent* versions of these if these methods are overridden.

Notes in the source code indicate that the ancestor management methods will be migrated to the *Component* class in a future release.

UI Delegation Methods

JComponent supports pluggable look-and-feels that can emulate the appearance of graphical interface of popular Java platforms or provide cross-platform and custom component presentations. The support for these features originates in the *JComponent* class.

JComponent contains what is perhaps the most important method in the entire architecture in its implementation of the *paint()* method. Unlike traditional custom JavaBeans, which rely on an override of this method to accomplish visual effects, the *JComponent* implementation delegates rendering of its graphics to a UI delegate object. These objects are implementations of a set of interfaces that describe the fundamental drawing operations for all JFC components. The job of the *UIManager* and the look-and-feel classes is to provide these delegate objects to components when they are created and to update them whenever the look-and-feel characteristics are modified.

The *updateUI()* method paints components on the screen. Subclasses of *JComponent* override the empty implementation of *updateUI()* to implement their desired paint behavior. This usually involoves acquiring a delegate object and passing the delegate object to the *setUI()* method. The *setUI()* method is responsible for ensuring that the support for a particular UI is installed (or uninstalled) and also fires a property change event to signal that a new UI is in place. This functionality is, in turn, provided by the *UIManager* class, which uses the results of the *getUIClassID()* method to determine what sort of UI delegate is required.

UI delegation, look-and-feel, and all related topics are covered in great detail in Chapter 9.

Focus Management

Focus usually refers to the component that is currently highlighted on a form. The purpose of this concept is to determine which component should be receiving keystroke events. Unlike a mouse-click event, which has a position, and can be targeted to a component by virtue of where it occurred on the screen, some alternate scheme is needed to process key events. The process is straightforward: Each active window specifies one of its components to be the focus component. The focus is transferred between two components in response to mouse clicks or when certain keystrokes are detected.

The mechanism that determines which component should have the focus is implemented partially in *JComponent* and partially in the class *FocusManager*. For each thread group, an instance of *FocusManager* is created to determine the component tab order. The class *DefaultFocusManager* is an implementation of the abstract class *FocusManager*. *DefaultFocusManager* provides methods that enable alteration of the focus propagation by programmatically specifying a tab order.

Some additional methods in *JComponent* interact with *FocusManager* to give even more flexibility over focus handling:

- *isFocusTraversable()*—This method determines if a component is capable of receiving focus. Certain components, such as *JLabel*, cannot receive any input events and never allow focus to be set. Other cases, such as the button controls, do not allow focus when they are in certain states, as when a button, menu, or check box is disabled. These controls return *true* for this method when focus is permissible.

- *getNextFocusableComponent()*, *setNextFocusableComponent (Component)*—These methods enable a component to override the *FocusManager* and specify what component should get the focus when it leaves the component. The reference to the component that is to receive the focus is stored in a client property dictionary that is accessible by the *FocusManager*. If no such component is specified, the *FocusManager* determines the component to receive the focus.

- *requestFocus(), grabFocus()*—These methods are used to cause focus to explicitly set to a particular component. The correct method of pro- gramatically assigning the focus is to use *requestFocus()*. The other method, *grabFocus()*, is intended to be used only by focus managers. In JFC 1.1, *grabFocus()* calls *super.requestFocus()*, which propagates the request to the *java.awt.Component* code, thus bypassing the Swing focus manager.

- *hasFocus()*—Returns *true* if the component currently has the focus. Only one component in each thread group can have the focus at any time.

- *setRequestFocusEnabled(), isRequestFocusEnabled()*—These methods manage an unbound property that controls whether a component is permitted to call *requestFocus()*.

- *isFocusCycleRoot()*—By overriding this method and returning *true*, it signifies to the *FocusManager* that the component has child components and that the focus will be moving among these and not to the next peer component in the tab order. The only JFC component that does this is *JRootPane*.

- *isManagingFocus()*—This method enables a component to specify that it desires to retain control over focus once it receives it. This is most often used by containers that use <Tab> characters as input, such as text or other editors, and by column-oriented components such as *JTable*, which uses the <Tab> key to change cell selections. When a class that extends *JComponent* overrides this method and returns *true*, the key events for <Tab> and <Shift>+<Tab> will be delivered directly to the component. <Control>+<Tab> and <Control>+<Shift>+<Tab> are implemented to override this feature and always cause focus to move to the next component in the focus cycle, regardless of the return value of this method.

- *requestDefaultFocus()*—Similar to the *requestFocus()* method except instead of directing focus to itself, the focus is directed to the component that is meant to have the focus by default.

The method iterates through the component tree until it finds a traversable component and calls *grabFocus()* on its behalf—heavyweight components are relegated to *requestFocus()* because it is the only supported method.

If the component is not traversable, the code checks if its implementation of *isManagingFocus()* returns *true*. If so, then a recursive call to *requestDefaultFocus()* is made on that component if it is lightweight, that is, a descendant of *JComponent*. If the component is neither traversable nor managing focus, the next child component is examined. If no suitable component is found, the method returns *false*. The method returns *true* if it manages to call *grabFocus()* or *requestFocus()* on one of its children. This does not guarantee that a component has actually received the focus, but simply indicates that a suitable component was identified.

ToolTips

ToolTips are a usability enhancement that enables users to acquire information about screen components without having to resort to invoking a help facility. ToolTips are supported for all JFC components through a set of properties and support classes.

The value of the ToolTip text for a component is stored as a client property of the component and is managed by the *getToolTipText()* and *setToolTipText()* methods. The mutator method comes in a parameterless version as well as a variant that takes a *MouseEvent* object. The parameterized version is used to show different ToolTip text depending on where the mouse position is within the bounds of a component.

JComponent provides an overridable method *createToolTip()* that enables creation of an alternate ToolTip component. If the default version is used, a component *JToolTip* is created. This component is added to the *POPUP_LAYER* of the root pane or created in a separate *JWindow* if necessary to ensure it is visible. Both the *JRootPane* and *JWindow* classes are described later in this chapter.

An infrastructural class, *ToolTipManager,* provides administration of all ToolTip activity. It provides the following features:

1. It supports a registration process whereby components are associated with ToolTip text.

2. It calculates the correct size and position for a ToolTip.

3. It manages a set of configurable timers that cause ToolTips to be created, displayed, and reshown when appropriate.

4. It manages a mouse motion listener to dismiss ToolTips when the mouse position changes.

5. It provides default keystroke bindings to display and hide ToolTip windows; <Ctrl+F1> toggles a ToolTip display, and <Esc> causes a ToolTip to hide.

6. It supports a *private interface* that enables ToolTips to be displayed as lightweight, mediumweight, or heavyweight windows and contains inner classes that support these three types:

   - *Lightweight*—Inherits from *JPanel*. Used for ToolTips that are guaranteed to be bound by a lightweight container. This type of ToolTip is not useful when the ToolTip area extends beyond this containment as it will be clipped by the content pane. The use of lightweight ToolTips can be managed by the method *setLightWeightPopupEnabled()*.

   - *Mediumweight*—Inherits from *java.awt.Panel*. This version is used when lightweight ToolTips are disabled, but the ToolTip will still fit inside its parent container. Because it is contained by a heavyweight (peered) component, it will always appear above all lightweight components.

   - *Heavyweight*—Inherits from *java.awt.Window*. This version is used when, in any case, a ToolTip cannot be bound by a parent container. Creating a *Window* enables the ToolTip to appear anywhere on the screen, but incurs the additional resources of a high-level standalone window. *ToolTipManager* only creates a heavyweight ToolTip as a last resort.

Scrolling and Autoscrolling

JComponent supports autoscrolling by implementing a timer-based object. This object, known as *Autoscroller*, creates mouse-drag events and propagates them to the container. Classes such as *JViewport*, which support scrolling of contents, can react to these additional messages and scroll contents automatically. The autoscroll capability is managed by the *getAutoscrolls()* and *setAutoscrolls()* methods. *JComponent* also provides an implementation of the *scrollRectToVisible()* method that forwards these requests to containers.

JFC Containers

JFC provides a set of containers that provide the basic support for the Model/View/Controller architecture as well as close compatibility with the AWT-based containers. JFC provides a set of peer-based window classes designed to furnish the foundation for developing lightweight applications. These classes serve as a bridge between the native components and the lightweight infrastructure.

Swing Window Classes

JFC has its own set of classes that inherit from their AWT counterparts. The Swing window classes provide additional support that helps implement the lightweight component architecture. Figure 2-2 shows the partial inheritance tree for these classes.

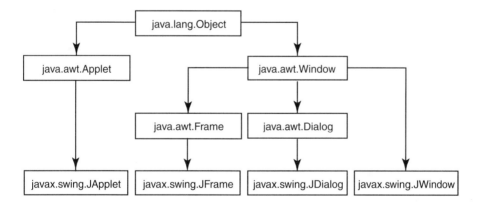

Figure 2-2. *Swing window classes*

It is important to remember that these window classes are technically heavyweight and do have peer counterparts (with the exception of *JInternalFrame*). Also significant is the fact that these classes do *not* inherit from *JComponent*, so the specific features of that class are not available.

Root Pane Containment

All of the Swing window classes implement the *RootPaneContainer* interface. The methods of this interface provide the mechanism for instances of these classes to provide a sophisticated containment hierarchy as well as support for lightweight menus. This hierarchy is described in the "JFC Containment Hierarchy" section later in this chapter.

JWindow Class

This class inherits from *java.awt.Window* and provides an undecorated window, that is, one without a caption bar and border. When a *JWindow* is instantiated, it is created with a root pane as its only direct child.

Because the *JWindow* does not have any control areas associated with it, it is not of much use on its own because it cannot be closed or moved. If this type of functionality is desired, it must be implemented manually. *JWindow* extensions seem to be best used for special-purpose windows such as splash screens and other floating windows.

JWindow is a full-fledged window in that it can exist on its own and takes up its own real estate on the desktop. It can be created as the child of any other window that inherits from *java.awt.Frame* or as a parentless window. If a parentless window is created, the class actually uses an invisible shared instance of a frame as a parent. This feature is provided by the method *getSharedOwnerFrame()*, which is a static method in the *SwingUtilies* class. Because this method has friendly access, it can only be invoked by classes that are in the *javax.swing* package.

JFrame Class

The *JFrame* class provides an application-level window that has a caption and control buttons as well as a potentially resizable border. It is an extension of the class *java.awt.Frame* that includes the special keytroke handling and other capabilities of JFC and provides the root pane that serves as a container suitable for lightweight components.

It is also interesting to note that *JFrame* does not inherit from *JWindow* in the same way that *java.awt.Frame* inherits from *java.awt.Window*. Because *JFrame* inherits from *java.awt.Frame*, *java.awt.Window* is in the inheritance hierarchy. *JWindow* does not have any value-added functionality that would benefit *JFrame*.

Close Event Support

JFrame has a significant advantage over its AWT counterpart in that it provides a mechanism for intercepting the close event from the frame controls. *JFrame* supports an integer property named *DefaultCloseOperation* that controls this behavior. Three options are provided for this feature:

- *DO_NOTHING_ON_CLOSE*—This option means that the implementor is responsible for handling the *windowClosing()* method of a *WindowListener* in order to catch the close event. When this occurs, code can be invoked in the listener to hide the frame and dispose of any discardable resources.

- *HIDE_ON_CLOSE*—This is the default option and causes a *setVisible(false)* to be invoked on the frame after all registered *WindowListeners* have been notified.

- *DISPOSE_ON_CLOSE*—This option calls not only *setVisible(false)*, but also a call to the *dispose()* method of the frame to release its resources.

These identifiers are defined in the *javax.swing.WindowConstants* interface, which is implemented by *JFrame*.

JDialog and JApplet Classes

These classes inherit from their AWT counterparts and provide similar functionality. The chief distinctions of the JFC version of these classes are that they support root pane containment and JFC-style lightweight menus. In addition, *JDialog* supports a default close operation that is identical to that of *JFrame*.

JInternalFrame Class

This class provides a 100-percent lightweight frame that can only be created within the bounds of a lightweight container. The use of this class is covered in the "Advanced Techniques" section.

JFC Containment Hierarchy

The chief distinction of the JFC window classes is that the ownership of child components is delegated to a container class that is derived from *JComponent*. Each window class provides a containment hierarchy that is encapsulated in a set of panes. The window classes all implement the *RootPaneContainer* interface; this specifies the methods used to access the various pane objects. All classes that implement this interface also require an indirection to perform container operations. In an AWT container, the *add* method is used to insert child components:

```
// The good old days
java.awt.Dialog dlg = new java.awt.Dialog();
dlg.add(new Panel());
```

This approach is fine for heavyweight controls because they use a peer component to manage its children. The lightweight world has no equivalent; there needs to be a separate set of containers to manage the content of the window.

The Root Pane

In Swing, the *RootPaneContainer* portion of the window classes manages child components and mediates between the heavyweight portion of the container and the *JComponent* capabilities. This approach requires a different strategy for inserting child components. For example, the following code causes a runtime exception:

```
javax.swing.JDialog dlg = new javax.swing.JDialog();
dlg.add(new JPanel()); // Down in flames!!
```

To access the content pane, use the *getContentPane* method specified by *RootPaneContainer*. Keep in mind that this rule only applies to the window classes; other container classes, such as the *JPanel* class, do not require this indirection because they are entirely implemented as lightweight components.

```
// Good to go!
javax.swing.JDialog dlg = new javax.swing.JDialog();
dlg.getContentPane().add(new JPanel());
```

The method that JFC containers use to catch illegal *add()* operations is managed by a property known as *RootPaneCheckingEnabled* and is managed by the methods *setRootPaneCheckingEnabled()* and *isRootPaneCheckingEnabled()*. The accessor method is called in the *add()* method; if the value is *true*, an exception is thrown. The principle purpose of the mutator method is to temporarily disable checking so that the root pane created for the container can be added. After the root pane is in place, root-pane checking is immediately re-enabled. It is recommended that this property not be manipulated as its purpose is to prevent accidental destruction of the containment structure.

This indirect technique must also be used for assigning a layout manager to a window class. What is happening in this case is the layout is being assigned to the content pane instead of the target container. Although the window classes are not themselves derived from *JComponent*, the content pane object returned by this method is. *RootPaneContainer* serves an additional purpose: It serves as a marker so Swing-enabled development environments can correctly identify these classes as having this indirect method of adding children.

Root Pane Organization

The root pane itself is implemented by a container class called *JRootPane*. This class is responsible for managing all of the content in the Swing window container. *JRootPane* contains a stratified set of subordinate containers that manage the contents of the window classes. Figure 2-3 describes each of these constituents.

Layered Pane

This component adds depth to JFC containers. It provides the capability to overlap components by assigning a z-axis position. These positions,

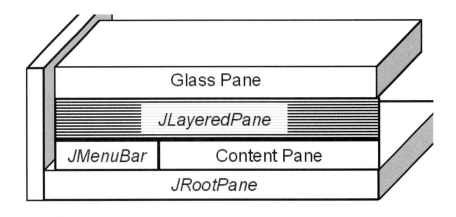

Figure 2-3. *Swing root pane components*

called layers, begin with zero representing the bottom-most placement. Higher numbered layers are drawn on top of those below. The implementing class, *JLayeredPane*, provides static constants for convenience and standardization as well as a set of methods to manipulate the layer in which a component might appear.

In many respects, *JLayeredPane* is similar to a container with a *CardLayout* manager. The essential difference is that *JLayeredPane* is intended to support the simultaneous viewing of all of its layers. This is accomplished by the way in which components are rendered inside the *JLayeredPane*: Each layer is rendered in turn starting from the lowest to the highest existing layer. The net effect is that components in the higher layer will conceal those below. These standard layers give an excellent picture of how the layered pane operates:

- *DEFAULT_LAYER*—This is the layer where components are added by default. The menu bar and content pane are the two components that make up this layer. The reason that this layer is segregated this way is to avoid inadvertently obscuring the menu bar when components are added to the content pane.

- *PALETTE_LAYER*—This layer is designated for any floating tool-bars, palettes, or any other window that needs to appear above the content without concealing popups or modal dialog boxes.

- *MODAL_LAYER*—Modal dialog boxes appear in this layer. This ensures that modal dialog boxes conceal content and palettes but are still below popup components. Note that palettes cannot be used with modal dialog boxes because the dialog box will obscure any components in that layer.

- *POPUP_LAYER*—This layer is where all components such as combo box drop-downs, popup menus, and ToolTips are positioned. This is to ensure that these elements function properly in modal dialog boxes.

- *DRAG_LAYER*—When components are being dragged into a container, they are assigned to this layer. This guarantees that they will not be obscured by any other component so long as they appear in a standard layer.

There is an additional layer known as *FRAME_CONTENT_LAYER*. This is the layer that the content pane and menu bar are placed in. It is generally not necessary to use this layer.

The default layout for the *JLayeredPane* class is *null*. This means that the *setBounds()* method must be used to manage the position of components. If a layout manager is asigned to *JLayeredPane* the layering effects are ignored.

Glass Pane

Sitting on top of all other components, including those in the *JLayeredPane*, is the glass pane. The glass pane is a transparent component whose primary function is to intercept keyboard and mouse events, but also serves a function in drag-and-drop. Any transparent component can be used as a glass pane. The default implementation is a nonopaque instance of *JPanel*.

The glass pane is invisible by default. It can be replaced by a component of your choice, but cannot be set to *null*. Components can be added to the glass pane; they will appear above all other components in the root pane container if the glass pane is visible.

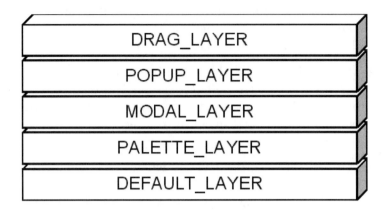

Figure 2-4. *Layered pane layers*

A useful example of glass-pane processing is given in the Advanced Techniques chapter.

Root Pane Layout

JRootPane uses a special layout manager called *RootLayout*. It is implemented as a protected inner class of *JRootPane*. It is responsible for ensuring that the subordinate components of *JRootPane* fill the viewable area. Its layout algorithm is straightforward:

- It constrains the glass pane and the layered pane to take up the root pane's entire viewable area.

- It positions the menu bar (if any) at the upper edge of the layered pane.

- It causes the content pane to use all remaining viewable space in the default layer of the layered pane less the area taken up by the menu bar.

Nothing prevents you from substituting your own custom layout for the root pane. Keep in mind that if you do so, you are responsible for managing the containment hierarchy yourself.

Creating a Root Pane

In some cases, it is advantageous to create a root pane. Although a root pane is created by default for the Swing heavyweights, there is no reason why a *JRootPane* could not be added to any lightweight container. This technique is especially useful when a layered pane, glass pane, or menu are to be added to a *JPanel* or other lightweight container. The container should be set to use a *BorderLayout* and the *JRootPane* instance added to the container, as would be any other component. A layered pane and glass pane are created (if needed) and associated with the new *JRootPane*.

Although this technique is useful, it does introduce a large amount of additional overhead on container processing. Thus, it should only be used when layering is required on a lightweight container. Also, lightweight containers will not delegate to the root pane when components are added. Components must be added to the default layer of the layered pane directly when this technique is used.

Default Button Support

The default button is a bound property of *JRootPane* that enables an instance of *JButton* to be designated as a default button. The way this is accomplished is by creating a keyboard binding to the <Return> key that maps to the specified button. The methods *setDefaultButton()* and *getDefaultButton()* manage this property. *JRootPane* also contains default action objects that are created and fired when the <Return> key is pressed and released.

I would not give a fig for the simplicity this *side of complexity, but I would give my life for the simplicity on the* other *side of complexity.*
—Oliver Wendell Holmes

Chapter 3

Basic Components Part 1

This chapter examines some of the simpler components that JFC provides, specifically, the label and button components. These components are considered to be the most straightforward to implement because they either have simple, straightforward model implementations or no model whatsoever.

This chapter explores the label and button components in detail, focusing on how these elementary components function in relation to each other and the *JComponent* base class.

In later chapters, where more complex components are examined, it will become clear how these elementary components serve as building blocks for more complicated functionality.

JLabel

The lightweight label control is one of the simplest components provided with JFC, but also serves as the principal mechanism for rendering portions of more sophisticated components. *JLabel* enables the display of text, an image, or both, and provides properties to control position and alignment.

Apart from providing static images and text in an application, *JLabel* provides the means by which data is rendered in the *JList*, *JComboBox*, *JTree*, and *JTable* components. For more information on how *JLabel* supports each of these, consult the applicable chapters.

Position and Alignment

Four bound properties control the relative position and alignment of text and icon components. These methods use constants defined in the *SwingConstants* interface.

The *HorizontalAlignment* property (see Figure 3-1) controls where the text appears relative to left and right edges of the label. Five values are supported of which three are listed in Table 3-1.

Table 3-1. *Horizontal alignment*

Value	Meaning
LEFT	Label contents are aligned with the left edge of the label. This is the default for text-only labels, that is, labels that have a null value for their icon and disabled icon properties.
CENTER	Content is centered in the label on the X-axis. This is the default for icon-only labels.
RIGHT	Content is right-justified, that is, aligned with the right edge of the label.

Figure 3-1. *Horizontal alignment example*

Another two constants that are usable for horizontal alignment are designed to support bidirectional languages. Because some languages read from right to left, such as Hebrew and Arabic, the meaning of "left" and "right" to describe relative positions are not meaningful. By using the values listed in Table 3-2, text justification can be described as relative to the direction of the current language.

Table 3-2. *Bidirectional alignment*

Value	Meaning
LEADING	Content is justified toward the beginning of the line, regardless of direction of language.
TRAILING	Content is justified toward the end of a text line, regardless of direction of language.

The *HorizontalTextPosition* property controls the position of text relative to its icon. This property is only meaningful for labels with both text and icon. Table 3-3 lists this property's values, and Figure 3-2 shows their results.

Table 3-3. *Horizontal text position*

Value	Meaning
RIGHT	Text appears to the right of the icon—this is the default.
CENTER	Text appears centered on the X-axis.
LEFT	Text appears to the left of the icon.

Figure 3-2. *Horizontal text position example*

The *VerticalAlignment* property controls where the text is centered with regard to the Y-axis. Table 3-4 lists the values that are accepted for this property, and Figure 3-3 shows the results.

Table 3-4. *Vertical alignment*

Value	Meaning
TOP	Text is aligned with the top of the label.
CENTER	Text appears centered on the Y-axis. This is the default.
BOTTOM	Text is aligned with the bottom of the label.

Figure 3-3. *Vertical alignment example*

Lastly, the *VerticalTextPosition* property controls the location of text relative to its icon in the Y-axis direction. Accepted values are listed in Table 3-5, and their results are shown in Figure 3-4.

As with its counterpart, this property is only meaningful when a label has both icon and text.

Label Mnemonics

JLabel cannot accept input events, but has a property that enables specification of an associated component. This component is directed to receive input focus when the mnemonic key associated with *JLabel* is struck. The methods *getLabelFor()* and *setLabelFor()* manage this property. If the target component is derived from *JComponent*, the *setLabelFor()* method also sets a client property to support accessibility.

Table 3-5. *Vertical text position*

Value	Meaning
TOP	Text appears above the icon.
CENTER	Text appears centered on the Y-axis. This is the default.
BOTTOM	Text appears below the icon.

Figure 3-4. *Vertical text position example*

Button Components

JFC provides many flavors of sophisticated, simple components that fall under the classification of button controls. Although button controls have many common characteristics, they are also diverse and provide valuable functionality to many more complex components.

To take proper advantage of object orientation, it is sensible to combine the common attributes of similar controls and package them in a highly reusable abstract class. The *AbstractButton* class serves in this role. *AbstractButton* provides a considerable number of features to the components that extend it, many of which are implemented by its support of a robust model common to all its subclasses.

JFC provides four basic buttons classes that inherit from *AbstractButton*: *JButton*, *JToggleButton*, *JCheckbox*, and the *JRadioButton*. Other components, such as menus and "popup" menus, also borrow some functionality from this class.

The fundamental purposes of *AbstractButton* are to provide a universal model, *ButtonModel*, that supports all required button functionality and to manage the properties that are specific to this family of components.

ButtonModel

ButtonModel is the interface that describes button components use to delegate much of its functional capability. The standard implementation of this interface is *DefaultButtonModel*, which, along with the other button model classes, is suitable for all but the most unusual cases. Perhaps the most interesting feature of *ButtonModel* is its dual-purpose nature, serving as both a data model and a state model. Although it is a departure from the strict paradigm, the type of data that a button is liable to contain is not sufficient to warrant a separate model. In general, buttons are used to initiate actions and selections, not to contain any data other than its selection state.

ButtonModel is an extension of the *java.awt.ItemSelectable* interface, which describes the fundamental methods needed to set up a listener for item selection. The concept of selection plays an important part in the functionality of many, but not all, button components. *ItemSelectable* requires the *addItemListener()* and *removeItemListener()* methods, which are used to manage listeners that are interested in when a selection state changes. Although another method, *getSelectedObjects()*, is also specified, it has a "no-op" implementation in *DefaultButtonModel* because it has no use in the context of button operation.

ButtonModel Properties

The *ButtonModel* interface specifies several properties that represent the data and state of a button component. It is understood that not all of these properties are applicable to every button component; it is at the discretion of the component designer to determine which properties are suitable and to implement them accordingly.

ActionCommand Property

This is a *String* property that supports the association of a text string to represent a momentary command that might be generated by a menu selection, push button, or keystroke binding. Using command strings enables sharing of listeners and event handlers, especially in cases where multiple components are expected to produce the exact same effect.

The fundamental example of the efficacy of action commands would be an application that has a menu item, a mnemonic keystroke, and a toolbar button that all perform identical functions. By assigning each of the components the same action command strings, more efficient and reusable code can be developed. This also enables action event handlers to segregate functionality by string comparison instead of comparing instances of control sources, which allows for more practical encapsulation and better hiding of implementation.

The *ActionCommand* property is not bound. This may seem unusual, but it must have been a design assumption that action commands are not generally altered during application execution. The default value for the action command is *null* (as implemented in *DefaultButtonModel*).

Mnemonic Property

The *Mnemonic* property is an integer that represents a character that is to be used as an actuator keystroke for a particular button component. *BasicButtonListener* is the UI support class that provides mnemonic and other property and event support. It is discussed in detail later in this chapter.

Other Features of ButtonModel

ButtonModel specifies several additional properties to support button functionality. As with the previously discussed properties, components that derive from *AbstractButton* will have different interpretations of these properties or, in certain cases, not implement them at all. These interpretations are included in the sections specific to these components.

State Properties

Four *boolean* properties are provided by *ButtonModel*: *Armed, Pressed, Selected,* and *Rollover*. The combination of these binary states reflects the selection condition of the button component. Inheritors of *AbstractButton* are free to implement these as necessary to describe the component's state. The specific meanings of these properties are discussed in the sections covering the button classes, but they do have prevalent meanings.

The Armed Property

The *Armed* property is *true* when the button is "capable" of being pressed. This behavior is most evident in the *JButton* and *JToggleButton* class, which implement the momentary and toggled versions of a push button. The buttons do not actually "click" until the mouse is released, although the button may actually appear to be depressed. The behavior of buttons is to not fire its action until the mouse is released, and only if it is released within the button's bounds. To see an example of this behavior, click and hold the mouse while over a *JButton* or *JToggleButton*. If the mouse is moved out of the bounds of the button, it reverts back to its "unpressed" state even though the mouse button is still pressed. In this case, the button's *Armed* state is *true* until the mouse button is released regardless of whether the component's other states change. This distinction is made to enable button UI delegates to correctly render buttons in this situation.

The Rollover Property

The meaning of the *Rollover* property is identical for all implementations of *AbstractButton* and has the value of *true* when the mouse cursor is over the button area. The property is managed by a listener delegate, *BasicButtonListener*, which is implemented differently according to the interpretation of the current look-and-feel. This property is implemented this way because the semantics of what constitutes being "over" the button may differ depending on how button views are rendered. The *Rollover* property is bound; the component will respond to changes in this property by swapping icons if rollover icons are specified.

AbstractButton Initialization

The *AbstractButton* class provides a *protected* method *init()* that is conventionally called in the constructors of all subclasses. This method can be overridden in the subclass, but it is vital to call the superclass version because it does some important initialization.

OverlayLayout

The first thing that the *init()* method does is set the layout of the button component to *OverlayLayout*. This is a constrained layout that is used exclusively by *AbstractButton* and some features of text component processing to provide a layout where child components can overlay each other at their specified alignment points. The *OverlayLayout* class calculates a preferred size based on the largest size of the child components found. It does not descend recursively down its child components.

Completing Button Initialization

After the layout is set, the values of the *Text* and *Icon* properties, which are the two parameters to the *init()* method, are examined to see if they are *null*. If not, the values are assigned to the properties using *setText()* and *setIcon()* that will cause property changes to be fired, although the button listener does not yet exist.

Next, the *updateUI()* method is called, which creates and assigns the UI delegate for the button according to the button's class and the current look-and-feel. Although this is implemented as a "no-op" in *AbstractButton*, inheritors are expected to override this method and set the UI property of the button with the delegate returned by the *UIManager*. This ultimately causes the *setUI()* method of *JComponent* to be called, which will deinstall the existing UI (if one exists), install the new UI, and fire a property change and request a revalidation and repaint of the control. This pattern is virtually identical in all JFC components.

Lastly, the *init()* method creates an anonymous inner class that serves as a *FocusListener* and adds it to the button's focus listener list. This seems redundant, considering that the *BasicButtonListener* is already listening for focus events. The listener methods *focusGained()* and *focusLost()* perform very little activity; they fire an accessibility state change when focus changes and request a repaint only when focus is lost. It may be implemented this way because the *BasicButtonListener* delegate does not support accessibility state changes. However, it seems a better idea to add this support in the proper place and eliminate additional focus listener methods from being created for every instance of *AbstractButton* components.

AbstractButton Properties

AbstractButton supports a number of additional properties beyond those provided by the model delegate. These mostly relate to visual characteristics of the button that are related to the various states of the model, but do not actually represent a "state."

Text Property

The standard button implementations support a *Text* bound property that represents the optional caption of the button. The property mutator, *setText()*, does not test the new value to see if it differs from the current caption, but uniformly issues a property change event. After firing the event, it checks the accessible context of the button to see if one is recognized and fires an accessible state property change. Lastly, the method checks the new value against the old and, if they differ, revalidates and repaints the button.

Button captions support underlining of the mnemonic character in the text string. Interestingly, the code that accomplishes this uses a peculiar method to determine which character to underline. Because mnemonics are not case-sensitive, the method *drawString()* in *BasicGraphicsUtils* looks for the first occurrence of the upper- and lowercase instances of the character in the caption string. Although one might expect that the uppercase instance of the character was preferable, the algorithm selects the lowercase character over the uppercase one if both exist.

Button Icons

AbstractButton supports the use of multiple button icons to serve as an additional visual aid to application users. These icons are dynamically displayed by the UI delegates when the button's state changes in particular ways. The base UI delegate *BasicButtonUI* provides a method *paintIcon()* where the icon type is determined and painted into the button. The algorithm for determining the icon type is as follows:

- If the button is not enabled, the icon is set to the value of the *DisabledIcon* property.

- If the button is pressed and armed, the icon is set to the value of *PressedIcon*. If this value is *null*, the default icon is used.

- If rollover is enabled and the *Rollover* property is *true*, the icon is set to the *RolloverIcon*.

- If the new value of the icon property is *null*, the default icon value is used.

Table 3-6 summarizes the algorithm by showing all of the icon types and the circumstances in which they are used.

A property of the UI delegate *TextShiftOffset* is used to make the button contents appear to move (in certain look-and-feel implementations) when the button is pressed. This value is used in the calculations to determine where the icon is to be painted.

Changes to the icon properties have similar ramifications. Each mutator explicitly fires a property change event as well as an accessible property change if an accessible context is associated with the button. The *setIcon()* method checks if the new icon value differs in the object reference before invoking a *repaint()*, and also checks if the icon's size has changed to determine whether to revalidate the component as well. The *setDisabledIcon()*, *setSelectedIcon()*, and *setPressedIcon()* methods will not cause the button to revalidate. They only invoke a repaint if the icon reference changes or if the button is in either the disabled, selected, or pressed states, respectively. The *setRolloverIcon()* and *setRolloverSelectedIcon()* methods check if the icon changed, but cannot determine the rollover state, thus always invoking a repaint request if the new property value differs from the current.

Table 3-6. *Icon types and usage*

Icon Property	Enabled	Pressed	Selected	Rollover
Icon (default)	true	false	false	false
PressedIcon	true	true	false	false
SelectedIcon	true	false	true	false
RolloverIcon	true	false	false	true
RolloverSelectedIcon†	true	false	true	true
DisabledIcon	false	false	false	false
DisabledSelectedIcon‡	false	false	true	false

†supported by *JRadioButton* and *JToggleButton* only
‡supported by Java (Metal) look-and-feel only

The *setDisabledSelectedIcon()* method, which only comes into play in the Java LAF, creates a disabled icon image from the selected icon if one is not provided. It also checks whether the size of the icon changed before invoking a revalidation of the component and whether the icon itself has changed to invoke a repaint operation.

An additional property is provided to optionally suppress rollover processing. If the value of *RolloverEnabled* is *false*, the UI delegate ignores the rollover state when determining which icon to use.

Text/Icon Position and Alignment

The text and alignment properties supported by *AbstractButton* are identical in behavior to that of the *JLabel* component, so their descriptions are not repeated here. In all cases of the mutator methods of these properties, a *protected* method of *AbstractButton* is invoked to check the validity of the property values. The methods *checkHorizontalKey()* and *checkVerticalKey()* will both throw an *IllegalArgumentException* if an invalid value is specified. All four of the methods, *setHorizontalAlignment()*, *setVerticalAlignment()*, *setHorizontalTextPosition()*, and *setVerticalTextPosition()*, fire applicable property change events when invoked and explicitly cause the button component to repaint.

Selection Property and Clicking

AbstractButton provides accessor and mutator methods for only one of the four *boolean* state properties managed by the *ButtonModel*. The *isSelected()* and *setSelected()* methods delegate to the *ButtonModel* instance, but there is an important distinction between setting this property and actuating a "click." The *setSelected()* method only fires a property change for the accessible state property, not for the *Selected* property itself. This makes it suitable for initializing the selection state of button components, but not suitable for programmatically actuating a button press. Calling *setSelected(true)* only sets that property; it does not affect the *Pressed* or *Armed* properties and thus will not cause the button's listeners to be notified of any state changes.

To provide the capability of generating an actual programmatic click, the *doClick()* method is provided. This method provides a parameterless version and a version that takes an integer that represents the amount of time the button is to remain pressed. The method delegates to the model to set the *Armed* and *Pressed* properties to *true*, which causes the usual flurry of property and state change events to be generated. The method then uses the *sleep()* method of *Thread* to wait the specified number of milliseconds before resetting the *Armed* and *Pressed* properties.

The parameterless version of the *doClick()* method invokes the parameterized version with a sleep time of 68 milliseconds. One can only imagine what dark secret this number might represent.

Button Borders and Margins

JFC buttons are implemented similarly to their *JLabel* counterparts in their capability to robustly arrange text and icons. The standard implementations of the look-and-feel delegates for button components are free to manage the interpretation of the contents of a button as well as what "decorations" are placed around the content to make it look like a button. Generally, the *Border* property specified by *JComponent* is used to provide these decorations.

AbstractButton supports an additional mechanism to suppress painting of border areas because some button implementations do not use borders to paint the button's view. The *setBorderPainted()* and *isBorderPainted()* methods mutate and access the *boolean* value of this property. *AbstractButton* overrides the *paintBorder()* method of *JComponent* and only invokes the superclass method, which actually paints the border using the border delegate specified by the *Border* property.

The capability exists to explicitly specify the margin between the button's border and its content. The *Margin* property is expressed as a *java.awt.Insets* object. As discussed in the first chapter on UI delegation, property values are tagged with the *UIResource* interface. This interface signals to the component that the *Insets* object used for the margin was set by a UI delegate. Thus, *AbstractButton* will attempt to cache the current margin value if it is an instance of *UIResource*. Setting the value of the *Margin* property to *null* will restore the original margin specified by the UI.

A property change event is fired every time the *Margin* property mutator is called, but the component is only revalidated and repainted if the new margin differs from the current value.

Button Focus

Buttons can optionally provide a visual indicator as to whether they currently own the keyboard focus. This is commonly rendered as a dashed rectangle around the button content. A property is provided by *AbstractButton* that enables suppression of the painting of focus indication on a per-component basis or by deriving from a button class.

The value of this property can be examined by the UI delegate when it determines whether to paint a focus indicator. The *BasicButtonUI* delegate implements the *paintFocus()* method as a "no-op," so it will have no effect on the base UI delegate.

Button Fill

Buttons derived from *AbstractButton* have a different mechanism for expressing their opacity because this quality differs in various LAF implementations. An additional property is provided, *ContentAreaFilled*, that takes the place of *isOpaque()* and *setOpaque()* for button components. The LAF-specific UI delegate can interpret this value in whatever way is desired. In the case of the *BasicButtonUI* class, the value of *ContentAreaFilled* is simply propagated to *Opaque*. Buttons found on the title bar of *JInternalFrame* have this property set to *false* to mimic the behavior of platform emulation LAFs.

Event Listeners

ButtonModel specifies three types of event listeners, *ActionListener*, *ChangeListener,* and *ItemListener*, each having its own corresponding event object and activation semantics.

Generally, *ActionListener* enables an event handler to be notified with the component's current action command string when the button's state is changed. *ChangeListener* provides a mechanism to detect when the state properties of a button component have changed, although the *ChangeEvent* object does not contain the actual properties that have mutated. It is included in the model for backward compatibility with AWT events, which do not provide this additional information. To partially compensate for this, you can use the *ItemListener* interface. The *ItemEvent*, unlike *ChangeEvent*, does contain one of the state property values, namely the *boolean* selection state. The *DefaultButtonModel* class also provides methods to fire each of these three events.

Button Listener Delegates

When a button component is created, additional objects are instantiated to support the interaction between the control and the user interface. All JFC components support a "UI" property that contains a reference to a delegate that manages the visual rendering and certain aspects of user interaction. Listener and other delegates are associated with a component by the pluggable look-and-feel (PLAF) facility of JFC, which is covered in great depth in two chapters of this book.

Although the complex issues surrounding delegation have not yet been covered, it is important to mention this particular aspect because it is so central to the function and capabilities of JFC button components. Button components use delegate objects that extend the *BasicButtonUI* class in the *javax.swing.plaf.basic* package to provide encapsulation of many of its capabilities including painting of the button interface. This package also contains a class *BasicButtonListener* that encapsulates all of the event handling capabilities into a single delegate. The method *createButtonListener()* is provided by *BasicButtonUI* and can be extended by PLAF classes. This method is responsible for providing a suitable implementation of *BasicButtonListener* that supports the look-and-feel-specific requirements. It takes a reference to an *AbstractButton* as a parameter and returns a reference to a instance of *BasicButtonListener*.

BasicButtonListener

BasicButtonListener implements the *MouseListener*, *MouseMotionListener*, *FocusListener*, *ChangeListener*, and *PropertyChangeListener* interfaces and provides a canonical implementation of all of the required methods.

Buttons use the *MouseListener* interface to detect mouse clicks, presses, and releases as well as rollover detection by interpreting enter and exit messages relative to the button's bounding rectangle. *MouseMotionListener* reports mouse movements and drag activities, although *BasicButtonListener* implements *mouseMove()* as a "no-op." The code for the *mouseDragged()* method contains a comment explaining how its use is a "hack" for the lack of reporting of *mouseEnter()* and *mouseExit()* events by *MouseListener* when the mouse button is down.

BasicButtonListener has implementations of *focusGained()* and *focusLost()* to manage the reassignment of the default button and to repaint the button when it loses focus. The default button is reassigned to the button receiving focus under the following circumstances:

- The button must be an instance of *JButton* because it's the only type of button that is capable of being a default button.

- The *JButton* must have its *DefaultCapable* property set to *true*. This property is discussed in the section detailing the *JButton* class.

- The *JButton* must have a *JRootPane* as a parent. This is because the method that supports assignment of the default button is handled by the *JRootPane* class. It is feasible to instantiate JFC components and add them to heavyweight containers, but it is not possible to make a button the default in this circumstance.

When focus is gained or lost, *BasicButtonListener* invokes the *repaint()* method to enqueue a repaint request. This behavior enables buttons to present different view characteristics when focus changes.

BasicButtonListener has an implementation of the *stateChanged()* method specified by the *ChangeListener* interface. When this event is received, a repaint request is enqueued using the *repaint()* method. This enables buttons to render changes in their armed, pressed, and selected states.

Finally, the *BasicButtonListener* class detects changes in two properties specified by *AbstractButton*: the *Mnemonic* property and the *ContentAreaFilled* property. The *ContentAreaFilled* property lets the opacity of buttons be controlled by the prevailing look-and-feel.

Button Keystroke Handling

Changes in the *Mnemonic* property are detected in *BasicButtonListener* and are used to trigger changes in the registered keystrokes for button components. These changes are actuated when the methods *uninstall KeyboardActions()* and *installKeyboardActions()* are invoked. The *uninstall KeyboardActions()* method resets all of the keyboard actions registered by

BasicButtonListener; installKeyboardActions() is invoked to register the new keystrokes specified by the new *Mnemonic* value and other applicable keystrokes.

The capability for handling these events is provided by two objects that inherit from *AbstractAction*. The *AbstractAction* class encapsulates a dictionary of information about programmable actions and is provided for simple keystroke action mapping as well as complex key sequences for editor components. The static inner classes that inherit from *AbstractAction* are *PressedAction* and *ReleasedAction*; they are defined as having "friendly" access.

The *actionPerformed()* method, which is invoked when these actions are triggered, delegates to the *ButtonModel* to manipulate its state properties. *PressedAction* sets the *Armed* and *Pressed* properties to *true*, which causes the button state to change as if is were clicked. In case the focus was lost during the processing of this action, it is once again requested. The *ReleasedAction* class sets the value of the *Pressed* property of the button to *false*, thus reversing the click action.

If a mnemonic is set, that is, if the integer value of the property is nonzero, the combination of the <Alt> key and the specified mnemonic keystroke is registered with the button for both the press and release of the mnemonic key sequence. A third keystroke is registered that handles the release of the mnemonic key if the <Alt> key was released during the actuation of the button.

All buttons are capable of being actuated by hitting the space bar when the button has focus. The <Enter> key is also a valid mechanism for invoking a button click unless the button is of type *JToggleButton*. <Spacebar> and <Enter> key actions are registered as only being active when the button has focus by specifying the *WHEN_FOCUSED* flag in the registration process. The same global action classes are used as for mnemonic keystrokes; the *PressedAction* and *ReleasedAction* objects for handling the spacebar are shared across all instances of *AbstractButton*.

AbstractButton Components

This section describes some of the specific characteristics of the components derived from *AbstractButton*.

JButton

JButton is a "momentary" button, meaning that its *Selected* state is directly linked to its *Pressed* and *Armed* states. *JButton* and its extensions are the only component that *JRootPane* recognizes as being capable of being a default button for a dialog box, window, or frame. Two properties are exclusive to *JButton*: *DefaultButton* and *DefaultCapable*. *DefaultButton* is a read-only *boolean* property that implements the *isDefaultButton()* method to query the enclosing *JRootPane* as to whether the button is the current default. The *DefaultCapable* property provides a *boolean* accessor and mutator that controls whether a button is allowed to become the default button for a root pane. This property does not change a button from being the default if this property is changed while it is the default button. It is used primarily by the *JToolbar* container to suppress setting of *JButton* objects it contains to be the default button.

JToggleButton

The other version of the push-button type of control is *JToggleButton*, which, unlike *JButton*, is not momentary and changes its selection state whenever it is pressed. To cause this specific behavior, *JToggleButton* implements a *public static* inner class that extends *DefaultButtonModel*. This class, *ToggleButtonModel*, overrides the *isSelected()*, *setSelected()*, and *setPressed()* methods to provide this alternate functionality.

The *setPressed()* method differs from that of the default model in that it fires its action command when the value changes, regardless of whether it is armed or not. In the *isSelected()* and *setSelected()* methods, the state of the button is delegated to an instance of *ButtonGroup* if one is associated with the component.

Button Group

ButtonGroup is a nonvisible object that manages groups of toggle-oriented buttons that need to have their selection states made exclusive. *ButtonGroup* is also commonly used with *JRadioButton* to create a mutually exclusive set of choices. *ButtonGroup* supports *add()* and *remove()* methods that take an *AbstractButton* as a parameter, allowing run-time assignment of buttons to groups. *ButtonGroup* also maintains a reference to the button model of the currently selected button that is delegated by implementations of *isSelected()* and *getSelected()*.

Because the components are managed by a *Vector*, *ButtonGroup* provides the capability of enumerating its contents using the *getElements()* method, which in turn invokes the *elements()* method of the managing *Vector*.

ButtonModel specifies a *setGroup()* method that is meant to be called by *ButtonGroup* when a button is added. This enables the button model to delegate to the *ButtonGroup* version of the appropriate model methods.

JCheckBox and JRadioButton

JCheckBox and *JRadioButton* are inherited from *JToggleButton* instead of directly from *AbstractButton*. Their function is virtually identical, although they are generally rendered with different selection state indicators. *JCheckBox* and *JRadioButton* both behave according to the rules of the *ToggleButtonModel*, although conventionally check boxes are used for nonexclusive choices and radio buttons for exclusive choices. Both have the capability of having their state managed by a *ButtonGroup* delegate.

These components rely completely on their UI delegates to implement their functionality and override very little of the support provided by *AbstractButton*. Both classes set the default value of *BorderPainted* to *false* and the *HorizontalAlignment* property to *LEFT*. An example of how to construct UI delegates for these components is described in the second chapter on UI delegation.

Fa-yen, a Chinese Zen master, overheard four monks arguing about subjectivity and objectivity. He joined them and said, "There is a large stone. Is this stone inside or outside your mind?" One monk replied, "The Buddha taught that everything is an objectification of mind, so I would say the stone is inside my mind." "In that case," observed Fa-yen, "your head must be very heavy indeed."

—Traditional Zen Aphorism

Chapter 4

JFC Containers

The Swing component set provides several very flexible and powerful containers. These containers are designed to aid in application design and to provide the capability to maximize the limited amount of screen real estate that an application is afforded.

This chapter examines these containers in detail. The discussions on each container's capabilities are accompanied by material from the UI delegate objects that render the interface for these containers.

JPanel

The implementation of *JPanel* is to serve as a *tabula rasa* (Lat. "empty drawing board"). It is a bare-bones implementation of *JComponent*. In other words, it is a JFC component in every way except that it does not paint anything other than its border and its background. However, because *JPanel* is a full implementation of *JComponent*, it can and does serve as the elementary JFC container.

In version 1.1 of JFC, *JPanel* is afforded all of the same capabilities from a UI delegate perspective as all other Swing components. Prior to this, *JPanel* did not have a UI delegate. This caused some unusual side effects in applications with dynamic layouts; because there was no UI delegate to calculate the preferred size, the panel layout manager's idea as to what the size should be was used. This was not always correct, especially in heavily nested sub-containers.

The default layout for *JPanel* is *java.awt.FlowLayout* and the default border is *null*. *JPanel* objects are initially created with double-buffering enabled and their *Opaque* property set to *true*. You can find more information on these properties in the chapter focusing on the *JComponent* base class.

Box and BoxLayout

Another general container, *javax.swing.Box*, is provided by the Swing component set. It is used to provide a canonical implementation of a JFC layout called *BoxLayout*. *Box* objects come in two flavors, which match the two directions in which a *BoxLayout* operates. Box does not inherit from *JComponent* and does not have a UI delegate. Its layout provides all of its containment functionality.

Creating a Box

The constant values *BoxLayout.X_AXIS* and *BoxLayout.Y_AXIS* define the two types of *Box* that can be created. One of these must be specified either in the *Box* constructor or by using the *createHorizontalBox()* or *createVerticalBox()* static methods in the *Box* class. The axis of a *Box* cannot be altered after it is created.

Although the *BoxLayout* is a legitimate layout manager that is suitable for any container class, *Box* does not allow changes to its layout manager and throws an *AWTError* exception if its *setLayout()* method is invoked. Multiple containers cannot share a single instance of *BoxLayout*. If this is attempted, an *AWTError* is thrown.

Box Components

The purpose of a *Box* object is not just to provide an easy method of instantiating a layout manager. *Box* and *BoxLayout* recognize certain child components as having special behavior with regard to layout management. Several *static* methods are provided to create these invisible components.

Glue Components

A "glue" is an invisible component that expands to take up as much space as possible between two components. Glue components can be created to suit the type of *Box* they are being used in or to behave in two dimensions.

The static method *createGlue()* creates a glue component that operates in two directions. It is suitable for use in either vertical or horizontal *Box* components. There are versions *createHorizontalGlue()* and *createVerticalGlue()*, also *static*, that provide components suitable for those type of boxes.

Strut Components

Whereas glue components shrink and expand to fit the leftover space between components, the strut is used to create an invisible component that has a fixed size in either the vertical or horizontal *Box* layouts. The *static* methods *createVerticalStrut()* and *createHorizontalStrut()* take an integer parameter representing the size, in pixels, that the strut will occupy. Struts are therefore used to maintain equal distance between box components when their containers are resized.

Rigid Area Components

Box enables the creation of a two-dimensional area whose maximum, minimum, and preferred sizes are immutable. The static method *createRigidArea()* takes a *Dimension* object as a parameter and returns an invisible component with these properties. Rigid areas are used to ensure a fixed rectangular space in a layout. Comments in the code suggest that the use of rigid areas could be eliminated by judicious use of strut components.

The Filler Component

Filler is a *public static* inner class of *Box* that provides a base class for the rigid area, strut, and glue components. It is an extension of the *Container* class. Although the direction of a *Box* cannot be changed, the sizes of its invisible subcomponents can be changed using the *changeShape()* method of *Box.Filler*.

In the strut implementation *Box.Filler,* vertical struts have zero width and a fixed height, and horizontal struts have a fixed width and zero height. Glue components have a maximum size of *Short.MAX_VALUE* in their specific direction and a minimum and preferred size of zero. Rigid areas have fixed minimum, maximum, and preferred sizes that can be any integer value.

How BoxLayout Operates

BoxLayout is an implementation of *java.awt.LayoutManager2*. Nonetheless, it provides empty implementations for both versions of *addLayoutComponent()* and also for *removeLayoutComponent()*. The *layoutContainer()* method, as usual for many layout managers, does the majority of the work.

Although *BoxLayout* functions differently for the two supported axes, its fundamental algorithm is the same. For a horizontal box, the layout height is calculated to be the largest height of all of its children. The width is calculated by adding up the widths of all components. For a vertical box, the opposite process occurs: the maximum width is established and the heights of all components totalled. *BoxLayout* caches as much of this information as possible, discarding it only when the *invalidateLayout()* method is invoked.

It is the fact that *BoxLayout* caches its preferred, maximum, and minimum sizes that makes it unsuitable for being shared by multiple containers.

Box Example

In many applications, a button bar is provided that centers buttons along the bottom of a dialog box or frame. Although the same effect could be achieved using *GridBagLayout* or perhaps *FlowLayout*, *BoxLayout* is an ideal alternative.

The requirements for this example are a container that supports three buttons. The buttons are to remain equidistant from each other, but should be centered on the X-axis. The following code produces just such a container:

import javax.swing.*;

```
    . . .
    // Create the box container
    Box box = Box.createHorizontalBox();
    // Add the first glue
    box.add(Box.createHorizontalGlue());
    // Add a button and a ten-pixel strut
    box.add(okButton);
    box.add(Box.createHorizontalStrut(10));
    // Add a button and a ten-pixel strut
    box.add(cancelButton);
    // Add a button and the last glue
    box.add(Box.createHorizontalStrut(10));
    box.add(retryButton);
    box.add(Box.createHorizontalGlue());
    this.getContentPane().add(box);
    . . .
```

This construction produces the effects shown in Figure 4-1 when a container is resized. The strut and button size remains constant and the "glue" components take up the extra space.

Scrolling

JFC components, unlike many of their heavyweight counterparts, do not have built-in support for scrolling their content. Instead, a more robust model-oriented approach is taken that enables not only pluggable look-and-feel but an entirely self-contained component hierarchy. This also

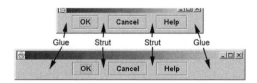

Figure 4-1. *Boxes: glues and struts*

allows support for additional value-added features such as row and column headers and "Autoscrolling" when the user drags the selection to the extents of the viewport.

JScrollPane

Scrolling capability is encapsulated in a container class called *JScrollPane*. Its primary child component is a "viewport" that, in turn, manages the component being scrolled. See Figure 4-2.

The viewport itself is implemented by the *JViewport* class. *JScrollPane* manages the main viewport and two additional viewports that serve as the row and column headers. Two scroll bars and four corner components make up the remainder of the direct children of *JScrollPane*. See Figure 4-3.

ScrollPane Constants

This interface defines many important constants that are used by *JScrollPane* and its related components. Some are apparently less important than others, as two constants are defined here that are not found anywhere in the JFC source. Table 4-1 lists the constants.

ScrollPaneLayout

This layout is designed specifically for the *JScrollPane* implementation. Its purpose is to manage the size and position of the subcomponents of the scroll pane.

Figure 4-2. *JScrollPane container*

ScrollPaneLayout implements the *java.awt.LayoutManager* interface and uses the "old" style of constraint specification, which supports only the *String* type.

The method *syncWithScrollPane()* is used when the layout manager is assigned to a scroll pane. Its single parameter is a reference to a *JScrollPane* component. When invoked, the code in *syncWithScrollPane()* queries the *JScrollPane* for references to its child components, of which copies are stored internally. This method can be overridden by classes that derive from *ScrollPaneLayout* to change its component storage characteristics. The *syncWithScrollPane()* is used in one other important place: It is invoked by the base UI delegate for the scroll pane when it detects a *ChangeEvent* from its contained viewport.

A protected method, *addSingletonComponent()*, is used by the implementation of *addLayoutComponent()*. Its function is to ensure that only one component of each of the specified children of *JScrollPane* is associ-

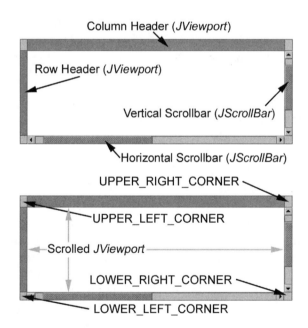

Figure 4-3. *JScrollPane schema*

Table 4-1. *JScrollPane constants*

Constant	Usage/Meaning
VIEWPORT	Layout constraint
VERTICAL_SCROLLBAR	Layout constraint
HORIZONTAL_SCROLLBAR	Layout constraint
ROW_HEADER	Layout constraint
COLUMN_HEADER	Layout constraint
LOWER_LEFT_CORNER	Layout constraint
LOWER_RIGHT_CORNER	Layout constraint
UPPER_LEFT_CORNER	Layout constraint
UPPER_RIGHT_CORNER	Layout constraint
VERTICAL_SCROLLBAR_POLICY	Not implemented
VERTICAL_SCROLLBAR_AS_NEEDED	Scrollbar Policy Value
VERTICAL_SCROLLBAR_NEVER	Scrollbar Policy Value
VERTICAL_SCROLLBAR_ALWAYS	Scrollbar Policy Value
HORIZONTAL_SCROLLBAR_POLICY	Not implemented
HORIZONTAL_SCROLLBAR_AS_NEEDED	Scrollbar Policy Value
HORIZONTAL_SCROLLBAR_NEVER	Scrollbar Policy Value
HORIZONTAL_SCROLLBAR_ALWAYS	Scrollbar Policy Value

ated with the container at any one time. The effect of this is that when a new component is added to the layout, the pre-existing one is automatically removed. The different component types are represented by static integers in the *ScrollPaneConstants* interface. It is recommended that *addLayoutComponent()* not be called directly and that the property mutator methods supported by *JScrollPane* be used instead.

An unusual pair of methods is contained in the *ScrollPaneLayout*: a property interface to the vertical and horizontal scroll bar policies. These are nearly identical to that of *JScrollBar* except the mutator is not implemented as bound. These methods are not actually used by the layout manager, so it is likely that they will be deprecated and should not be used.

Also found in the class are accessor versions of the component properties that are used internally by the layout. Again, it is recommended that these operations be performed on the *JScrollPane* itself. The basic reason for this is that it is possible for *ScrollPaneLayout()* to be over-ridden to provide alternate layout behavior. Addressing these property values in a derived version of the layout may cause unpredictable results.

The Scrollable Interface

Although the *JScrollPane* component operates on any component contained in a suitable viewport, an interface exists that components may implement to deliver additional communications between the scroll pane and its content. The scrollable interface specifies methods that a component can use to set specific scrolling characteristics that are conventionally defined within each component. It is implemented by the JFC components that are generally expected to be used in a scroll pane, namely *JList, JTree, JTable,* and *JTextComponent* (the base class for JFC editing components).

The *Scrollable* interface enables a component to define scrolling increments for both axes. Two forms of scrolling are defined: unit and block. Although these terms are free to be interpreted by the implementing component, unit scrolling is roughly equivalent to a single row in a list or table, whereas block scrolling is a larger increment that could represent a page of rows or a paragraph.

The methods that are used to report this information, *getScrollableUnitIncrement()* and *getScrollableBlockIncrement(),* take the same parameters. The first parameter is an instance of *Rectangle* that represents the amount of pixels in either direction that the unit or block increment will scroll. The second parameter is the orientation of the scroll operation. This is provided to enable specification for horizontal and vertical scrolling with the same method. The allowed values for orientation are either *VERTICAL* or *HORIZONTAL* as defined in *SwingConstants.* The last parameter represents the direction of the scroll operation. It conventionally has a negative value to specify increments for scrolling up and left, and positive values for down and right. This enables a component to specify different increments for different scroll directions if so desired.

The method *getPreferredScrollableViewportSize()* looks similar to the *getPreferredSize()* method of *java.awt.Component* and is analogous. Both methods return an object of type *Dimension* that represents a preferred size.

The version in *Component* and its subclasses is used to inform a container what size a component wishes to be, while the *getPreferredScrollable ViewportSize()* method is used by a scrollable component to inform a scroll pane what the preferred size of the viewport should be. Obviously, these concepts are different in practice; setting the preferred size of a component is not effective in determining the required size of its viewport.

Two other methods are defined by the Scrollable interface, *getScrollableTracksViewportWidth()* and *getScrollableTracksViewportHeight()*, both of which return a *boolean*. Although the names are daunting, their purpose is straightforward. If a component returns *true* to one of these methods it means that the component is tracking the viewport's height or width for the purpose of determining its own size. In other words, when the component returns *true* for these methods, it means it is not scrollable in that direction because it will take up exactly the size of the viewport for whichever direction is specified. An example of where this method returns *true* is in the implementation of *JTable*. *JTable* has a flag that sets the column widths to be "autosized." When this flag is set, the table gives equal space to each column, taking up the exact width of the viewport and inhibiting scrolling. Perhaps more sensible names for these methods might be *isTrackingViewportHeight()* and *isTrackingViewportWidth()*.

Scroll Pane UI Delegation

The class *BasicScrollPaneUI* contains the base class used as the UI delegate for *JScrollPane*. Apart from providing the typical features of a UI delegate class, such as installation of defaults and painting of the component, *BasicScrollPaneUI* also manages several listener interfaces that are important to the coordination of scroll pane components.

BasicScrollPaneUI installs listeners that listen for changes in the *BoundedRangeModel* objects managed by its two scroll panes and for any *ChangeEvent* objects generated when certain characteristics of the viewport change, such as the size of its content or a change in its extent. These properties are covered in depth in the section of this chapter focusing on the *JViewport* component, which is JFC's implementation of a scrollable viewport.

The base UI delegate also installs several keyboard actions by default. Because the orientation of a scroll bar is modifiable, actions are implemented that have meaning in either scrolling direction. The six actions implemented use a private abstract class *ScrollPaneAction* that extends *AbstractAction* to provide targets for the keystroke registration.

By default, the <Page Up>key is mapped to the *ScrollUp* and *ScrollLeft* actions and the <Page Down> key to *ScrollDown* and *ScrollRight*. Additional keystrokes are registered for the <Home> and <End> keys to the *ScrollHome* and *ScrollEnd* actions. Because scroll bars rarely change their orientation dynamically, it is worthwhile to consider the merit of only registering for the appropriate actions when the orientation of the scroll bar is set. This is detectable by the UI because the *Orientation* property of *JScrollBar* is bound.

A protected method *syncScrollPaneWithViewport()* is provided by the UI delegate, which is analogous to the *syncWithScrollPane()* methods of *ScrollPaneLayout*. This method is called by the viewport change handler and refreshes the UI's references to the scroll pane components much in the same way that *syncWithScrollPane()* refreshes the layout.

Several protected methods are provided to handle property changes for the scroll bar policies and the content of the three viewports: the main viewport, the row header, and the column header. The *updateViewport()* method is invoked when a new viewport object is added to a scroll pane. This method switches the change listener to the new viewport and updates the view position as needed. The *updateRowHeader()* and *updateColumnHeader()* are called when those components are changed. The UI delegate adjusts the viewport and scroll bars to accommodate the new header components. When the scroll policy is changed for either scroll bar, the protected method *updateScrollBarPolicy()* is invoked; this method revalidates and repaints the entire scroll pane.

JScrollBar

The scroll bar component is used by *JScrollPane* to provide a user the ability to change the viewport position and, consequentially, the appearance of its content. Scroll bars are a familiar paradigm to users acquainted with graphical interfaces. The primary function of a scroll bar is to provide a continuous set of values for selection. In the case of the scroll pane, these values are represented by the minimum and maximum positions of the content of the viewport.

JScrollBar can be operated in two orientations, *Horizontal* or *Vertical*. The *Horizontal* orientation enables a user to select a value along the X-axis; the *Vertical* orientation manages the Y-axis. The orientation of the scroll bar can be changed dynamically (although there is rarely a reason to do so) or set with a constructor parameter.

Because *JScrollBar* does not support labeling or tick marks, the *JSlider* component is generally considered to be more useful than a standalone scroll bar. For this reason, scroll bars are rarely used outside the scroll pane container.

The *JScrollBar* component defines five areas that are treated as sub-components (see Figure 4-4). At the end of the scroll bar are two scroll buttons, that serve to move the scroll position one increment in the direction of the button. If the button is clicked while the scroll bar is in the maximum or minimum position, the button has no effect. The buttons are separated by a track that serves as the area in which the scroll thumb moves.

The thumb is used for three purposes: It serves to denote the scroll position by its proximity to the ends of the track and also as a drag handle for arbitrarily positioning the scroll content when the mouse button is clicked, held, and dragged inside its borders. The size of the thumb also signifies the amount of visible content relative to the scroll container: If the content is much larger than the viewport, the thumb appears smaller, thus informing the user that a larger number of scroll bar movements are needed to traverse the data. When the content is only slightly smaller than the scroll pane, the thumb may take up nearly all of the area allowed for its track.

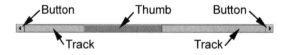

Figure 4-4. *JScrollBar component*

The track itself is aware of mouse input. A mouse click on the track, as opposed to the scroll button itself, causes a block scroll, equivalent to a page up/page down sequence for a vertical scroll, but operable in the horizontal direction as well. Most scroll bar implementations highlight the track when it is clicked for additional user feedback.

BoundedRangeModel

This interface defines a data and state model for *JScrollBar* as well as *JSlider* and *JProgressBar*. JFC provides a canonical implementation of this model called *DefaultBoundedRangeModel*. Its fundamental purpose is to define four integer properties, *minimum*, *maximum*, *extent*, and *value*. The combination of these values represents both the available set of data as well as additional information defining selection characteristics. A *BoundedRangeModel* is required to maintain the following relationship among these values such that

minimum <= value <= value + extent <= maximum.

The *minimum* and *maximum* values represent the inclusive range of allowed integer values. The *value* property must have a value somewhere between the two. Another property called *extent* is defined; its purpose is to show how much of a range is visible. It is used in the implementation of the *JScrollBar* class to control the relative size of the thumb button. The implementation of the model must either adjust these four values as necessary to preserve the specified relationship or throw appropriate exceptions.

Properties

The model's values are managed by a set of properties that, in the default implementation, are not bound; changes in these values are reported as *ChangeEvents* and detected using a *ChangeListener* implementation. The model supports *Minimum*, *Maximum*, *Value,* and *Extent* properties that are expected to have values according to the rules of *BoundedRangeModel*.

Another property is available called *ValueIsAdjusting;* its purpose is to clarify the state of the component as to why the values are changing. Basically, the *ValueIsAdjusting* property is set when the model is undergoing a rapid set of incremental changes. A listener can decide whether to ignore events generated when the value of this property is *true*, because there is high likelihood that it will change again soon. When the value of this property is false, the change can be expected to be permanent. The archetypal use of this property is by the *JScrollBar* component. When a user clicks and drags the scroll bar "thumb," events are continuously generated with the *ValueIsAdjusting* property set to *true*. When the user lets go of the thumb, the value is set back to *false* and the thumb stays in its position.

Another method is required by the interface. The *setRangeProperties()* method enables the setting of all five properties with a single method call. In the *DefaultBoundedRangeModel* implementation, all of the property changes are ultimately done with this method. This is a convenient place for the firing of the change event.

Lastly, the model provides two methods that are used to maintain a list of interested listeners for *ChangeEvent* activity. Note that the *ChangeEvent* object does not report the changed values of the model, as is the case with a bound property change. The event is used to signal a listener to examine the model values manually when the event arrives. Because a listener must have a reference to the model to add itself to the interest list, it is presumed it has access to the values as well. In the case of a bound property change, the receiver may or may not have actual access to the property value.

JScrollBar Value Properties

JScrollBar provides several methods that delegate to the *BoundedRangeModel* that represents both the data and the state of the component. A method is provided, *setValues()*, that updates each of the four elements managed by the model interface, namely the current value, the extent, the maximum value, and the minimum value. The *ValueIsAdjusting* property, which is bound, is also supported and represents a state in which additional changes to the model are expected immediately.

In the *JScrollBar* component, the *Value* property is bound, although it is not bound by the default implementation of the model (*DefaultBoundedRangeModel*). The methods *getValue()* and *setValue()* retrieve or update the current position of the scroll thumb. The *VisibleAmount* property represents the *extent* value of the model, which, in the case of

JScrollBar, is defined as the proportional size of the thumb to the range of the model. If the extent is closer in value to the maximum, the scroll button appears larger. The *Minimum* and *Maximum* properties manage the minimum and maximum allowed values of the scroll bar. See Figure 4-5.

The *ValueIsAdjusting* property signifies whether the current *Value* property is likely to change again in a short time. Generally, this property will be *true* when the scroll bar thumb is being dragged. Many implementations ignore value changes until the value of this property changes to *false* to avoid multiple redrawing of contents when unnecessary. The accessor method for this property is *getValueIsAdjusting()*.

JScrollBar relies on the model implementation to ensure that the specified relationships of values are maintained. See the section on *BoundedRangeModel* for an explanation of this dependence.

Other JScrollBar Properties

The *Model* property accesses a scroll bar's data model or supplies it with a new one. *JScrollBar* uses *BoundedRangeModel* as its data and state model. Many of the properties of *JScrollBar* delegate directly to the model associated with the component. The model property is bound to enable interested listeners to add themselves to a new model when it becomes active.

The *Orientation* property of the scroll bar can have the value *HORIZONTAL* or *VERTICAL*. This value does not affect its behavior with

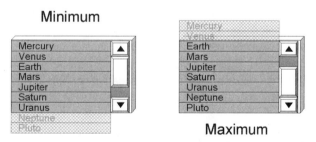

Figure 4-5. *Scrolliing positions*

regard to how it interprets model data and user interaction, except in the differences among the keystrokes that are generally bound, such as the left–right or up–down arrow keys.

JScrollBar supports *UnitIncrement* and *BlockIncrement* properties that control how much a scroll bar will scroll depending on whether it was changed by a click on the scroll buttons or track, or through the use of a keystroke binding. The unit increment controls how much the scroll bar will change when the arrow keys are used or when the scroll bar buttons are pressed. The default value of this property is 1.

The block increment is intended to represent a large change in the scroll bar position. It is used when the page-up/page-down keys are used or when a user clicks inside the scroll track. Its default value is set to the initial *extent* of the scroll bar, if it is greater than zero, or 1 if the *extent* is zero. Bear in mind that the *JScrollBar* component does not do any value checking on the unit or block increment properties, so be cautious that it is not set to a value that may confuse a user.

Backward Compatibility with AWT

According to the design principles of Swing, compatibility with AWT was to be preserved wherever feasible. In the case of *JScrollBar,* it was deemed appropriate to retain the AWT event structure because many pre-existing classes might have written code around it. So, for at least the foreseeable future, the *AdjustmentListener* mechanism will be retained. *JScrollBar* provides a private inner class that serves to reflect the model changes as reported through the *ChangeListener* interface to those implementing *AdjustmentListener*. Note that there is an imperfect mapping of the two event types.

Also, two additional versions of property accessors are provided: parameterless implementations of *getUnitIncrement()* and *getBlockIncrement()*. It makes little difference which one is used because version 1.1 of JFC ignores the *direction* parameter.

ScrollBarUI Delegate

The base class that provides the UI delegate, *BasicScrollBarUI*, is discussed in detail in the second chapter in the UI delegation section. In this section, an example of an alternative rendering of a scroll bar is provided; this is a much more appropriate place to discuss these complex details.

JViewport

The *JViewport* class is one of the most interesting and robust components in the JFC architecture. Its primary purpose is to provide a "window" through which the content of a scroll pane can be viewed. When the scroll bars are moved, it is *JViewport* that actually moves over the rendered image of the scroll pane content. *JViewport* is also uniquely designed to take advantage of some substantial performance enhancements.

Although *JViewport* is an extension of *JComponent* and has its own UI delegate, it does provide its own version of the *java.awt.Component* version of the *paint()* method. Although this breaks the pattern of JFC components, this alternate painting mechanism enables *JViewport* to operate on an off-screen image of its content. This capability is known as a backing store and it supersedes the normal double-buffering capability. The use of a backing store is manageable through a *boolean* parameter called *BackingStoreEnabled.* The method *isOptimizedDrawingEnabled()* is overridden to return *false,* disabling *JComponent* and other code from using double-buffering. See Figure 4-6.

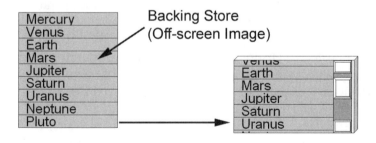

Figure 4-6. *Backing store example*

JViewport does not support the use of a *Border* and throws an exception if one is set. Due to this characteristic, the *Insets* of *JViewport* are hardcoded to return zero insets. Both implementations of *getInsets()* are *final,* so this behavior is not modifiable.

JViewport manages only a single child component, which is manipulated with the help of a specialized layout, *ViewportLayout.* To ensure that only one component is contained in a *JViewport,* the protected *addImpl()* method of *java.awt.Container* is overridden.

JViewport Properties

The *View* property represents the component that the viewport is managing. The *getView()* method returns *null* if the viewport is empty. The *setView()* method updates the current viewport contents by first removing any child components from the container, adding the new view component and lastly initializing a *ComponentListener* to detect size changes in the content.

Two properties control the size and position of the view relative to its content. The *ViewSize* property is used to manage the size. It delegates to the component contained by the viewport to retrieve its size using *getSize()* if the size is explicitly set, or the preferred size if not. Using *setViewSize()* changes the size of the view component explicitly, setting a flag indicating that the preferred size should not be used. This flag is set to *false* by default and does not appear to have any mechanism to reset its value once it has been triggered by *setViewSize()* short of reinvoking *setView().* Both methods check if the view is *null* before performing these operations.

The *ViewPosition* property specifies the view coordinates in the upper-left corner of the viewport. When *setViewPostion()* is invoked, the position is adjusted to ensure that it lies within the bounds of the view. Both *setViewPosition()* and *getViewPosition()* change the signs of their integer components to make them conventionally consistent. Another method *getViewRect()* returns the size and position as a *Rectangle.*

A property called *ExtentSize* also provides methods to alter the actual size of the visible part of the view. The *getExtentSize()* and *setExtentSize()* methods are used by the *JScrollPane* to adjust the scroll bar extent characteristics. This is reflected in a change of the scroll thumb size relative to the track.

JViewport Methods

An alternative method can be used to cause a particular area of a viewport to be made visible. *JViewport* overrides the *scrollRectToVisible()* method implemented in *JComponent* to adjust the position of the view so that the specified *Rectangle* is visible.

Additional Painting Support

JViewport provides an overridden version of *repaint()* as an alternative to that of *JComponent*. Its purpose is to ensure that when the *RepaintManager* is called, its dirty region is in the parent coordinate system. This is accomplished by deriving the parent of the viewport through *getParent()* and calling *repaint()* on the parent object. The effect of this procedure is that *RepaintManager* is invoked only once. If the viewport has no parent, the superclass version is invoked.

The *reshape()* method is also overridden. The version of the method in *JViewport* checks if the size (not the position) of the bounds has changed. If so, it sets an internal flag and sets the reference to the backing store to *null*, thus disabling use of the off-screen image used to cache the view of the content. After calling the superclass version of *reshape()*, it checks the flag again and fires a state change event if it is *true*.

View Coordinate Conversion

Two methods of *JViewport* are designed to be implemented in a subclass that interprets its content coordinates differently. These methods enable the establishment of a "logical" coordinate system that differs from the physical coordinate system. A logical coordinate system can behave in any conceivable way, including scaling, logarithmic calculations, or with any deterministic set of conversion rules.

To implement a logical coordinate system, override both versions of the method *toViewCoordinates()*. One version takes a *Dimension* parameter and returns a *Dimension* object with its values converted to the values specified by the conversion algorithm; the other takes a *Point* object and returns a converted *Point*. The *Dimension* version is used primarily to implement size conversions; the *Point* version generally reserved for location calculation. It is essential to implement these methods consistently if they are overridden.

The default implementation of *toViewCoordinates()* returns their parameters unaltered, thus enforcing the physical coordinate system.

JSplitPane

The splitter pane is a commonly used method to help components effectively share screen real estate. The *JSplitPane* class is JFC's implementation of splitter panes; it is implemented primarily by a base UI delegate and a set of inner classes that implement two special layout managers.

The *JSplitPane* component supports the management of two child components and manages the amount of size allocated to each with a divider. The divider can be dragged with a mouse click to change the relative sizes and can also be modified programmatically to give a proportional or fixed amount of space to its children. See Figure 4-7.

Split Pane Orientation

The *JSplitPane* operates in a horizontal or vertical orientation, which can be dynamically modified by the *Orientation* property. In the horizontal orientation, which is the default, the components are displayed side-by-side and referred to as the "left" and "right" components. In the vertical orientation, the child panes are oriented on top of one another and referred to as the top and bottom components. If the orientation changes, the left component becomes the top and the right becomes the bottom (and vice versa). The *Orientation* must have the values *JSplitPane.HORIZONTAL_SPLIT* or *JSplitPane.VERTICAL_SPLIT* or an exception is thrown. The property is also bound so the component and the UI delegate can make the necessary layout changes.

Specifying Child Components

JSplitPane has many mechanisms to assign components to the two panes provided. The constructors of this class provide the capability to assign the two components, and several additional methods are provided to enable dynamic modification of these.

The methods *setLeftComponent()* and *setTopComponent()* are interchangeable, as are *setRightComponent()* and *setBottomComponent()*. These methods also have interchangeable analogs to retrieve references to the child components. These methods do not map to bound properties because they use overridden versions of the *add()* and *remove()* methods of *Container*, which automatically causes the layout of the split pane to be recalculated. Either or both components can be set to *null*.

The behavior of the split pane with regard to its children is defined almost exclusively by the UI delegate (*BasicSplitPaneUI*) and the two layout managers that it implements.

Split Pane Redrawing

Some of the constructors of *JSplitPane*, have the capability to set a property that causes the child components of the split pane to be continually updated as the position of the divider changes. This *boolean* property, which is bound, can also be modfied using the *setContinuousLayout()* method and its value determined with the *isContinuousLayout()* accessor. If the value of this property is *false*, the sizes of the child components are updated only after the divider drag operation ends.

The Split Pane Divider

An additional component is provided by *JSplitPane* that enables the relative sizes of the panes containing the child components to be changed. This divider responds to both mouse and keyboard operations to enable adjustment of its position. When the divider position is adjusted, the proportionate size of the child windows is changed accordingly. Properties are provided for manipulation of many different visual and behavioral characteristics of the divider.

The divider is actually derived from *Container* and not *JComponent*. It is created by the split pane UI delegate using an overridable method, and can thus have alternative implementations in different look-and-feels. It is not considered a heavyweight component even though it implements the AWT-style *paint()* method.

Moving the Divider

The divider is moved by the application user by a mouse click and drag sequence. Clicking and holding the divider activates it, causing it to change position as the mouse position changes. When the mouse button is released, the divider deactivates and the panes are resized according to the new position. If *ContinuousLayout* is *true*, the panes are continually resized as mouse motion events are received.

The keyboard can also be used as an alternative to the mouse. The base UI delegate for the divider registers actions for the four arrow keys, the <Home> key, and the <End> key. These actions are activated when the <F8> key is toggled and the input focus is in any child component of *JSplitPane*. When <F8> is pressed, the divider changes color to denote that it has the input focus. The arrow key moves the dividers in the specified direction. The <Home> and <End> keys move the divider to its minimum and maximum positions. When <F8> is pressed again, the divider reverts to its normal appearance.

Divider Size

The divider generally takes up the entire width or height of the split pane depending on the orientation. The thickness of the divider is controlled by a bound property *DividerSize*. Both the UI delegate of the split pane as well as the divider register interest in this property change. The split pane readjusts its children according to its layout algorithm, taking into account the change to the divider size.

Divider Location Property

The location of the divider can be set programmatically as well as through keyboard and mouse input. The *DividerLocation* property controls the position of the divider; it represents a distance (in pixels) from the edge of the split pane to the edge of the divider. The layout managers in the UI delegate ensure that the actual position of the divider is reasonable. If the value is negative, for example, the actual value is recalculated by the layout and propagated to the UI.

An alternative version of the mutator method is provided that takes a *double* as a parameter. The parameter is used as a proportional value to determine the divider position instead of a pixel count. The method enforces the range of the value to be between 0.0 and 1.0; an *IllegalArgumentException* is thrown if an unacceptable value is passed. The proportion represents the relative size of the left component in a horizontal orientation or the top component in a vertical. This method is the best way of ensuring a divider is completely exposing one or the other component.

It is important to remember that the *DividerLocation* property is not bound. When its mutator property is invoked, no event is fired. A call to *revalidate()* causes the layout manager of the split pane to recalculate the new cell sizes and divider position. This is probably necessary because of the rapid location changes that could occur with the continuous layout mode. If this property were bound it would have to go through at least one event handling cycle before the UI delegate would be notified of the change. It would probably just invoke a *revalidate()* anyway, so a potentially expensive step is avoided.

The location of the divider is initially set to accommodate the preferred size of the left or top component.

Last Divider Location

The split pane component also supports tracking of the last location where a splitter's divider was found. This is used in an important calculation: When a divider is dragged, it is ghosted, meaning that the divider itself stays in place and a gray rectangle (or whatever the UI provides) is superimposed over the child panes. The *LastDividerLocation* property is bound because it is not a value that will change rapidly when a drag operation is in progress. To be specific, it is changed to the position at the beginning of the drag operation after the *revalidate()* and *repaint()* methods are invoked. This actually leads to the introduction of an error, because the location of the beginning of the drag is not exactly the same as the divider position. This two-pixel defect is introduced because the calculation does not take into account the width of the border of the divider; its default is one pixel, multiplied by two for symmetry.

The one-touch expandibility feature of the *JSplitPane* uses the last divider location as does the keyboard interface. Both of these mechanisms need to remember where the divider was before it was moved to the edge of the split pane.

Two additional location-related properties are supported by *JSplitPane*. The *MinimumDividerLocation* and *MaximumDividerLocation* properties are of *integer* type and are read-only. This method is delegated to the *SplitPaneUI* delegate and its purpose is to report the smallest and largest allowable values for the divider given the current child component bounds. It main purpose seems to be a mechanism that supports an *Accessibility* property for returning the screen position as a selectable number. It is read-only because it is not a useful capability to alter these values.

It is also suggested that it would be irresponsible to mention that the names of these properties should use the adjectives *Minimal* and *Maximal* instead of the noun versions.

One-Touch Expandability

A bound *boolean* property is provided that gives an extra interface feature. When this property is set to *true*, the UI delegate for the divider provides two child components that can serve to move the divider all the way to the minimum and maximum divider locations.

In the same fashion as the keyboard mechanism for moving the divider, the one-touch mechanism moves the cursor to the edge if the divider is anywhere in the center of the split pane. If the divider is already on the edge, clicking the one-touch button to move the divider in the opposite direction causes the divider to return to the *LastDividerLocation* position. Another click brings the divider to the opposite edge of the container.

SplitPaneUI Delegates

Most of the actual work done by *JSplitPane* is done in its UI delegate classes. The base class *SplitPaneUI* is unusual in that it defines some additional abstract methods. It specifies the UI version of the *DividerLocation* property that takes a reference to a *JSplitPane* as an additional parameter. This, of course, is the interface that the component delegates to manage these values. The same holds true for the read-only property methods *getMinimumDividerLocation()* and *getMaximumDividerLocation()*; they require a reference to the split pane component to operate at the UI level.

Two additional methods are specified, *resetToPreferredSizes() and finishedPaintingChildren()*. The first method is specified because it is an additional method provided by the layout managers implemented within the *BasicSplitPaneUI* class, which serve to delegate this feature. The second is used to provide the ghost rectangle that appears above the child panes when the divider is in a drag operation. The UI needs this signal to ensure that the child windows do not obscure the "ghost" divider.

This *BasicSplitPaneUI* delegate provides most of the functionality used to implement the *JSplitPane* features, but it cooperates with the divider component and its UI delegate, *BasicSplitPaneDivider*. The divider itself, which is a component created for each instance of *JSplitPane*, is created by the method *createDefaultDivider()* invoked when the UI defaults are installed. Overridding *createDefaultDivider()* enables the capability for look-and-feel implementations of different divider components. The component must inherit from *BasicSplitPaneDivider*, but is free to implement any interface characteristics that can be supported.

Another divider is provided internally for the UI delegate. The *NonContinuousLayoutDivider* is actually a created as an extension of *java.awt.Canvas,* a heavyweight component. This is only used in dragging operations on split panes with their *ContinuousLayout* property set to *false*. When it is set to *true*, the divider is not ghosted during drag operations; the divider itself is repainted in as the mouse drags occur.

UI Delegate Listeners

The basic delegate for split pane installs several event listeners that it uses to provide its behavior. Each of these listeners is instantiated by a *protected* method that may be overridden in a class that extends *BasicSplitPaneUI*.

The method *createPropertyChangeListener()* returns an instance of *PropertyChangeListener* and registers it with the split pane instance that is associated with the delegate. The default implementation creates an instance of an inner class *PropertyHandler*. The property changes that are being listened for in the basic implementation are the *Orientation* and the *ContinuousLayout* properties. If the orientation dynamically changes, the associated layout managers must also be changed. The method *resetLayoutManager()* is invoked to create a layout manager suitable for the new orientation.

The *createFocusListener()* method is used to provide a *FocusListener* that is added to the split pane. The default implementation listens only for the *focusLost()* event. When the split pane loses focus, it is used as an indicator that the keystroke toggle should be reset. This prevents steal-

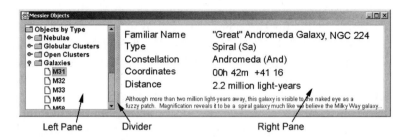

Figure 4-7. *JSplitPane example*

ing of registered keystrokes from child components after the use has finished resizing the split pane with the keyboard.

Lastly, the UI installs five keyboard listeners that listen for the split pane resizing keystrokes. The five methods *createKeyboardUpLeftListener()*, *createKeyboardDownRightListener()*, *createKeyboardHomeListener()*, *create KeyboardEndListener()*, and the tersely named *createKeyboardResizeToggle Listener()*. Each of these methods returns an instance of an *ActionListener* that is used to register the keystroke actions that provide the keyboard interface. The *protected* method *installKeyboardActions()* performs these registrations.

Split Pane Layouts

The two inner classes that *BasicSplitPaneUI* provides are the place where the split pane calculates the result of changes to its child components or in the location of its divider. These classes represent the layout rules for a horizontally or vertically oriented split pane, and the *Orientation* property is implemented as bound just for this reason. *BasicHorizontalLayoutManager* is a *public* inner class that implements the *java.awt.LayoutManager2* interface. This layout interface provides the capability of specifying layout constraints that are of the *Object* type. The layout manager is essentially hardcoded to contain three components: the left and right child components and the divider. The *layoutContainer* method is responsible for setting the bounds of each of its child components. *BasicVerticalLayoutManager* inherits from *BasicHorizontalLayoutManager* and replaces the functionality in that superclass to perform a version of the layout that operates along the Y-axis.

Both layouts rely on the old version of *addLayoutComponent()* that is defined in *java.awt.LayoutManager*. It uses only five specific values for its string constraint: *JSplitPane.RIGHT*, *JSplitPane.LEFT*, *JSplitPane.TOP*, *JSplitPane.BOTTOM* or *JSplitPane.NON_CONTIGUOUS_DIVIDER*. Any other value causes an *IllegalArgumentException* to be thrown.

The Basic Divider

As previously discussed, the divider is a special type of component that actually inherits from *java.awt.Container*. It provides a number of important features that contribute to the behavior of the split pane. A divider is always created for each instance of *JSplitPane* and the reference to that object is kept as a *protected* member of the *BasicSplitPaneDivider* class. Because a UI delegate for the split pane is created on a per-instance basis, it is responsible for creating the divider and providing a reference to both the split pane component and itself. The divider mirrors the *Orientation* property of the *JSplitPane* component by adding itself as a property change listener; hence, the implementation of the *PropertyChangeListener* interface. The properties monitored by the divider are the *Orientation* property and the *OneTouchExpandable* property. The latter property is observed by the divider because if its value becomes *true*, the divider is expected to provide a control area for the one-touch commands to be actuated.

One-touch Support

A *protected* method in the divider code, *oneTouchExpandableChanged()*, is invoked by the *propertyChange()* method if a change in that property is received. It causes two anonymous extensions of *JButton* to be created that serve as the one-touch acutators. These buttons have their *FocusPainted* and *BorderPainted* properties set to *false*.

Strangely, no code exists to remove the buttons when the *OneTouchExpandable* property changes its value back to *false*. It is suspected that this was thought to be a rare enough occasion in typical user interfaces that it was deemed simpler to destroy and reinstantiate a new divider when the UI detects the property change.

BasicSplitPaneDivider provides a *protected* layout manager that manages the size and position of the one-touch buttons within the divider container.

Divider Drag Capabilities

Although the implementation that performs the layout of child components resides in the UI delegate, the divider component is responsible for providing the implementations of *MouseListener* and *MouseMotionListener* that enable drag operations. The divider uses three methods to signal its associated UI object when changes in drag state occur. The first of these methods is *prepareForDragging()*, which invokes the method *startDragging()* in the UI delegate. This operation occurs when the user clicks the mouse within the divider's bounds. The *dragDividerTo()* method calls the method with the same name in the UI. It occurs whenever a *mouseDragged()* event is received by the *MouseMotionListener*. The method *finishDraggingTo()* provides the UI with the final position of the divider after the drag operation is complete.

The divider is also responsible for changing the mouse cursor when it is within its bounds. The *mouseMoved()* method is used as a mechanism to determine when the unclicked mouse is over the divider and changes the cursor to the vertical or horizontal double arrows depending on its orientation.

Inside a Drag Operation

When the divider received a *mousePressed()* event, several things must occur before the UI is signaled that a drag is occurring. First, the heavyweight ghost version of the divider is created. Besides being guaranteed to appear on top of all lightweight child components, the hidden divider can instantly react to cursor changes without the well-known problems caused in the lightweight world. The mouse and mouse motion listeners are redirected to the new hidden divider so it may serve to generate mouse-related events. Lastly, just before the *prepareForDragging()* method is invoked, a state management object is created, an instance of either *DragController* or

VerticalDragController. These objects serve as delegates for additional incoming mouse and mouse motion events. Within these objects, the state graphs that they implement are used to determine which methods should be called and if the drag session has completed. *Vertical DragControllerI* inherits from *DragController* and implements the Y-axis version of the drag state machine.

When a drag is occurring, the UI and divider will receive *mouseDragged()* events instead of *mouseMoved()* events. Instead of altering the cursor, the *mouseDragged()* event ultimately causes a *dragDividerTo()* method to be called with the new divider position. This is invoked unconditionally by the *continueDrag()* method of *DragController*.

When the release of the mouse button is detected, the *completeDrag()* event of *DragController* is invoked, which signals the divider and the UI with a *finishDraggingTo()* method. This method, among other things, updates the *LastDividerPosition* property value.

Tabbed Pane

Another useful container JFC provides is encapsulated by the *JTabbedPane* class. This class emulates the multilevel tabbed pane components found in many GUI platforms, enabling the user to select a set of overlapping panes by a keyed tab. See Figure 4-8.

Brightest Stars	Nearest Stars				
Name	**Dist (lt-yrs)**	**Spec Type**	**Vis Mag**	**Abs Mag**	
Sun	8 lt-mins	G2 V	-26.72	+4.85	▲
Sirius	8.6	A1 V	-1.46	+1.42	
Canopus	80	A9 II	-0.72	-2.5	
Alpha Centauri	4.3	G2 V	-0.01	+4.37	
Arcturus	34	K2 III	-0.04	+0.2	▼

First Tab Selected

Brightest Stars	Nearest Stars				
Name	**Dist (lt-yrs)**	**Spec Type**	**Vis Mag**	**Abs Mag**	
Sun	8 lt-mins	G2 V	-26.72	+4.85	▲
Alpha Centauri	4.2	M5.5 V	-0.01	+4.37	
Barnard's Star	6.0	M4 V	+9.54	+13.22	
Wolf 359	7.7	M6 V	+13.53	+16.65	
BD+36 2147	8.2	M2 V	+7.50	+10.50	▼

Second Tab Selected

Figure 4-8. *JTabbedPane example*

The lightweight version has the advantage of providing icons and other formatting capabilities in the tabs themselves and also has the capability of rendering the set of tabs in four different positions: at the top, bottom, left, or right of the pane. A constructor is provided for *JTabbedPane*, along with a parameterless version, that takes an *int* as a parameter. This integer can have the value *JTabbedPane.TOP* (the default), *JTabbedPane.BOTTOM, JTabbedPane.LEFT,* or *JTabbedPane.RIGHT.* These values are defined in the *SwingConstants* interface, which is implemented by *JTabbedPane.* See Figure 4-9.

JTabbedPane also supports a bound property called *TabPlacement* that controls the tab position dynamically. In either case, an *IllegalArgumentException* will be thrown if an invalid value is specified.

JTabbedPane Features

The *JTabbedPane* has a tab area and a content area. The UI delegate for the *JTabbedPane* component is responsible for managing the layout of these areas and painting the visual appearance of the tabs. *JTabbedPane* does not supply a renderer delegate for drawing customized tabs, but it does allow an icon in each label. The UI uses the static method *layoutCompoundLabel()* in *SwingUtilities* to draw tabs, thus at least leveraging that capability. It is compelling to consider a future version of this component that supports a tab renderer delegate, although some of the complex calculations involved with drawing multilevel tabs is an understandable mitigation for its absence.

JTabbedPane provides container operations that enable users to add, insert, and remove tabs; to disable and enable tabs; to change the

Figure 4-9. *Bottom tab placement*

enabled and disabled icons for a tab; and change the foreground and background color on a per-tab basis.

The *JTabbedPane* component supports keyboard and mouse operations to select tabs, and also provides several programmatic methods to change the currently selected tab. Also supported are per-tab ToolTips with an important caveat: They can only be set when a tab is added and not modified thereafter. There is a *getToolTipText()* method, but no analogous mutator for this property.

Anatomy of a Tab

Information about the tabs that are contained in an instance of *JTabbedPane* is kept in a *java.util.Vector*. The contents of this dynamic array contain an object of type *Page*, a private inner class of *JTabbedPane*; it also serves as the target for *Accessibility* as it is an extension of *AccessibleContext*. The information kept in this class maps each pane to its title, icon, colors, and enabled state.

Inserting Tabs

The components that map to each tab are added to the *JTabbedPane* using the *public* method *insertTab()* that takes five parameters: a title string, an *Icon*, a *Component* instance that the tab represents, a ToolTip string, and an index representing the position of the tab. The index value must be less than or equal to the current number of tabs in the container. Giving an index that is either too large for the current vector (or negative) generates an *ArrayIndexOutOfBoundsException*.

Several convenience methods are provided to add tabs to the *JTabbedPane*. Each one enables the automatic specification of default values. Three versions of *addTab()* are provided; these automatically calculate the next valid tab index and enable default specification for the ToolTip and icon parameters. Also provided are overridden methods for the five versions of *add()* specified by *java.awt.Container*.

As for the parameters of *insertTab()* and its relatives, the title, the icon, and the ToolTip may all be specified as *null*. The *Component* cannot be *null*, so an empty tab cannot be added in this manner. To add an empty tab, call *insertTab()* or any of the related methods with code similar to this:

```
. . .
JTabbedPane tabbedPane = new JTabbedPane();
tabbedPane.addTab("Empty Tab", new JPanel());
. . .
```

Selecting Tabs

Most of the labor of managing the tab selection is done by the state model *SingleSelectionModel*. Methods that delegate to the model are provided by *JSplitPane*. These methods are expressed as property interfaces, of which there are two ways to refer: by tab index number or by the contained component itself. The *SelectedIndex* property returns the *integer* index of the currently selected tab using *getSelectedIndex()*. If no tabs exist in the container, the value (–1) is returned. Specifying an index to *setSelectedIndex()* that is unreasonable is not checked, and an *ArrayIndexOutOfBoundsException* could be thrown.

The *SelectedComponent* property behaves similarly to the index version except it is of type *Component*. If no components exist, a *null* value is returned by *getSelectedComponent()*. Attempting to select a component that is not actually found in the Tab pane causes an *IllegalArgument Exception* to be thrown.

Counting and Identifying Tabs

The mechanism for determining the number of tabs currently in a *JTabbedPane* is to use the *getTabCount()* method. This method delegates to the internal *Vector* containing the *Page* objects to determine how many elements exist. The number of tab "runs," that is, the number of rows of stacked tabs, can be retrieved by using the *getTabRunCount()* method.

Because tabs are identified primarily by their index in the *Vector*, three versions of the method *indexOfTab()* are provided to facilitate the determination of a tab index by its title, icon, or contained component.

Allowing the identification of tabs by their component prevents having two or more tabs from sharing a component. This is an important side-effect. Although it may seem like a reasonable constraint, it means that in cases where two or more tabs do happen to refer to the same component, the component must be cloned for each tab. Attempting to add a component twice to a *JTabbedPane* results in an *ArrayIndexOutOfBoundsException* being thrown.

Changing Tab Properties

Some additional indexed property methods are provided to enable programmatic alteration of a tab's properties (see Table 4-1). An indexed property is one that specified an initial parameter of type *int* that serves to indicate which tab to modify.

All of these methods cause an *ArrayIndexOutOfBoundsException* to be thrown if the specified index is less than zero or greater than the highest index, which is always one less than the count returned by *getTabCount()*.

The accessor methods for the tab properties, with the exception of *getBoundsAt()*, delegate to the *Page* vector to retrieve their information. The *getBoundsAt()* method delegates to the tabbed pane UI to determine the bounds of a particular tab.

The mutators for these properties have various effects. Changing the title of a tab, its icon, or its disabled icon (if the tab is disabled) generates calls to *revalidate()* and *repaint()* because the tab sizes and run counts may have changed. Changing the background or foreground colors or the enabled state causes a repaint to be done on the area of the tab

Table 4-1. *Changing tab properties*

Property	Type	Accessor	Mutator
TitleAt	String	getTitleAt()	setTitleAt()
IconAt	Icon	getIconAt()	setIconAt()
DisabledIconAt	Icon	getDisabledIconAt()	setDisabledIconAt()
BackgroundAt	Color	getBackgroundAt()	setBackgroundAt()
ForegroundAt	Color	getForegroundAt()	setForegroundAt()
ComponentAt	Component	getComponentAt()	setComponentAt()
EnabledAt	Boolean	isEnabledAt()	setEnabledAt()
BoundsAt	Rectangle	getBoundsAt()	N/A

bounds; thus the need for the *getBoundsAt()* method. The *revalidate()* call is invoked without a repaint when the *setComponentAt()* method is called because the tabs are not themselves affected.

Removing Tabs

JSplitPane provides methods for removing tabs as well. In addition to the *remove()* and *removeAll()* methods specified by *Container*, a version of *remove()* is provided that refers to the tab component itself and not the containment index. An additional method *removeTabAt()* is provided that enables specification of a tab by its index number.

Tabbed Pane Selection Model

JTabbedPane uses *SingleSelectionModel* as its state model. This is the same model used by *JMenuBar* and *JPopupMenu* to handle the menu selection state. As such, the *ChangeListener* interface is used to register interest in when the tab selection is changed. The constructor of *JTabbedPane* installs an instance of *DefaultSelectionModel* as the intial model delegate. The *Model* property of *JTabbedPane* is bound to enable listeners to be migrated to newly specified models.

Tabbed Pane UI Delegate

The *BasicTabbedPaneUI* class, which extends *TabbedPaneUI*, provides most of the mechanics of the tabbed pane component. Along with providing the mechanism for graphically rendering the tabs, the UI delegate is also responsible for layout of the tabs and the calculation of required sizes for both the tabs and the tab components.

UI Delegate Listeners

When *BasicTabbedPaneUI* installs its defaults, it creates four listeners that are added to the *JTabbedPane* instance: a property change listener, a tab change listener, a mouse listener, and a focus listener. Each of these listeners is instantiated by a *protected* method of *BasicTabbedPaneUI* and could be substituted in a subclass.

The *ChangeListener* portion of the UI is listening to the *SingleSelectionModel* implementation as to when tab changes occur. This adapter causes a revalidation of the *JTabbedPane*, which in turn is the mechanism that actually reorganized the tabs in their new configuration. A call to *repaint()* is issued to cause the tabs to appear in the new state and to make certain the newly selected tab component is visible.

A mouse handler is used to trap *mousePressed()* events that occur within the tab area of the container. The handler uses the *public* method *tabForCoordinate()* that returns the tab index where the mouse press occurred or (–1). This index is used as a parameter for a call to *getSelectedIndex()* if the tab is enabled.

Focus events are also tracked, apparently as a workaround for a bug in JDK 1.1.5. Both the *focusGained()* and *focusLost()* methods unconditionally repaint the currently selected tab. The property change listener has a *null* implementation. It is likely present for future expansion, but it also wastes a little execution time in the *JTabbedPane* operation.

TabbedPaneLayout

As with the other container classes, *BasicTabbedPaneUI* provides an inner layout manager for arranging its child components and calculating the position and size of its tabs. The layout can be said to perform two fundamental functions. First, it examines the preferred and minimum heights of each of the tab components in order to calculate the dimensions of the largest component. This is accomplished by iterating through the children of the container and requesting their preferred and minimum sizes. The width and height of the maximum size component must be tracked as separate variables because one component may have the largest height and the other the largest width. The second task it performs is the actual calculation of the size requirements for each tab, and the fitting of these sizes into tab runs that fit within the allowed size of the container. Both of these processes are encapsulated in the *protected* method *calculateSize()*, which is invoked by the *preferredLayoutSize()* and *minimumLayoutSize()* methods specified by the *LayoutManager* interface.

The actual setting of component bounds is performed in the *layoutContainer()* method, also specified by *LayoutManager*. This method not only takes the placement of tabs into consideration, it also makes the currently selected tab component fill its available space and visible, while all other tab components remain hidden underneath.

BasicTabbedPaneUI is a complex class and contains additional methods relating to the navigation among tabs and tab runs, calculation of tab sizes, the assignment of tabs to tab runs, and the painting of each tab's borders and focus indicators.

Chapter 5

The JList Component

The *JList* is one of the fundamental components provided with the Swing component package. Its purpose is to present a set of items for presentation or selection. The *JList* component uses the *ListModel* interface, which is the simplest of the standard JFC data models. Because *JList* also supports UI delegation and custom rendering, it also has a tremendous amount of flexibility concerning how data are displayed.

Unlike the heavyweight version of the list control, *java.awt.List*, *JList* does not provide methods for inserting individual entries. Instead, *JList* expects its data to be contained in a *ListModel* object, which is a type of data model.

A data model is an object that furnishes JFC components with data as well as information about the available data. This information is accessed by the *JList* and other controls with a series of callback methods encapsulated in a Java interface. The methods of data model interfaces generally provide the quantity of data available, the relationship among data elements, such as sequence or parent/child hierarchy, and the data elements themselves. Models also generally provide special methods whereby interested listeners can register for model change events.

ListModel Methods

This *getSize()* method reports the number of available data elements to the list component. If the list contains no elements, this function should return zero. A negative number is treated as if it were a zero, but this behavior should not be depended on. The value returned by this method less one represents the last data element available in the model.

To access the model elements, use the *getElementAt()* method, which takes an integer index as a parameter and returns the element as an opaque *Object* type. Because the list does not paint itself, but depends on a renderer delegate to do so, the *Object* type can be interpreted in any suitable way. The behavior of the default list renderer, that is, the one that is used if no alternate is specified, is to invoke the *toString()* method on the object and represent the value as a string. Much more powerful and flexible capabilities are available by recognition of more complex objects. Depending on how much of the list is visible, *getElementAt()* is called for each list cell that requires repainting when the list is scrolled or a change is detected in the data.

List Data Changes

The *ListModel* interface describes two additional methods that are used to add and remove listeners from an interest list. The *addListDataListener()* and *removeListDataListener()* methods both take a *ListDataListener* object as a parameter. It is the task of the model implementation to manage the list of active listeners and to invoke the proper event methods when a change occurs.

Because these methods are part of an interface, these methods always need to be implemented, but they can be constructed without any body in cases where the list data is guaranteed never to change. This type of model is known as a constant data model.

The *ListDataListener* interface is implemented by objects that request notification of data changes. Along with the accompanying event object, it is covered later in this chapter in detail.

AbstractListModel

JFC provides two implementations of the *ListModel* interface in its API. The *AbstractListModel* class is an abstract implementation of a list data model. It requires implementation of both the *getSize()* and *getElementAt()* methods. It also provides code for adding and removing data listeners and three value-added functions for firing the supported event types.

Listeners are managed by the *AbstractListModel* through the implementation of a class known as *EventListenerList* implemented in the *javax.swing.event* package. This class stores the reference to the listener object along with the class of event for which the listener is intended, thus enabling one list to support multiple types of events. The lists themselves are stored as a one-dimensional array of type *Object*; by convention the references are paired such that even indices always contain the class reference and the successor the listener reference. Access to the internal array is synchronized to prevent events from being fired while the list is being modifed.

When events are fired by the *AbstractListModel* (and other implementations), the list is always traversed from the last entry to the first; this ensures that the most recently added listener is notified before all others.

DefaultListModel

The second base implementation of *ListModel* is the *DefaultListModel* class. It extends *AbstractListModel*, delegating the management of list data to a private instance of a *Vector*. *DefaultListModel* is most useful in cases where a *Vector* is the most suitable place to store list elements; it can also be extended for more specialized handling of *Vector* data. It also exposes several value-added methods for maintaining the data, most of which delegate to the contained *Vector* after firing the appropriate events.

Some of the methods *DefaultListModel* provides are wrappers for the equivalent methods provided by *Vector*, such as *copyInto()*, *trimToSize()*, *ensureCapacity()*, *setSize()*, *capacity()*, *isEmpty()*, *elements()*, *contains()*, *indexOf()*, *lastIndexOf()*, *firstElement()*, and *lastElement()*. It is important to remember that these methods will only be implemented by models that inherit from *DefaultListModel*; one cannot assume that they are implemented for every model.

Associating a Model with a List

To populate a list with items, a data model object is created either direct-ly or generates a default list model with the *JList* control. A list data model object can be associated with the control in three ways:

- The *Model* property and a version of the constructor allow the assignment of any object that implements the *ListModel* inter-face as the data model. The object can be a default model, an extension of *AbstractListModel, DefaultListModel,* or any class that implements the *ListModel* interface.

- Constructors exist that take either an array of *Object* or a single *Vector* as a parameter. These cause an anonymous extension of *AbstractListModel* object to be created internally by the control. The source array and *Vector* are not copied.

- There are a pair of methods called *setListData()* that take an array of *Object* or a single *Vector*. These also cause an *AbstractListModel* extension to be created without copying the source data instance.

Creating a Constant List Model

On occasion, the list data is very unlikely to change so a constant model is appropriate. The *AbstractListModel* and *DefaultListModel* classes both assume that data is mutable and provide model event listeners and methods to fire model events. Under some circumstances, it may be important to distinguish which models are mutable and immutable. The *ConstantListModel* class is an alternative base class that you can use instead of *AbstractListModel* to denote that a model is immutable.

```
public abstract class ConstantListModel {
    public abstract int getSize();
    public abstract Object getElementAt(int index);
    public void addListDataListener(ListDataListener l) {
    }
    void removeListDataListener(ListDataListener l) {
    }
}
```

Using models derived from this class enables code to detect whether a model is mutable using the instanceof expression. Here is an example:

```
public class SecurityListModel extends ConstantListModel {
    String[] securityLevels = {
        "public", "protected", "private"
    };
    public int getSize() {
        return securityLevels.length;
    }
    public Object getElementAt(int index) {
        return securityLevels[index];
    }
}
```

Extending DefaultListModel

Although not the ideal way to provide this feature, *DefaultListModel* can be extended to provide simple manipulations of the data it contains. This example provides a simple method of numbering a list using this technique:

```
. . .
NumberedListModel model = new NumberedListModel();
model.addElement("Huey");
model.addElement("Dewey");
model.addElement("Louie");
JList list = new JList(model);
. . .
class NumberedListModel extends DefaultListModel {
    public Object getElementAt(int index) {
        Object element = super.get getElementAt(index);
        String result = Integer.toString(index) +
                ")   " + element.toString();
        return result;
    }
}
```

This will produce the results illustrated in Figure 5-1.

List Model Events

All list models must implement methods that enable interested listeners to subscribe to change events. When a list model is assigned or changed, an event is fired to interested listeners on the control. Objects intended to listen for these events must implement the *ListDataListener* interface, which requires three methods, each expecting a single parameter of type *ListDataEvent*:

- ***intervalAdded()***—Called when elements are added to the model. The *ListDataEvent* object will contain the closed interval of indexes added.

- ***intervalRemoved()***—Called when elements are removed from the model. The *ListDataEvent* object will contain the closed interval of indexes removed.

- ***contentsChanged()***—Called when the value of elements change. The *ListDataEvent* object will contain the closed interval of indexes where changes took place.

Note that these events do not have any affect on listeners interested in selection changes. Although removal of items may cause the selection to change, a different mechanism known as a "selection model" supports firing of selection events.

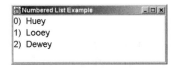

Figure 5-1. *Extending DefaultListModel*

AbstractListModel provides the implementation of the methods that add and remove model listeners along with three methods to fire the events supported by the model listener. If you extend *AbstractListModel* you must remember to fire those events when the data changes. *DefaultListModel* provides this capability automatically, but you must call the superclass for any overriding methods to ensure that the event firing takes place.

Here is an example of a list data listener:

```
JList list = new JList(new DefaultListModel());
list.getModel().addListDataListener(new ListDataListener() {    public void
intervalAdded(ListDataEvent event) {
    System.out.println("intervalAdded: " + event);
  }
  public void intervalRemoved(ListDataEvent event) {
    System.out.println("intervalRemoved: " + event);
  }
  public void contentsChanged(ListDataEvent event) {
    System.out.println("contentsChanged: " + event);
  }
});
```

List Model Filtering

This seems like an excellent time to introduce a very useful concept—model filtering. Model filtering is another way to add significant value to the MVC application architecture.

Model filtering is founded on this principle: JFC controls do not pay much attention to how data is provided. As long as the *ListModel* interface is implemented, *JList* is perfectly happy. Because of the blissful way in which *ListModels* are treated, additional classes can be devised to interpret the data in a model differently than would ordinarily occur.

Life Without Filters

In the ordinary case, the elements in the list are displayed in whatever order they are represented by the model. The *JList* control invokes methods on the

ListModel object currently associated with the object. Thus, the order of data returned by the *getElementAt()* method will be directly reflected in the list. The following code for a constant data model will be used as an example:

```
public class DwarfListModel extends ConstantListModel {
    String[] dwarves = {
        "Sleepy", "Sneezy", "Doc", "Grumpy"
        "Dopey", "Bashful", "Happy"
    };
    public int getSize() {
        return dwarves.length;
    }
    public Object getElementAt(int index) {
        return dwarves [index];
    }
}
```

When associated with a list using code such as this,

```
JList dwarfList = new JList(new DwarfListModel()};
```

the results look like Figure 5-2. Nevertheless, a problem occurs: The person paying for this information wants to see a numbered list. You have a few ways to approach this problem, but using a model filter is probably the most flexible and powerful solution.

Structure of Model Filters

The way model filters work is similar to the way the fuel filter works in an automobile. The filtering device is placed between the source of the data and the manipulator of the data in the same way a filter intercepts all of the gasoline flowing from your fuel tank to your engine. Both the engine and driver only care whether the tank contains gas.

The best thing about model filters is that they can be made as powerful as necessary and still remain completely transparent to the operation of the list control. By implementing classes derived from a simple base class, data can be manipulated in many different ways, including the prefixing of a number to a list.

Figure 5-2. *Unsorted list model*

List model filters are created by extending an abstract model filter class. A design pattern that should be adopted suffixes the word *Filter* to the model being filtered. Thus, the name for the filter base class of the *ListModel* is *ListModelFilter*. All models supported by JFC can be filtered in this way, as can any custom data or state models that might be devised.

This is the code for the *ListModelFilter* class:

```
public abstract class ListModelFilter extends AbstractListModel {
    // reference to model being filtered
    protected ListModel model;
    // force use of parameterized constructor
    private ListModelFilter() {
    }
    // constructor - model can be null if not
    // available when filter constructed
    public ListModelFilter(ListModel model) {
        this.model = model;
    }
    // from ListModel interface, return number of list rows
    public int getSize() {
        return this.model.getSize();
    }
    // from ListModel interface, retrieve data element
    public Object getElementAt(int index) {
        return this.model.getElementAt(index);
    }
```

```
// return reference of model
public ListModel getModel() {
    return this.model;
}
// set new model reference
public void setModel(ListModel newModel) {
    this.model = newModel;
}
} // end of ListModelFilter
```

To create a filter that essentially does nothing, extend the *ListModelFilter* class without overriding any methods. The default behavior of the class is to delegate model activity to whichever model is associated with the filter.

To create a filter that is useful, override the *getSize()* and/or the *getElementAt()* methods with something that alters the underlying behavior. For example, this class adds the ordinal prefix and makes the list numbered. This is not the fanciest way to do it, but it serves as a good example:

```
public class NumberedListModelFilter extends ListModelFilter {
    public Object getElementAt(int index) {
      return Integer.toString(index + 1) + ") " +
            this.model.getElementAt(index).toString();
    }
}
```

To implement the model, just use the provided model as the argument to the filter constructor:

```
DwarfListModel model = new DwarfListModel();
NumberedListModelFilter filter
                = new NumberedListModelFilter(model);
JList dwarfList = new JList(filter};
```

The result of the filtered operation is a numbered list. This is not a perfect solution, because if the list were longer, the text would not line up due to the number of ordinal digits. The section on List Cell Rendering covers another approach to numbered lists that overcomes this obstacle.

Sorting Filters

You can also use filters to change the order in which data appears in a list. It turns out that the list is still not exactly right: The users want to see the dwarves in alphabetical order. But, by devising a more robust filter that changes the order that elements are depicted, sorting can be accomplished with total transparency. The code for *AlphaSortListModel* demonstrates a straightforward example of a sorting filter:

```
public class SortedListModelFilter extends ListModelFilter {
    // Vector to hold sorted dynamic array
    protected Vector sortedList;
    // constructor - takes model as parameter
    public SortedListModelFilter(ListModel model) {
        super(model);    // I love this line of code!
        sortModel();
    }
    // delegate element fetch to vector
    public Object getElementAt(int index) {
        return sortedList.elementAt(index);
    }
    // return size of vector
    public int getSize(){
        return sortedList.size();
```

Use an insertion sort to create a vector of sorted references to the model elements. Insertion sort is the best sort for these small tasks. Anything bigger than a few dozen or couple of hundred elements needs a stack-based sort (such as Shell sort) for decent performance.

The insertion sort is a simple algorithm that is essentially a bubble sort with a very important shortcut. The algorithm examines each input element in relation to the items already in the sorted list. When it finds an element in the sorted vector that is higher in value than the one being examined, it inserts the input element into the sorted array. The *Vector* class is ideal because it supports the insertion operation as a method.

```
private void sortModel() {
    sortedList = new Vector();
    nextElement:
```

```
        for (int x=0; x < model.getSize(); x++)
        {
            for (int y=0; y < x; y++)
            {
                if (model.getElementAt(x).toString().
compareTo(sortedList.elementAt(y).toString()) < 0)
                {
                    sortedList.insertElementAt(
                            model.getElementAt(x), y);
                        continue nextElement;
                }
            }
            sortedList.addElement(model.getElementAt(x));
        }
    }
} // end of SortedListModelFilter
```

To use this filter, create an instance using a list data model and set
the filter to be the model property of the list (see Figure 5-3):

```
DwarfListModel model = new DwarfListModel();
SortedListModelFilter sortFilter =
            new SortedListModelFilter(model);
 JList dwarfList = new JList(sortFilter};
```

Because they are transparent to the control and to each other, filters can be stacked arbitrarily. This enables us to build a list that is not
only alphabetized, but sorted as well:

```
DwarfListModel model = new DwarfListModel();
SortedListModelFilter sortFilter =
             new SortedListModelFilter(model);
NumberedListModelFilter numberFilter =
             new NumberedListModelFilter(sortFilter);
JList dwarfList = new JList(numberFilter};
```

This code produces the results shown in Figure 5-4.

Sorting filters need not be based on alphabetic sequence, but could
be used to evaluate any qualitative or quantitative aspect of list data elements. This is one of the reasons why data models return elements as

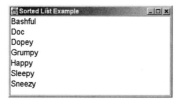

Figure 5-3. *Sroting with a filter*

type *java.lang.Object*: it becomes the responsibility of the implementor to decide what the data actually means. In most cases, calling *toString()* on the data model element will be sufficient. However, in the event that more powerful processing is needed, these robust features are available to the JFC programmer.

List Selection

In common with most other components in the Swing architecture, the *JList* component supports not only a data model but also a state model. A state model works in conjunction with a data model to encapsulate a component's state-related properties. In the case of components such as *JList*, the models that describe the state are known as selection models.'

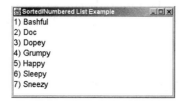

Figure 5-4. *Combining, sorting, and numbering*

Selection models serve many purposes. Chiefly, they contain methods to report on the current state of a component, such as which of its entries might be currently selected. The most significant advantage to this approach is that it is possible to overcome the AWT limitation of single selection. Selection models can enable algorithms of arbitrary complexity to be used to determine list control behavior.

Selection models also provide methods to control the rules of selection; these options are known as a selection modes or selection strategies.

List Selection Events

To figure out when a selection changes, the selection model provides a hook that enables registration of selection listeners. Selection listeners must implement the *ListSelectionListener* interface, which contains a single method *valueChanged()*. The parameter to this method is a *ListSelectionEvent* object that contains information on what selection changes have occurred.

It is important to remember something when list selection listeners are constructed. When a selection changes, more than one event may be generated. In the case of a single selection, an event is generated for the deselection of an index and the selection of the new index. Fortunately, there is a way of telling whether the event was a part of a series of selection changes or an actual change. The *ListSelectionEvent* class and the *JList* component provide access to the *ValueIsAdjusting* property through use of the *getValueIsAdjusting()* method. When this method returns *true* the event is going through a sequence of changes. Thus, in the case of the single selection change, the first event received for the deselect will have the *getValueIsAdjusting()* set to *true*. This means the event can probably be ignored. The second event will return *false* for *getValueIsAdjusting()*, so it is recognized as an actual change in selection state.

Selection Modes

The *JList* control supports three standard selection modes, each represented by a static final integer on the *ListSelectionModel* interface. Each mode reflects a deterministic selection strategy:

- **SINGLE_SELECTION**—When this mode is specified, only one row in the list can be selected. If a new row is selected, the previously selected row is unselected.

- **SINGLE_INTERVAL_SELECTION**—If this mode is specified, any number of indices can be selected so long as they lie within the same interval. Selecting a row outside of an interval deselects all selected indices and a new interval is created.

- **MULTIPLE_INTERVAL_SELECTION**—This is the default selection model for *DefaultListSelectionModel*. This is a free-for-all mode where any combination of selection intervals can be combined. As with *SINGLE_INTERVAL_SELECTION*, the default behavior is to toggle the selection of indices between the anchor and lead points, depending on the initial state of the anchor point.

These selection modes are certainly the most commonly required strategies, but it is possible to conceive of other reasonable requirements.

The *JList* component also supports keyboard navigation to select indices. You can use the arrow keys to change the index pointer, and the space bar serves as the toggle key.

The ListSelectionModel Interface

This interface contains the methods for an object intended to represent the state of a *JList* control. The following is a description of those methods and their default behaviors:

- **void clearSelection()**—Sets the selection to the empty set.

- **boolean isSelectionEmpty()**—Returns *true* if the selection set is empty.

- **boolean isSelectedIndex(int index)**—Returns *true* if the item with the specified index is selected.

- **int getSelectionMode()**—Returns the current selection mode.

- **void setSelectionMode(int selectionMode)**—Assigns a new selection mode; an illegal mode causes an *IllegalArgumentException* to be thrown. Note that changing the mode does *not* change the selection state, only the rules of selection from that point forward.

- *int getMaxSelectionIndex()*—Returns the highest currently selected index or (–1) if no elements are selected. In the case of *SINGLE_SELECTION* mode, the currently selected index or (–1) is returned.

- *int getMinSelectionIndex()*—Returns the lowest currently selected index or (–1) if no elements are selected. In the case of *SINGLE_SELECTION* mode, the currently selected index or (–1) is returned.

- *void setSelectionInterval(int start, int end)*—Sets the selection set to be the specified contiguous interval. In the case of *SINGLE_SELECTION* mode, the second (end) index is ignored and the first (start) index is toggled. For the other modes, the indices between the two intervals are toggled. If the end index is less than the start index, the interval is still valid. If either value is (–1), no action is taken.

- *void addSelectionInterval(int start, int end)*—In the case of *SINGLE_SELECTION* mode, the second (end) index is ignored and the first (start) index is toggled. For *SINGLE_INTERVAL_SELECTION*, the behavior is identical to *setSelectionInterval()*. For *MULTIPLE_INTERVAL_SELECTION*, the items in the set are added to the existing selection set. Those items in the range that are already selected are deselected and those not selected are selected. If either value is (–1), no action is taken.

- *void removeSelectionInterval(int start, int end)*—Removes the specified contiguous interval from the selection set. If either value is (–1), no action is taken.

- *void insertIndexInterval(int index, int length, boolean before)*—Inserts a new set of selection indices to the model. This is primarily used when the data model changes.

- *void removeIndexInterval(int start, int end)*—Removes the set of selection indices from the model. This is primarily used when the data model changes.

- *int getAnchorSelectionIndex()*—The anchor selection index is the initial cell selected in a multiple select operation. The anchor is so called because it remains selected on the same cell while the user clicks additional cells.

- *void setAnchorSelectionIndex(int index)*—This method sets a new anchor position (see *getAnchorSelectionIndex()*). The selection state of indices are unchanged by this call. The value (–1) has the meaning of unassigned.

- *int getLeadSelectionIndex()*—The lead index is the last cell in a multiple select operation. Unlike the anchor index, it can be moved around with the mouse or keyboard.

- *void setLeadSelectionIndex(int index)*—This method sets a new lead position (see *getLeadSelectionIndex()*). If the anchor cell is selected, this call will select all the values in the range between the anchor and lead. If it is not selected, the values will all be deselected. The value (–1) has the meaning of unassigned.

- *boolean getValueIsAdjusting()*—This property is true when the selections occurring are part of a multiple set of selection changes for a single operation. When a single selection changes, two events are generated: one for the deselection of the previous instance and one for the new selection. The value is set to *true* when the deselect operation is occurring. Also, when intervals are selected and deselected, a situation often occurs where indices are temporarily selected and deselected. To summarize: This value indicates to an interested listener that an operation may have occurred. It is not one that will permanently affect the selection state.

- *void setValueIsAdjusting(boolean valueIsAdjusting)*—This flag is used to manually set the *ValueIsAdjusting* property of the selection model (see *getValueIsAdjusting()*).

- *void addListSelectionListener(ListSelectionListener listener), void removeListSelectionListener(ListSelectionListener listener)*—Adds and removes selection listeners from a listener list.

DefaultListSelectionModel

The default implementation of the list selection model is *DefaultList SelectionModel*. It provides support for the three standard selection modes.

DefaultListSelectionModel is an interesting class. To keep track of the selection status, it uses a class of the *java.util* package called *BitSet*, which manages an arbitrary-sized set of bit values. *BitSet* has advantages of being able to manage a large set of bits in a condensed area of storage, but it does have some extra overhead in access. *BitSet* does not provide any shifting methods (oddly enough) so these operations need to be written when this class is used.

Custom List Selection Models

Suppose a requirement for a list strategy only allowed a user to select one or two items from a list box. In theory, it would not be that difficult to construct listener code that alters selection behavior, but that would require copying of code or additional subclassing to integrate that feature. A better way is to create a customized list selection model.

Although not too often needed, it is interesting to look at what goes into making a customized list selection model. Just to make this effort even more worthwhile, two examples cover two very different requirements.

RestrictedListSelectionModel

The idea behind this example is to come up with a way of selecting only a specified number of items. Although the same could be done programmatically, the ability to use a selection model is much more desirable. As an additional advantage, this model provides a way to configure the number of selectable items through a property called *SelectionLimit*.

```
package.com.ketherware.ListSelection;
import java.awt.*;
import java.awt.event.*;
import javax.swing.*;
import javax.swing.event.*;
```

```java
public class RestrictedListSelectionModel implements
      ListSelectionModel {
   // value of selection limit property
   protected int selectionLimit = 0;
   // Array of selected items
   protected int[] selectionArray;
   // Value is adjusting value
   protected boolean valueIsAdjusting = false;
   // Event listener list
   private EventListenerList listenerList =
         new EventListenerList();

   // Constructor: sets initial value of selection limit
   public RestrictedListSelectionModel(int initialLimit) {
      setSelectionLimit(initialLimit);
   }

   // Mutator for SelectionLimit property
   public void setSelectionLimit(int selectionLimit) {
      this.selectionLimit = selectionLimit;
      if (!isSelectionEmpty())
         clearSelection();
      selectionArray = new int[selectionLimit];
      for (int h=0; h < selectionLimit; h++)
         selectionArray[h] = -1;
   }
   // Internal method used to change shift array when
   // new index selected
   private void shiftAndSelect(int newIndex) {
      if (isSelectedIndex(newIndex))
            return;
      int lastIndex = selectionArray[0];

      // Bump everything down the list. This will cause
      // the index of the earliest selection to be
      // bumped off into outer space
      for (int h=0; h < selectionLimit - 1; h++) {
```

```
            selectionArray[h] = selectionArray[h + 1];
        }
        selectionArray[selectionLimit - 1] = newIndex;

        // Two events are fired, one for the deselect and
        // one for the new selection
        fireValueChanged(lastIndex, lastIndex, true);
        fireValueChanged(newIndex, newIndex, false);
    }

    // Selection Limit property accessor
    public int getSelectionLimit() {
        return this.selectionLimit;
    }

    // When a new selection comes along, pass it to the
    // internal routine to handle the array changes
    public void setSelectionInterval(int index0, int index1) {
        shiftAndSelect(index0);
    }

    public void addSelectionInterval(int index0, int index1) {
        // No op
    }

    public void removeSelectionInterval(int i0, int i1) {
            // No op
    }

    // Calculate the lowest selected index
    public int getMinSelectionIndex() {
        int min = Integer.MAX_VALUE;
        for (int h=0; h < selectionLimit; h++) {
            if (selectionArray[h] < min)
                min = selectionArray[h];
        }
        if (min == Integer.MAX_VALUE)
```

```java
        min = -1;
    return min;
}

// Calculate the highest selected index
public int getMaxSelectionIndex() {
    int max = -1;
    for (int h=0; h < selectionLimit; h++) {
        if (selectionArray[h] > max)
            max = selectionArray[h];
    }
    return max;
}

// Determine if a particular index is selected
public boolean isSelectedIndex(int index) {
    for (int h=0; h < selectionLimit; h++) {
        if (selectionArray[h] == index)
            return true;
    }
    return false;
}

// Return the earliest selection as the anchor
public int getAnchorSelectionIndex() {
    return selectionArray[0];
}

public void setAnchorSelectionIndex(int index) {
        // No op
}

// Return the latest selection as the lead
public int getLeadSelectionIndex() {
    return selectionArray[selectionLimit - 1];
}
```

```
public void setLeadSelectionIndex(int index) {
   // No op
}

// Clear all selections by iterating through the array
// and setting all values to (-1). Also, fire an event
// to inform any listeners
public void clearSelection() {
   if (selectionArray == null)
      return;

   for (int h=0; h < selectionLimit; h++) {
      if (selectionArray[h] != -1) {
         selectionArray[h] = -1;
         fireValueChanged(selectionArray[h],
            selectionArray[h], true);
      }
   }
}

// If there is no array or all values are (-1)
// the selection is empty
public boolean isSelectionEmpty() {
   if (selectionArray == null)
      return true;
   for (int h=0; h < selectionLimit; h++) {
      if (selectionArray[h] != -1)
                return false;
   }
   return true;
}

public void insertIndexInterval(int index,
         int length, boolean before) {
   // No op
}
```

```java
public void removeIndexInterval(int index0, int index1) {
   // No op
}

// Property mutator
public void setValueIsAdjusting(boolean valueIsAdjusting) {
   this.valueIsAdjusting = valueIsAdjusting;
}

// Property accessor
public boolean getValueIsAdjusting() {
   return this.valueIsAdjusting;
}

public void setSelectionMode(int selectionMode) {
   // No op
}

// Just return this instead of a bogus value
public int getSelectionMode() {
   return ListSelectionModel.
         MULTIPLE_INTERVAL_SELECTION;
}

// Helper method to propagate events to the listeners.
// This method 'lazily' creates the event object and
// sends it to all of the registered listeners
protected void fireValueChanged(int firstIndex,
      int lastIndex, boolean isAdjusting)   {
   Object[] listeners = listenerList.getListenerList();
   ListSelectionEvent event = null;
   for (int i = listeners.length - 2; i >= 0; i -= 2) {
      if (listeners[i] ==
            ListSelectionListener.class) {
      if (event == null)
         event = new ListSelectionEvent(this,
                        firstIndex, lastIndex,
```

```
                    isAdjusting);
            }
            (ListSelectionListener)listeners[i+1]).
                    valueChanged(event);
        }
    }

    // add a listener to the interest list
    public void addListSelectionListener(
            ListSelectionListener l) {
        listenerList.add(ListSelectionListener.class, l);
    }

    // remove a listener from the interest list
    public void removeListSelectionListener(
            ListSelectionListener l) {
        listenerList.remove(
            ListSelectionListener.class, l);
    }
}
```

It seemed more sensible that the selection would be cleared when the *SelectionLimit* changed; this is because the number of selections could decrease, and you have no way to decide which selections to keep.

FrozenListSelectionModel

This selection model is extremely useful. An interface must often display a list of selected items but not let the selections be changed. Ordinarily, setting the *JList* control to a disabled state would do this. The problem is that when it is disabled, the text is grayed out and can be difficult to read.

The *FrozenListSelectionModel* example shows an alternative to disabling a control by constructing what amounts to a model filter on a selection mode. *FrozenListSelectionModel* retains whatever selection state is already present, but does not allow any changes. It takes an existing selection model as a parameter to its constructor.

```
package com.ketherware.ListSelection;

import java.awt.*;
import java.awt.event.*;
import javax.swing.*;
import javax.swing.event.*;

public class FrozenListSelectionModel
    implements ListSelectionModel {

  // Instance of existing model
  protected ListSelectionModel existingModel;

  // Constructor - takes a selection model as a parm
  public FrozenListSelectionModel(
      ListSelectionModel existingModel) {
    // Store reference to filtered model
    this.existingModel = existingModel;
  }

    public void setSelectionInterval(int index0, int index1) {
        // No op
    }
    public void addSelectionInterval(int index0, int index1) {
        // No op
    }
    public void removeSelectionInterval(int index0, int index1) {
        // No op
    }
    public int getMinSelectionIndex() {
        // Delegate to filtered model
        return existingModel.getMinSelectionIndex();
    }
    public int getMaxSelectionIndex() {
        // Delegate to filtered model
        return existingModel.getMinSelectionIndex();
    }
```

```java
public boolean isSelectedIndex(int index) {
    // Delegate to filtered model
    return existingModel.isSelectedIndex(index);
}
public int getAnchorSelectionIndex() {
    // Delegate to filtered model
    return existingModel.getAnchorSelectionIndex();
}
public void setAnchorSelectionIndex(int index) {
    // No op
}
public int getLeadSelectionIndex() {
    // Delegate to filtered model
    return existingModel.getLeadSelectionIndex();
}
public void setLeadSelectionIndex(int index) {
    // No op
}
public void clearSelection() {
    // No op
}
public boolean isSelectionEmpty() {
    // Delegate to filtered model
    return existingModel.isSelectionEmpty();
}

public void insertIndexInterval(int index,
    int length, boolean before) {
    // No op
}

public void removeIndexInterval(int index0, int index1)  {
    // No op
}
public void setValueIsAdjusting(boolean valueIsAdjusting) {
    // No op
}
```

```java
    public boolean getValueIsAdjusting() {
        // Delegate to filtered model
        return existingModel.getValueIsAdjusting();
    }

    public void setSelectionMode(int selectionMode) {
        // No op
    }

    public int getSelectionMode() {
        // Delegate to filtered model
        return existingModel.getSelectionMode();
    }
    public void addListSelectionListener(
            ListSelectionListener l) {
      // Delegate to filtered model
      existingModel.addListSelectionListener(l);
   }

    public void removeListSelectionListener(
            ListSelectionListener l) {
        // Delegate to filtered model
        existingModel.removeListSelectionListener(l);
    }
}
```

It is compelling to contrast this approach with that of data model filtering. It also seems that an abstract selection model would probably simplify both of these classes.

List Selection Sample Code

As is traditional with sample code, a Chinese restaurant menu serves as an excellent example of restricted selection. This sample program shows how both the previously described selection models can be implemented:

```java
package com.ketherware.ListSelection;

import java.awt.*;
```

```
import java.awt.event.*;
import javax.swing.*;
import javax.swing.event.*;
import javax.swing.border.*;

public class ListSelectionFrame extends JFrame {
    String[] dishes = {
        "Roast Pork Lo Mein", "Twice Cooked Pork",
        "Buddha's Delight", "Orange Beef",
        "Shrimp with Lobster Sauce", "Szechuan Duck",
        "Kung Pao Chicken", "Chili Shrimp",
        "Beef with Broccoli", "Sa Cha Lamb"
    };
    public ListSelectionFrame() {
        setTitle("Restricted List Selection");
        setLocation(100, 100);
        JPanel selPanel = new JPanel(new BorderLayout());
        TitledBorder border =
            new TitledBorder("Select two dishes:");
        border.setBorder(new LineBorder(Color.black));
        border.setTitleColor(Color.black);
        border.setTitleJustification(TitledBorder.CENTER);
        selPanel.setBorder(border);
        this.getContentPane().add(selPanel, "Center");

    JList list = new JList(dishes);
        selPanel.add(list);
        final RestrictedListSelectionModel selModel =
                    new RestrictedListSelectionModel(2);
        list.setSelectionModel(selModel);

        final FrozenListSelectionModel frozenSelModel =
                new FrozenListSelectionModel(selModel);
        final JToggleButton button = new
            JToggleButton("Freeze");
        this.getContentPane().add(button, "South");
```

```
button.addActionListener(new ActionListener() {
    public void actionPerformed(ActionEvent event) {
        if (button.isSelected()) {
        list.setSelectionModel(
        frozenSelModel);
            button.setText("Unfreeze");
        }
        else {
        list.setSelectionModel(selModel);
            button.setText("Freeze");
        }
    }
});
this.pack();
Dimension size = this.getSize();
size.width *= 2;
this.setSize(size);

// Catch the frame when it closes and end the process
this.addWindowListener(new WindowAdapter() {
    public void windowClosing(WindowEvent event) {
        System.exit(0);
    }
});
}

public static void main(String[] args) {
    new ListSelectionFrame().show();
}
}
```

List Cell Rendering

So far, this book has covered two of the three aspects of MVC architecture, namely the controller and the model. The view portion of the architecture, which represents how data is actually displayed in the user interface, is also a highly customizable feature of the Swing control set. One of the ways that view delegation is implemented is with the use of renderer objects to draw portions of complex controls.

Rendering Nostalgia

In the good old days of AWT, there was plenty of capability to create lightweight components. All one had to do was subclass a component such as a *Canvas* object and override the *paint()* method. Although the task in itself was a trivial undertaking, it resulted in several implications when looking at customization from an architectural standpoint. For example, imagine how long it would take to create a list box from the *Canvas* class. Code would have to be written to store and retrieve the list data in a useful way, and methods to manipulate list data and generate events would be required.

A related issue is this: If aspects of customized controls are desirable in other components, how can they be cleanly reused? Creating additional subclasses of components for every type of custom component is not only a chore, but also a maintenance ordeal, especially when trying to propagate custom interface changes throughout the architecture.

Rendering Delegates

The solution to this dilemma is, of course, the MVC architecture. One of the benefits of separating component functionality into delegate objects is that the appearance and behavior of components such as list boxes can be modified with great ease and a minimal amount of additional class creation.

The *JList* control supports a property called *CellRenderer*. This property contains a reference to an object that implements the *ListCellRenderer* interface. Although a default renderer is provided by Swing, it is a straightforward matter to create an alternate way of interpreting and displaying list data.

The *ListCellRender* interface contains only a single method, *getListCellRendererComponent()*. The single job of this method is to interpret the list item data and return an object that represents how the cell is to be rendered. This return value must be derived from *java.awt.Component*.

To state it a little differently, the responsibility of the renderer object is to generate objects that paint themselves into the place that the control designates. This is what actually causes the list items to appear in the list. It is important to note that the components created by renderers cannot participate in event handling or other operations.

The default list cell renderer is a class known as *BasicListCellRenderer*. It is implemented by the default pluggable look and feel apparatus (see PLAF). The class is itself derived from the *JLabel* class. This gives list items a fair amount of flexibility with regard to text and icon representations. It is possible to return any component type from a renderer class, but because they do not participate in event handling, it is generally not useful. In the case of other controls that support rendering, such as *JTree* and *JTable*, additional classes to provide in-cell editing are also provided. When these classes are used, access to events is available. Unfortunately, the *JList* class does not support this type of editing.

ListCellRenderer Interface

The rendering interface has only a single method:

```
public Component getListCellRendererComponent(JList list, Object value,
int index, boolean isSelected, boolean cellHasFocus)
```

This method takes the following parameters:

- *JList list*—This is a reference to the *JList* component being rendered. The presence of a reference to the control makes this a stateful delegate. This parameter is necessary because renderer objects can be shared by multiple list components simultaneously. It may be necessary for the renderer to have access to the data model or other list control properties.

- *Object value*—This is the actual value that is to appear in the list cell. As stated before, the default behavior of renderers is to use the *toString()* method of *Object* to generate a string value.

- *int index*—This value represents the index into the data model and *not* the row in which the element appears on the screen.

- *boolean isSelected*—This is *true* when the cell being rendered is marked as selected by the selection model. Default behavior is to highlight the cell.

- **boolean cellHasFocus**—This is *true* when the cell being rendered has the focus within the component. This is mostly used for keyboard navigation and selection; also to support multiple selection modes. Default behavior is to draw a focus rectangle within the cell.

A Simple Renderer Example

An alternative approach to using a list model filter as a method to number cells is to use a simple renderer. Keeping in mind that default renderers use a subclass of *JLabel* to represent cells, we can construct an example that prefixes the index to the *Text* property of the label control. This same principle will be used later to add icons to the list cell.

To perform the changes we need to make, we still need a *JLabel* to work with. It makes most sense to enable the default renderer to provide the instance of the label because it will already be created with the attributes of the current look and feel. To preserve these characteristics in the custom-rendered cell, we need to keep track of a reference to the existing renderer before it is swapped out for a new one. Note that the constructor for the custom renderer takes a reference to a *ListCellRenderer* as a parameter. This is used as a method for storing the pre-existing renderer and using it to generate the initial component (see Figure 5-5).

Figure 5-5. *Numbering with a renderer*

```
public class NumberedListCellRenderer implements ListCellRenderer {
    protected ListCellRenderer oldRenderer;
    public NumberedListCellRenderer(
            ListCellRenderer oldRenderer) {
        this.oldRenderer = oldRenderer;
    }
    public Component getListCellRendererComponent(JList list,
            Object value, int index, boolean isSelected,
            boolean cellHasFocus) {
        JLabel cell = (JLabel) oldRenderer.
            getListCellRendererComponent(list, value,
            index, isSelected, cellHasFocus);
        String text = cell.getText();
        cell.setText(Integer.toString(index + 1) +
                ") " + text;
        return cell;
    }
}
```

Adding Icons to List Cells

Because the default list cell renderer returns a component that is an instance of *JLabel*, it is possible to use some of its label-specific functionality, such as support for an icon. This can enable the addition of a tremendous amount of visual information to a list box that can be of much more value than ordinary text.

Consider the following simple class as an example—it represents the name of a type of chili pepper and associates it with a particular level of hotness:

```
public class ChiliInfo {
    public String name;
    public int hotness;
    public static final int MILD = 0;
    public static final int MEDIUM = 1;
    public static final int HOT = 2;
    public static final int BLAZING = 3;
```

```
    public ChiliInfo(String name, int hotness) {
        this.name = name;
        this.hotness = hotness;
    }
};
```

An object of this class might represent an item of data in a list box. It would be very useful to have the name of the chili and an indication of hotness available to a user so he or she can select an appropriate condiment. A model can be created that returns values of this object to a list control:

```
public class ChiliListModel extends ConstantListModel {
    String[] names = {
        "Jalapeno", "Piquin", "Habanero", "Ancho"
        "Serrano", "Pasilla", "Tepin", "Cubanelle"
    };
    int[] hotness = {
        ChiliInfo.MEDIUM, ChiliInfo.BLAZING,
        ChiliInfo.BLAZING, ChiliInfo.MILD,
        ChiliInfo.HOT, ChiliInfo.MEDIUM,
        ChiliInfo.HOT, ChiliInfo.MILD
    };
    public int getSize() {
        return name.length;
    }
    public Object getElementAt(int index) {
        return new ChiliInfo(names[index],
                hotness[index]);
    }
}
```

Two options that could be used are a model filter or renderer to interpret the *ChiliInfo* object and prefix or append the heat level to the name of the chili. A more sophisticated approach might even map the chili name to a string version of the hotness scale, so there is no confusion about whether a zero represents the mildest or hottest chili.

However, a more effective and appropriate technique would be to use a picture to depict the hotness of a chili and have that picture accompany the name of the chili in the list. The icons themselves can be created as GIF files. GIF files are ideal for this purpose because they support transparency—that is, the format of the file supports areas through which the background will show. See Figure 5-6.

All that remains to be done is to create a renderer that understands the object we are interested in depicting. As before, we keep a reference to the old renderer in the new one to preserve the effects of the current look and feel.

```
public class HotnessListCellRenderer implements ListCellRenderer {
    protected ListCellRenderer oldRenderer;
    protected static ImageIcon icon[] = new ImageIcon[4];
    static {
        icon[0] = new ImageIcon("mild.gif");
        icon[1] = new ImageIcon("medium.gif");
        icon[2] = new ImageIcon("hot.gif");
        icon[3] = new ImageIcon("blazing.gif");
    }
    public HotnessListCellRenderer (
            ListCellRenderer oldRenderer) {
        this.oldRenderer = oldRenderer;
    }
    public Component getListCellRendererComponent(JList list,
```

Figure 5-6. *Using icons with a renderer*

```
        Object value, int index, boolean isSelected,
          boolean cellHasFocus) {
      JLabel cell = (JLabel) oldRenderer.
          getListCellRendererComponent(list, value,
          index, isSelected, cellHasFocus);
      ChiliInfo info = (ChiliInfo) value;
      cell.setIcon(icon[info.hotness]);
      return cell;
    }
  }
```

Naturally, it would be responsible to make sure that the old renderer really did return a *JList* and that the value was really of type *ChiliInfo*.

More Complex Cell Rendering

The label technique is only the default way of rendering list cells. There
is no restriction on the type of component used to render a cell. This also
extends to containers that contain additional components inside them.
A little additional work needs to be done to get the list items to appear
consistent with look-and-feel, but in many cases, it is straightforward.

Multicolumn List Cells

Often, it is desirable to contain data in a list box and have the information in separate columns. Although the same effect could be achieved by
a table or grid component, in many cases a specially rendered *JList* is
more appropriate.

For example, a requirement might be to produce a list of accounts
on a network with some added information, such as whether the user is
suspended. Although this could be denoted by an iconic representation
as previously discussed, a multicolumn list cell might is a good alternative. This is the data class for the example:

```
public class ExpirationInfo {
  public String userName;
  public boolean isSuspended;
  public ExpirationInfo (String userName,
```

```
                   boolean isSuspended) {
              this.userName = userName;
              this.isSuspended = isSuspended;
          }
      };
```

The goal of this exercise is to print out the user name and an indicator if the user is suspended. The name will be left-justified and the indicator will appear right-justified. In the case of a user who is not suspended, there is no reason to use an alternate renderer at all, and the name string can be used as-is.'

```
      public class ExpirationListCellRenderer
              implements ListCellRenderer {
          protected ListCellRenderer oldRenderer;
          protected JLabel indicator;
          protected JPanel panel;
          public ExpirationListCellRenderer (
                  ListCellRenderer oldRenderer) {
              this.oldRenderer = oldRenderer;
              ListCellRenderer indicatorRenderer =
                  oldRenderer.clone();
              indicator = (JLabel) indicatorRenderer.
                  getListCellRendererComponent(list,
                  "*SUSPENDED*", index, isSelected,
                  cellHasFocus);
              indicator.setColor(Color.red);
              indicator.setHorizontalAlignment(JLabel.RIGHT);
              panel = new JPanel(new GridLayout(1, 2));
          }
          public Component getListCellRendererComponent(JList list,
                  Object value, int index, boolean isSelected,
                  boolean cellHasFocus) {
              ExpirationInfo info = (ExpirationInfo) value;
              JLabel cell = (JLabel) oldRenderer.
                  getListCellRendererComponent(list,
                  info.userName, index, isSelected,
                  cellHasFocus);
```

```
        if (!info.isSuspended)
           return cell;
        else
           return createPanelCell(cell);
     }
     protected Component createPanelCell(Component cell) {
        panel.removeAll();
        panel.add(cell);
        panel.add(indicator);
        return panel;
     }
  }
```

Notice that an additional renderer had to be created to generate the additional cell. This is because it cannot be known whether the renderer class internally creates a separate instance for each cell it renders, or if a single instance exists per renderer instance. It so happens that the default renderer does not create a new cell so there would be unusual side effects if another renderer was not created.

Multiline List Cells

The same technique could be used to provide cells that are of varying height. One of the uses for a feature such as this is to implement a multiline list cell. One of the properties of the *JList* control is the *FixedCellHeight* property. This, along with its counterpart, the *FixedCellWidth* property, controls the way in which *JList* calculates the height and width of each cell. If the fixed height or width is less than zero, the preferred size of the rendered cell is used to determine the height. If either or both is greater than zero, that dimension becomes fixed and the preferred size is ignored. The default value for both is (–1) so the preferred width and height always comes into play unless otherwise specified.

This technique produces an interesting capability, because list rows of arbitrary height can now be employed. This is extremely useful for packing a great deal of useful information into a list row, which can sometimes be more prudent than a table or tree approach.

Scrollability

As with many Swing components, the responsibility for scroll bar processing is externalized. A special *JScrollPane* container was designed to provide this functionality in a manner compatible with the MVC and look-and-feel architectures.

The JScrollPane Component

The purpose of the *JScrollPane* component is to manage a series of child components. These are as follows:

- The viewed component itself. Any subclass of *java.awt.Component* can be used, and a set of constructors with a *Component* parameter is provided.

- A viewport that represents the field of view of the scroll pane. When the viewport is smaller than the component being viewed, scroll bars can be used to control the position of the component.

- Two additional viewports that serve as row and column headers.

- Four *Component* objects that serve as the four corners of the scroll pane.

- One horizontal and one vertical scroll bar of type *JScrollBar*—the appearance of these components is controlled by *JScrollPane* through the use of the *VerticalScrollBarPolicy* and *HorizontalScroll BarPolicy* properties. The values of these properties can be one of the following values in *JScrollPane*:

  - *VERTICAL_SCROLLBAR_AS_NEEDED, HORIZONTAL_SCROLL BAR_AS_NEEDED*—These are the default values. Scroll bars will appear if the size of the scrollable component is larger than the supplied viewport.

  - *VERTICAL_SCROLLBAR_ALWAYS, HORIZONTAL_SCROLLBAR_ ALWAYS*—These settings cause the specified scroll bar to be displayed no matter what the size of the scrollable component.

  - *VERTICAL_SCROLLBAR_NEVER, HORIZONTAL_SCROLLBAR_ NEVER*—These settings cause the specified scroll bar to be suppressed regardless of the size of the scrollable component. Scrolling can still be performed programmatically even if the scroll bars themselves are not visible.

Invalid values cause an *IllegalArgumentException* to be thrown, so be careful not to mismatch the vertical and horizontal values because they do differ. These and other constants are defined in the *ScrollPaneConstants* interface, which *JScrollPane* does implement.

Figure 5-7 visually illustrates the relationships of the child components. Any of the components can be substituted by a subclass of the particular component type. This is rarely necessary, given that these components are managed adequately by the default components.

A special layout manager called *ScrollPaneLayout* is responsible for managing the position and state of all the components of *JScrollPane*. You can substitute a layout, but *JScrollPane* only accepts a layout manager that derives from *ScrollPaneLayout*.

The Scrollable Interface

JFC components that require scrolling must implement the *Scrollable* interface. This is the contract between the component and the *JScrollPane* container. A component that implements this interface provides information to the *JScrollPane* (via the *JViewport*) as to its scrolling requirements.

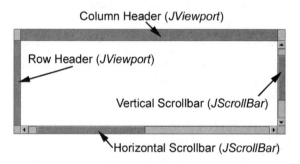

Figure 5-7. *Viewports and scroll bars in JScrollPane*

Components that do not provide this interface can still be scrolled, but they cannot communicate any information on how that scrolling is to occur. In that case, *JScrollPane* calculates the scroll intervals based on the difference in sizes between the viewport and the viewed component.

The interface defines these methods:

- *Dimension getPreferredScrollableViewportSize()*—This is the way in which a *Scrollable* component tells its scroll pane how big it wishes the viewport to be. It is at the discretion of the layout manager of the parent container as to how this request should be treated. When the calculation is made, the scroll bar policy is taken into consideration. This method is called each time *ScrollPanelLayout* is invalidated.

- *int getScrollableUnitIncrement(Rectangle visibleRect, int orientation, int direction)*—This method is the means by which the size of a scrollable unit is determined. The size returned is the number of pixels that need to be scrolled to expose an entire row or column. The semantics of what constitutes a row or column depends on the implementation of the component. The values of the *orientation* and *direction* parameters dictate which size is being requested.

- *int getScrollableBlockIncrement(Rectangle visibleRect, int orientation, int direction)*—This method is used to communicate to the *JScrollBar* the amount of scrolling that will expose an entire block of rows or columns in either the horizontal or vertical directions. The semantics of what constitutes a block depends on the implementation of the component.

- *boolean getScrollableTracksViewportHeight()*—This method should return *true* if the height of the component should be forced to match the viewport height.

- *boolean getScrollableTracksViewportWidth()*—This method should return *true* if the width of the component should be forced to match the viewport width.

Other Methods of JList

A few additional features of *JList* are notable:

- *int getVisibleRowCount()*—Requests that the viewport be sized to display the specified number of rows. This value is used in conjunction with the row height to calculate the *PreferredScrollable ViewportSize* property for the *Scrollable* interface.

- *public int getFirstVisibleIndex()*—This method retrieves the index of the cell in the upper-left corner of the *JList* even if it is only partially visible. If nothing is visible or the list is empty, a (–1) will be returned.

- *public int getLastVisibleIndex()*—This method retrieves the index of the cell in the lower-right corner of the *JList* even if it is only partially visible. If nothing is visible or the list is empty, a (–1) will be returned.

- *public void ensureIndexIsVisible(int index)*—This method can be used to guarantee that a particular list item is visible. The viewport is automatically scrolled to accommodate the request. This method has no effect on *JList* components not contained in a *JScrollPane*.

- *public int locationToIndex(Point location)*—This method returns the index of the list cell that contains the specified location (relative to the *JList*). If the point is not within the bounds of any index, (–1) is returned.

- *public Point indexToLocation(int index)*—This method returns the origin (top left pixel) of the specified index. If the index is not valid, *null* is returned.

- *public Rectangle getCellBounds(int index1, int index2)*—Returns the bounds of the rectangle that contains the specified indices. If the range is not valid, *null* is returned.

Exercises

1. Add sorting capability to the chili list application to sort by hotness or to exclude chilis based on their hotness value.

2. Develop a sorting list filter that accepts a pluggable sort algorithm. Develop a delegate interface and several examples of different sort algorithms. This mechanism could be used to test different sorting algorithms against each other or to tweak algorithms when used in concert with an optimizer or other profiling tool.

3. Create a list model and renderer that supports a multiline list renderer based on *JPanel* and *GridLayout*.

The world has traditionally been divided into the animate and the inanimate. Inanimate things do not have feelings or wills of their own, and can therefore be smashed, burned, or harnessed by animate ones without the animate ones having to feel guilty.
—Douglas R. Hofstadter, *Metamagical Themas: Questing for the Essence of Mind and Pattern*

Chapter 6

JFC Components Part 2

Now that the essential constituents of the Swing architecture have been discussed, it is sensible to discuss some of the additional features that JFC provides. This chapter discusses the following topics:

- JFC menu bars, popup menus, and *JToolbar* components

- The *JSlider* and *JProgressBar* components

- The *JToolTip* and *Timer* classes

- The dialog box classes provided by JFC: *JFileChooser*, *JcolorChooser*, and *JOptionPane*

Menus

Menus are a familiar sight to users of graphical interfaces. It is a fairly well-proven paradigm for offering a hierarchical list of actions from which a user can make a selection. The menu mechanism employed by AWT provides access to the native menu implementation, thus suffering from the lack of robustness caused by least-common-denominator capabilities.

JFC replaces the AWT menu mechanism with a lightweight menu component that extends *JComponent*. Using this alternative, the rendering and other characteristics of menu processing can be implemented in UI delegates. This produces almost limitless possibilities in developing customized menus with images or other graphical content.

Menu Organization

Three menu components are provided, each of which implements the *MenuElement* interface. Menus are organized in a hierarchical fashion with a single *JMenuBar* as the root. *JMenuBar* supports an *add()* method that supports the addition of menus. Menus are encapsulated in the *JMenu* class. *JMenu*, in turn, serves as the container for *JMenuItem* objects. These are the objects that are mapped to programmatic actions. See Figure 6-1.

JMenuItem extends *AbstractButton*; although this may seem unusual, it is fundamental to the operation of Swing menus. Actually, many of the features of the JFC button controls are very closely related to those desirable for menu processing. Inheriting from *AbstractButton* gives menu

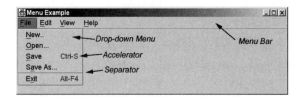

Figure 6-1. *Parts of a Swing menu*

items the capability to have associated action commands, mnemonics, selection, and other states. Code from the button UI delegates for the *JButton, JRadioButton,* and *JCheckBox* components is used to provide alternative menu item types that support exclusive and nonexclusive selection. See Figure 6-2.

JMenu inherits from *JMenuItem*; this gives the capability to create cascading menus by adding a *JMenu* to a *JMenu. JPopupMenu* is analogous to *JMenu* in this hierarchy, except it is not itself a *MenuElement.* Popup menus are covered in detail later in this chapter.

JMenuBar Class

JMenuBar is the container that is recognized by *JRootPane* as comprising a menu. Thus, any container that implements *RootPaneContainer* is able to provide a menu. In the case of *JApplet, JDialog, JFrame,* and *JInternalFrame,* a set of property methods is provided that delegate to the root pane, where the reference to the menu bar is actually stored. These methods, *setJMenuBar()* and *getJMenuBar(),* delegate to the identical methods in the *JRootPane.* The *JWindow* class is the exception; to add a *JMenuBar* to a *JWindow,* add the menu bar directly to the *JRootPane.*

JMenuBar supports the *SingleSelectionModel* interface as its data model, the same model implemented by *JTabbedPane.* The other menu components use *ButtonModel* for their state information; an effect of extending *AbstractButton.*

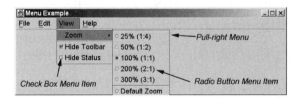

Figure 6-2. *Optional menu components*

Managing Menu Bar Children

Because *JMenuBar* is a descendant of *JComponent* and, therefore *java.awt. Container*, menu components are inserted into the menu bar by the *add()* method. A version of *add()* is provided that takes a *JMenu* as a parameter and returns the passed *JMenu* reference. The code simply calls the super-class version of *add()*. An implementation of *ContainerListener* registers each child that is added to the menu bar with a *ChangeListener* if, and only if, the new child is an instance of *JMenu*. Being identified as a *JMenu* implies that a *SingleSelectionListener* model is available and that sub-menus can be supported. Items other than a *JMenu* can be added to a menu bar, but their menu-like behavior will not operate because their state models will be ignored.

The *Container* syntax can be used to perform operations on a menu bar's children, but some additional methods are provided to simplify these operations.

The *getComponentAtIndex()* method is provided as an alternative to the *getComponent()* method of *Container*. Unlike *getComponent()*, *getComponentAtIndex()* returns *null* if an index is specified that is out of range. A complementary method *getComponentIndex()* is provided that takes a child component reference as a parameter and returns its index. A value of (–1) is returned if the specified component is not a child of the *JMenuBar*.

Two methods are provided for compatibility with the AWT version of *MenuBar*. The *getMenuCount()* method calls the superclass implementation of *getComponentCount()* instead of relying on a peer implementation. The method *getMenu()* takes an integer index as a parameter and returns the *JMenu* child component at that index. If the index is invalid or the child is not *JMenu*, the method returns *null*.

For selection support, *JMenuBar* provides the *setSelected()* method, which supports selection of any descendant of the menu bar by providing its object reference. The *isSelected()* method returns *true* if any descendant of the *JMenuBar* is selected when the method is invoked.

Menu Item Compatibility

A menu bar is not descended from *AbstractButton* nor does it implement the *MenuElement* interface. For simplicity in referring to menu components, certain methods of *AbstractButton* and *MenuElement* are provided by *JMenuBar*.

JMenuBar, as any *JComponent*, can have a border optionally set with the *Border* property. *AbstractButton* provides a *boolean* property *BorderPainted* that controls whether a border will be painted. This property is mimicked in *JMenuItem* with *setBorderPainted()* and *isBorderPainted()* methods. The default value for this property is *true*. Also, as in *AbstractButton*, a *Margin* property is supported that is implemented as an *Insets* object. The margin represents the space between a menu bar's border and its content. Neither of these properties is bound; *invalidate()* is called when the *setMargin()* method is called.

The MenuElement Interface

The common thread that binds the menu bar with its menu items is that they all implement the interface *MenuElement*. *MenuElement* defines the methods that enable the different menu components to communicate using a consistent API. Methods specified by this interface are used to process mouse and keyboard events, handle menu selection changes, and provide access to the children of menu containers.

The methods of *MenuElement* that process events are *processMouse Event()* and *processKeyEvent()*. These methods take three parameters, an event, an array of *MenuElement* objects, and a reference to a *Menu SelectionManager* object.

The MenuSelectionManager Class

MenuSelectionManager is a singleton object, meaning one instance is provided for all operating menus to share. Generally speaking, it is not directly invoked, but a brief description of its functionality is relevant.

MenuSelectionManager is the delegate for processing mouse events within a menu bar and its child components. It is responsible for determining which menu item the mouse is in while a menu operation is taking place. The public method *processMouseEvent()* is used for processing mouse menu operations. Another event-related method is *processKeyEvent()*, which supports menu accelerator key processing.

MenuSelectionManager implements multiple selection of menu items using an internal *Vector*. This lets menu selection be viewed as a path instead of as a singly selected item. The path of menu selection is represented as an array of menu components, starting from the *JMenuBar* reference and ending with the selected menu item. The elements in between represent the potentially cascading *JMenu* items. *MenuSelectionManager* treats the selection path as a property with a type of *MenuElement()*, providing the *getSelectedPath()* and *setSelectedPath()* methods to query and modify the current selection.

Other Methods of MenuElement

The *MenuElement* interface is responsible for telling a menu item when a descendant is selected or deselected. The *menuSelectionChanged()* method is invoked by *MenuSelectionManager* as the selection path changes to select and deselect menu items that are in or out of the selection path.

The *getSubElements()* method is used primarily by *JMenuBar* to report its child components. It returns an array of *MenuElement* objects representing the menu's children. The implementation for *JMenuItem* is to return an empty array; *JMenu* returns an empty array if it does not represent a popup for another menu.

The last method specified is *getComponent()*, which takes no parameters and returns an instance of *Component*. This method is defined to return the component that is to be used to render menu items; in all cases the method is coded to return a reference to *this* (the component itself).

The JMenu Class

The *JMenu* class, which inherits from *JMenuItem*, is used to add menus to a *JMenuBar*. Because *JMenuItem* inherits from *AbstractButton*, these capabilities are also present in *JMenu*. The model used for *JMenu* is *ButtonModel*; the property mutator, *setModel()*, adds a *ChangeListener* to the specified model. This listener checks if the item representing the menu is selected and propagates the selection to its submenus using a call to *fireMenuSelected()* or *fireMenuDeselected()*, which cause the submenu to either appear or disappear.

Managing JMenu Child Components

JMenu is designed to be a container for *JMenuItem* objects. Because it is itself a *JMenuItem*, cascading menus can be constructed by adding *JMenu* objects to another *JMenu*. In any case, *JMenu* is where the containment support must be provided for menu elements. *JMenu* supports several different mechanisms to access, add, insert, and delete its subcomponents.

JMenu Popup Characterstics

The *JMenu* class and the *JPopupMenu* class are very closely coordinated. The *JPopupMenu* is used to provide floating menus that do not have an associated menu bar and can thus appear anywhere on the screen. *JMenu* renders itself using the code provided in *JPopupMenu*. The chief difference is that the popup implementation for *JMenu* is automatically drawn in the correct position so as to appear to be a child menu of the menu bar. The implementation of *JPopupMenu* that is created for each *JMenu* is also used for storing the menu's subcomponents.

JMenu provides a *boolean* property *PopupMenuVisible* that controls the visibility of the associated popup menu, and a method *setMenuLocation()* that invokes a *setLocation()* on the popup portion of the *JMenu*. The *JMenu* portion also creates a window listener that listens for the *windowClosing()* event that occurs when the popup is closed. It uses this event to trigger an unconditional deselection of the popup menu.

Because it has other features not related to normal menu processing, the *JPopupMenu* class is covered in its own section later in this chapter.

Accessing Menu Components

The *getItem()* method takes an integer parameter that represents the item's index. If the specified component is *not* a *JMenuItem*, the method returns the reference to the *JMenu* itself. It is not clear why this is necessary; the documentation claims that this represents detection of a menu separator. A negative index generates an *IllegalArgumentException*.

The methods *getMenuComponentCount()* and *getMenuComponent()* both delegate to the contained *JPopupMenu*. The first method returns the number of contained components, the second returns the *JMenuItem* at the specified integer index. Another method *getItemCount()* is an alias for *getMenuComponentCount()*.

Adding Menu Components

JMenu supports four different overloaded methods named *add()*. Each of these methods eventually performs the exact same function: that of appending a subcomponent to a *JMenu* container.

The first version is an override of the *java.awt.Container* method, which takes a *Component* as a parameter and returns the reference to that component. The *JMenu* version redirects the add to *JPopupMenu* that serves as the container and view delegate. The second version takes a *JMenuItem* as a parameter; it also returns a *JMenuItem* reference. Unlike the other version, this version offers a little more type control than the *Component* version. It also delegates to the popup instance to perform the actual append operation.

The other two versions are much more robust and can be invaluable in reducing significant amounts of code. As described in the next section—covering *JMenuItem* in detail—a *JMenuItem* is an *AbstractButton* and therefore a *Text* property that supports firing of *ActionEvent* to interested listeners. *JMenu* provides a version of *add()* that supports an initial value for the *Texts* property and another that takes an *Action* object as a parameter. Both of these methods return the *JMenuItem* that is automatically generated.

Action is an extension of *ActionListener* that encapsulates an action command. It supports a set of properties that represent the text, description, representative icon, or other information.

Inserting Menu Components

Inserting menu components is similar to adding them, except an additional integer parameter is included that represents the position. Each of these methods delegates to the contained *JPopupMenu*, which stores its children in a temporary *Vector* in order to shift the existing elements. Any of these three methods may throw an *IllegalArgumentException* if the supplied index is negative.

The first version of *insert()* takes a *String* parameter and an integer index parameter. For some reason it returns *void* and not the *JMenuItem* created from the supplied *String*. The reason for this is not documented in the source code, and it seems a trivial change to return the instantiated *JMenuItem* instead.

The two additional *insert()* methods take a *JMenuItem* and an *Action* object respectively, with the inclusion of the index parameter. These methods do return the inserted *JMenuItem*.

Deleting Menu Components

Menu components are removed from a *JMenu* using the *remove()* method. Three versions of this method are provided. The first is an override of the *Container* version of the method and takes a single *Component* parameter. The two other versions take a *JMenuItem* and an integer index respectively. The *java.awt.Container* method *removeAll()* is also provided to delete all components from a menu.

Note that if the child of a *JMenu* is itself a *JMenu,* the *removeAll()* method only removes the direct descendents; it is not a recursive operation.

Listening for Menu Events

JMenu provides the capability for registering interest in changes in menu selection. Methods are provided that enable association of objects that implement the *MenuListener* interface. These methods, *addMenuListener()* and *removeMenuListener(),* both take a single argument that is an object of type *MenuListener.*

MenuListener defines three methods, each of which returns an event object of type *MenuEvent. MenuEvent* inherits from *java.util.MenuObject,* which only contains information about the source of the event, usually the *JMenu* itself.

The *menuSelected()* and *menuDeselected()* methods are invoked by the *MenuChangeListener* inner class of *JMenu.* This implementation of *ChangeListener* invokes *menuSelected()* when the model for the *JMenu* is selected and *menuDeselected()* otherwise. The third method, *menuCanceled(),* seems to be provided for compatibility with popup menu processing. A method is provided to fire the method, but no code anywhere in JFC actually seems to invoke it.

JMenu Properties

JMenu supports a *Delay* property that is used to tune the mouse drag characteristics. The base UI delegate for *JMenu, BasicMenuUI,* sets this value to 200 milliseconds. This time lapse represents the hesitation before a cascading menu is displayed, which is designed to give some time for users to move the mouse to a final destination before the selection is triggered. The timer is set when the mouse enters a *JMenu* object; the cascading effect is only apparent when the mouse remains in the menu object for the entire delay time.

JMenu provides the convenience methods *setSelected()* and *isSelected()* that delegate this *boolean* property to the state model. Another convenience method provided is *addSeparator()*, which creates a horizontal divider within a menu.

A method *isTearOff()* is provided and hardcoded to return *false*. This is presumably for future expansion that would enable conversion of *JMenu* objects to floating palettes. An alternative constructor for *JMenu* also supports the initialization of this property, but it has no effect.

Menu Items

Menu items are based on the class *JMenuItem* and represent both the branch and the leaf elements in a menu hierarchy. Because the behavior of the container portion has already been discussed in the previous section on *JMenu*, it remains only to talk about *JMenuItem* in its role as an endpoint of menu selection.

It is convenient to think of a menu as a hierarchical set of button components. Whereas *JMenu* serves as a container to enforce the structure, the *JMenuItem* elements that terminate the tree structure are where the user interaction actually happens. Because these elements are all light-weight, they are supported by external UI delegates. Thus, a powerful capability to customize menus exists, from both a rendering and an event-processing standpoint.

The JMenuItem Class

JMenuItem is an extension of *AbstractButton*, so it inherits the capabilities already discussed: encapsulation of a *ButtonModel*, text and iconic content, programmable action capability, mnemonic key assignment, and delegation to button UI classes.

Another benefit of being derived from *AbstractButton* is that subclasses of *JMenuItem* can adapt many of the features of the standard JFC button classes for use in menu processing. Later in this section, the standard JFC implementations of the radio button and check box components—themselves implemented as *AbstractButton* extensions—will be discussed.

Subclasses of *JMenuItem* are limited by the restriction that menu item states conform to those states supported by *ButtonModel*. This is not a serious restriction as it is not advisable to create menu items that exhibit behavior that is strikingly different from existing menus users are familiar with.

JMenuItem Constructors

The standard menu item object supports five constructors. A default constructor is provided, which creates a menu item with *null* values for the *Text* and *Icon* properties. Another two versions take a single *Icon* or a *String* parameter; another takes both a *String* and an *Icon*. This version is the one ultimately called by the first three. It creates a *DefaultButtonModel* instance for use as its state model, and then calls an internal method *init()* passing the text and icon specified by the parameters. This is analogous to the constructor for the other button classes.

Next, the constructor sets the *BorderPainted* and *FocusPainted* properties to *false*. These properties are provided by the *AbstractButton* implementation. They determine whether the UI delegate will paint a menu item's borders and focus indicator; these are generally not desirable on a menu item. Next, the default horizontal text position and alignment are set; the text is usually to the right of an icon and left-justified. Lastly, the *updateUI()* method is invoked to associate the component with a UI delegate. The last constructor takes a *String* text parameter and an integer mnemonic key value. This constructor behaves the same as does the *String* and *Icon* version, with two important differences: The *Mnemonic* property, which is implemented by *AbstractButton*, is initialized and the horizontal text position is set to have the text on the left of the icon. This is done because mnemonics are not compatible with a branch version of a menu item that would be used for a cascading menu. If this constructor is used, the icon is managed by the UI delegate to insert an arrow icon indicating a cascading menu.

Focus Listening

During the initialization of *JMenuItem*, a *private static* class is used as a focus listener. This listener merely requests that the focus be painted when focus is lost. Because focus is not painted by default, the addition of this listener to every created menu item seems unnecessary. Perhaps binding the *FocusPainted* property and adding the listener when the value was set to *true* would be a better idea. This type of focus listener does make sense in the normal button components because there are accessibility issues related to button focus.

The accessibility interface for menus is related to the *Armed* property of the menu, and the *setArmed()* and *isArmed()* methods are overridden in *JMenuItem* to interact with the menu accessibility context. Both methods ultimately delegate to the button model associated with the menu for this information. In a related matter, the *setEnabled()* method is also overridden to ensure that the menu item's *Armed* property is *false* when the menu item is disabled.

Another property-like method that *JMenuItem* implements is *alwaysOnTop()*, which returns *true*. As with ToolTips, *JMenuBar* and *JPopup* menus return *true* for this method, overridding the default value of *false* returned by *JComponent*. The purpose of this method is to serve as a callback for an internal version of the *paintImmediately()* method in *JComponent*.

It seems tempting to treat this more like an actual property and give any lightweight component the opportunity to return *true* for the *alwaysOnTop()* method, thus saving the effort of getting involved with *JLayeredPane* or the glass pane (see Chapter 4). Supposedly, this was not advisable because it would be difficult to reconcile what might happen if two overlapping components returned *true* for this method. Because ToolTips and menus are functionally coordinated, it is safe to allow those to coexist as high *z*-order components. But, because anyone who cares to do so can simply inherit from any component and return whatever they like, it seems tenable to offer it as a property. A suggestion: add *setAlwaysOnTop()* and *isAlwaysOnTop()* to *JComponent*; deprecate *alwaysOnTop()*.

Accelerators and Menu Events

Because the *Mnemonic* property of menu items is limited to combinations of the <Alt> key and a single character, the concept of supporting other keystroke combinations was implemented as the *Accelerator* property of *JMenuItem*. This property has the type *KeyStroke*, thus enabling it to encapsulate any supported combination of keys and modifiers. When the property is modified with the *setAccelerator()* method, a keyboard action is registered that consists of an anonymous inner class that extends *AbstractAction*. The flag for the registration is *JComponent. WHEN_IN_FOCUSED_WINDOW*, so the accelerator will be effective anywhere on the menu bar or popup menu's highest-level container, such as a *JDialog* or *JInternalFrame*. The *Accelerator* property is not bound; it seems sensible that it should be, and that the accelerator actions could be registered by a property change. This could enable, for example, look-and-feel-defined default actions.

The implementation of the base UI delegate for menu items paints additional text in a menu item with an accelerator to inform a user of the availability of the keystroke combination. This text is presented to the right of the menu caption itself and is in a noticeably smaller font.

Also, *JMenuItem* overrides the *processKeyEvent()* of *JComponent* to give it an opportunity to process key events generated by the *MenuSelectionManager*. It passes control to a public method of *JMenuItem* called *processMenuKeyEvent()* and forwards that to an instance of a *MenuKeyEvent* object. This object is the parameter of the methods defined in the *MenuKeyListener* interface, which describes an event supported by *JMenuItem*.

MenuKeyListener and MenuKeyEvent

An instance of *MenuKeyListener* is passed to the methods *addMenuKeyListener()* and *removeMenuKeyListener()*, implemented in *JMenuItem*. The interface defines three methods, all of which process keystrokes that are delivered by *MenuSelectionMananger*. These methods are *menuKeyTyped()*, *menuKeyPressed()*, and *menuKeyReleased()*, each of which passes a *MenuKeyEvent* as a parameter. They are activated under the same circumstances as their AWT analogs.

MenuKeyEvent is an extension of *java.awt.event.KeyEvent* and provides some added value in the form of two read-only properties. The *getPath()* method returns an array of *MenuElement* objects representing the current menu selection path. The method *getMenuSelectionManager()* returns a reference to the instance of the active selection manager.

JMenuItem Mouse Events

JFC defines an additional event called *javax.swing.event.MenuDragMouseEvent*, which is similar to a *MouseEvent*, which is used by both *MouseListener* and *MouseMotionListener*. It is used to coordinate the various mouse activities that menus use to operate. The *MenuDragMouseListener* interface is used to enable interest to be registered in these changes. *JMenuItem* provides the *addMenuDragMouseListener() and removeMenuDragMouseListener()* methods to provide this feature. This facility is primarily designed as a method of communicating mouse operations to the menu item UI delegate from the *MenuSelectionManager*.

Menu Item Mouse Listeners

The *MenuDragMouseListener* interface reduces the AWT-style mouse events into the four operations generated for the UI delegate by the selection manager. This interface is implemented along with the AWT mouse events by all menu items. This may seem peculiarly complex, but it is an effective workaround for an unusual situation.

Two mouse listener interfaces are defined by AWT: *MouseListener* and *MouseMotionListener*. *MouseListener* provides information about when a mouse button is pressed, released, and clicked, and when it enters or exits a component's bounds. *MouseMotionListener* provides two methods that report the motion of the mouse when the button is pressed (a drag operation) or not. Although this is a satisfactory arrangement for the most part, a side effect is that *mouseEnter()* and *mouseLeave()* events are not received while a drag operation is taking place. This means an alternate method needs to be implemented for menus, which need to coordinate both listener types.

UI Delegate Mouse Handling

BasicMenuItemUI defines the default handler for these events in a private inner class *MenuDragMouseHandler*. The methods *menuDragMouseDragged()* and *menuDragMouseReleased()* cause the menu selection manager to set and clear the current selection path. The methods *menuDragMouseEntered()* and *menuDragMouseExited()*, also defined by *MenuDragMouseListener*, have no-op implementations in the basic UI.

Interestingly, *BasicMenuUI* also registers listeners for the *MouseListener* and *MouseMotionListener* events. These events process mouse events before the *MenuDragMouseHandler*. The inner class defined as the listener is called *MouseInputHandler*. It provides an implementation of *MouseInputListener*, which extends *MouseListener* and *MouseMotionListener* for a total of seven required methods.

The *mouseEntered()* method causes the menu selection manager to recalculate the current menu selection path. The *mouseExited()* function removes the current menu element from the end of the selection path. The *mouseDragged()* method delegates to the *MenuSelectionManager* implemenation of *processMouseEvent()*, which then invokes the *MenuDrag MouseEvent* process.

The *mouseReleased()* method performs a very important function: If the mouse is released within the bounds of the menu item, the menu selection is cleared and the *doClick()* method of the *AbstractButton* ancestor class is invoked. This, in turn, causes the action listener to be notified with an *ActionEvent*, thus generating the activity associated with the menu item. These are the same two methods invoked by the anonymous action class that is instantiated when an *Accelerator* is set on a *JMenuItem*.

BasicMenuItemUI.MouseInputHandler provides no-op implementations for the *mouseClicked()*, *mousePressed()*, and *mouseMoved()*. Using the mouse click to activate the action mechanisms is not needed; the methods the underlying *AbstractButton* implementation signals the UI with a *ChangeEvent*, which is as a signal that a menu's selection state has changed.

The Menu Item UI Delegate

The *BasicMenuItemUI* class provides the two typical features of a UI delegate: painting the component using the interpretation of its properties and using that information to calculate the preferred size of a component.

Menu Item Size Calculation

This method takes into account look-and-feel default properties as well as any properties set programmatically. The delegate returns a *null* for the minimum and maximum sizes, as menus tend to transcend traditional component layout.

A *protected* method *getPreferredMenuItemSize()* is called by the *getPreferredSize()* implementation of *BasicMenuUI*. It calculates the required size of a menu item, taking in to account the menu text, alignment, position and font, the accelerator text and font, the icon size, and the pixel gap between icon and text.

Menu Item Painting

The *paint()* method defined *BasicMenuItemUI* delegates to a public method *paintMenuItem()* that takes seven parameters. It is evident that this method was intended to serve as the paint method for the *JMenu* and checked versions of the menu items as well. The method takes the *Graphics* object and the *JComponent* reference passed to it from *paint()*, along with a check icon, an arrow icon, the background and foreground colors, and the text/icon gap in pixels. This makes the same painting code usable by any extension of *JMenuItem* that supports these parameters.

The UI delegate uses a private method *layoutMenuItem()* that forwards the layout of the text and icons to the *SwingUtilities.layoutCompoundLabel()* method. This is the standard mechanism to calculate the required size for a text and icon pair, taking into account the string length, icon size, fonts, and so on. This version also accounts for the accelerator text and the additional arrow icon that is used for cascading menus. The mechanism that calculates the preferred size of the menu item uses a similar set of methods.

JCheckBoxMenuItem and JRadioButtonMenuItem

JMenuItem has two additional versions that provide somewhat different behavior. If a regular menu item is considered to be stateless, that is, only selected while it is pressed, then the alternatives provide menu items that possess state with nonmomentary states. These menu items are conceptually derived from their analogous components: the radio button and the check box. Their difference is primarily in their use of a UI delegate derived from *BasicMenuItemUI*. The delegate *BasicCheckBoxMenuItemUI* and its slightly lengthier-named cousin, *BasicRadioButtonMenuItemUI*, use icons to represent their different selection states. The icons that are used to simulate the radio and check states are determined by the UI defaults.

Both of these classes install UI defaults that are particular to their mode of operation. Also, their implementations of *processMouseEvent()*

are altered to suit their nonmomentary states. Both use identical code to change icons as the menu item's selection state changes; it is invoked in either case by the menu selection manager.

JSeparator

This is not actually a menu item, but is a *JComponent* used to provide a horizontal or vertical bar in a menu. Separators help organize a menu into compartments that can help a user understand the relationships among different menu items. A UI delegate that inherits from *SeparatorUI* is provided to enable the look-and-feel to provide rendering characteristics.

JSeparator can be added to a *JMenu* using its *Component* version of *add()*. It can also be used in nonmenu containers as a convenient way of displaying a separating line that is compatible with the current look-and-feel and color theme.

JPopupMenu

The *JPopupMenu* component is one of the most complex and robust classes that JFC provides. It performs the duty of not only standalone right-click menus, but also serves as the drop-down and drag-right menus that are associated with a menu bar and as the drop-down portion of the *JComboBox* component. *JPopupMenu* uses the same methods to manage children as *JMenu*, for which it serves as the delegate responsible for administrating its submenus and menu items.

Anatomy of a JPopupMenu

JPopupMenu is an unusual component because it is never actually added to the component that it is created for. The code in *JPopupMenu* and its UI delegate manage an additional container that serves to parent the popup (see Figure 6-3).

The implementation of popup menus is complex because of issues related to the implementation of lightweight components. For example, how can a lightweight popup be implemented in a mixed environment of heavyweight and lightweight components? Also, how can a lightweight menu be displayed in an area outside its container? In order to

Figure 6-3. *Popup menu example*

accommodate the various scenarios that arise in these and other similar situations, *JPopupMenu* supports being hosted by different container classes. The three supported popup scenarios are named lightweight, mediumweight, and heavyweight. The decision of which particular container to use is made dynamically, but a user can alter the behavior somewhat by disabling the use of lightweight popup menus.

Lightweight menus are hosted by a *JPanel*, which means that lightweight menus are restricted to appearing inside the bounds of its container. Although it is the preferred weight (by default), many situations will cause a lightweight menu to be automatically implemented as a medium or heavy version. One obvious case is where a popup extends outside the boundaries of the root pane container. Code exists in *JPopupMenu* to detect this condition and change to a different container on the fly.'

Heavyweight popups are contained by a *JWindow* instance, which means they have their own real estate in which to operate. If a menu exceeds its parent's bounds, it is automatically converted to a heavyweight or mediumweight, even if the original container was lightweight. Heavyweight components will always obscure peer-level components that are lightweight, so the visibility is guaranteed.

Mediumweight popups inherit from *java.awt.Panel*, so they are heavyweight components, but they are not hosted by their own real estate. Mediumweight popups are used in the case of popups occurring in modal dialog boxes or if lightweight popups are explicitly disabled by the user. The mediumweight popup is hosted by the layered pane portion of the root pane container in a layer that ensures it is visible over modal dialog boxes and components.

Each type of container has its own caching characteristics all of which are internal to the *JPopupMenu* class code. These caches are implemented to speed the creation and operation of popup containers and attempt to reduce the number of resources required to do so.

One of the most impressive things about this class is the way in which it hides the complexity of these implementations. No matter what sort of popup is created, they all respond to a consistent API.

Disabling Lightweight Popups

JPopupMenu provides a static property that controls whether the use of lightweight popups is disabled. This situation arises mostly from situations of mixing light- and heavyweight components or from some uses of the glass and layered panes. The method *setDefaultLightWeightPopupEnabled()* takes a *boolean* parameter and places that value in JFC's private application content hashtable. If the value is set to *false*, mediumweight popups are used in all cases where a lightweight one would have been created. The accessor method *getDefaultLightWeightPopupEnabled()* returns the value stored in the application context. The name of this method might be more correctly implemented as *isDefaultLightWeightPopupEnabled* according to property method naming guidelines.

JPopupMenu Methods

The support for popup menus requires some additional functionality beyond that of fixed ones. Popup menus all register themselves with a parent component that represents the coordinate space in which the menu operates. This capability is performed automatically for those popup menus used in displaying *JMenuBar* and *JMenu* components.

Displaying a Popup Menu

The *show()* method is used to display a popup menu. It takes three parameters: a *Component* reference, an *x*-axis position, and a *y*-axis position. The component represents the invoker of the popup; the axis positions are given as relative to that component's coordinate system. The popup menu converts the given coordinate to screen coordinates when it positions the popup window. If the invoker is *null* the popup uses screen coordinates.

JPopupMenu supports an *Invoker* property that manages the reference to the invoker. When the *setInvoker()* method is invoked, it checks to see if the new reference is different from the existing value. If so, the UI delegate is uninstalled and reinstalled. In either case, the *invalidate()* method is invoked on the popup to recalculate its layout.

Changing Size and Location

The *setSize()* and *getSize()* methods are not usable on *JPopupMenu* because the popup menu itself is hosted by a parent window. It is the size of this encapsulated container that dictates the dimensions of the menu. An additional pair of methods is provided to modify the menu's size; *setPopupSize()* provides a version that takes a *Dimension* object and another that takes a separate width and height as integers. The *setPopupSize()* version—as opposed to the *setSize()*—checks if the popup delegate is not *null* and calls *getSize()* on that container, not the *JPopupMenu* component itself. The *setLocation()* method is overridden to delegate to the popup delegate as well.

Popup Menu Events

JPopupMenu supports an event listener that allows detection of changes in a popup menu's visibility. The methods *addPopupMenuListener()* and *removePopupMenuListener()* both take a reference to a *PopupMenuListener* object and enable registration of popup menu events.

PopupMenuListener and PopupMenuEvent

This listener interface supports three methods, each of which contains a single parameter of type *PopupMenuEvent*. The first method, *popupMenuWillBecomeVisible()*, is invoked in the *JPopupMenu* version of *setVisible()* when the property is set to *true*. It gives an interested listener an opportunity to make changes before the menu displays. The analog to this method is *popupMenuWillBecomeInvisible()*, which is called by *setVisible* when its parameter is *false*. It gives listeners an opportunity to know when a popup is about to be closed. The mysterious *popupMenuCanceled()* is never invoked in the JFC library, so it is difficult to say under what condition it is supposed to get fired.

PopupMenuEvent inherits from *java.util.EventObject* with no changes, so the only piece of information available is the read-only *getSource()* property, which will contain an *Object* reference to the menu for which the event was fired.

Other Methods of JPopupMenu

The method *isPopupMenu()* returns *true* if the *JPopupMenu* it is invoked on is a standalone menu, that is, its invoker is not a *JMenu* or *null*. A side-effect of this test is that popups with *null* invokers are not considered popups, at least according to the functionality of this method.

Two methods are provided, *setLabel()* and *getLabel()*, that support a *Label* property that is associated with the popup instance. It is a bound property and also fires a property change to the accessibility context. This value is for optional use by the popup menu UI delegates.

Lastly, a method *addSeparator()* is provided that adds a look-and-feel-specified separator bar to a popup menu.

JToolBar

JToolBar is an alternative mechanism to menus for presenting users with different action choices. Instead of the pull-down/pull-right or popup paradigm, *JToolBar* is capable of being docked in a fixed position on a container or floating in a layer above the root pane's content. See Figure 6-4.

The *JToolBar* component is designed to be able to dock into a container that supports *BorderLayout*. When the toolbar is dragged around

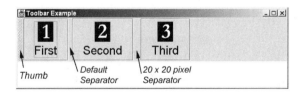

Figure 6-4. *JToolBar: docked position*

its container, the orientation of the toolbar is automatically changed depending on the side of the container (north, south, east, or west), it is dragged to. The toolbar docks with the closest side. See Figure 6-5.

Managing Toolbar Components

The *JToolBar* component is a rather typical container that uses *BoxLayout* to manage its children. Any component can be added to a toolbar; its layout can be changed to whatever might be more suitable.

Adding Components

An additional version of *add()* is provided that takes an object that implements the *Action* interface, such as *AbstractAction*. This method constructs an instance of *JButton* using the text and icon values stored in the *Action* object. It adds the action as a listener, changes a few of its properties, and adds it to the toolbar. A benefit of using this mechanism is that the generated action listener is managed in a registry that automatically destroys these support classes when the button is removed. A disadvantage is that the buttons need to be indirectly accessed to be customized beyond its *Text* and *Icon* properties.

As an encapsulation of the *BoxLayout* implementation, *JToolbar* provides a mechanism to add separators that can occupy space between components. Unlike the menu system's rendition, toolbar separators are invisible. They are created using the *addSeparator()* methods provided with *JToolbar*. One version takes a *Dimension* as a parameter, creating an

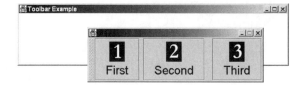

Figure 6-5. *JToolBar: floating position*

invisible component of the specified size. The parameterless version creates a separator of a standard size, whose dimensions are determined by look-and-feel defaults.

The separator is defined in a *public static* inner class that extends *JSeparator*. This class, *JToolBar.Separator*, is a lightweight component that occupies an index position in the toolbar.

Accessing and Removing Components

JToolbar supports two additional convenience methods that provide access to the child components; these are similar to those implemented in the menu classes. The same information is available using methods of *java.awt.Container*, but *getComponentIndex()* and *getComponentAtIndex()* encapsulate these calls in a way that avoids index exceptions. Using the *getComponentIndex()* method, a caller can identify the containment index for the component specified as its single parameter. If the component is not a direct child of the toolbar, the method returns (–1).

The *getComponentAtIndex()* method takes an integer parameter and returns the component at that index. The component may be of any extension of *java.awt.Component*, so it is not dependable that the reference returned might necessarily be a *JButton*; it may, for example, be a *JToolBar.Separator*. The method returns *null* (without throwing an exception) if the index is invalid—that is, the index is nonnegative and outside the bounds of the child component count.

JToolBar provides its own implementation of the *remove()* method specified by *java.awt.Container*. This version initially calls the superclass method, and performs the extra duty of emptying any listener registry entries that have been generated for automatically generated toolbar buttons.

Toolbar Properties

A *JToolBar* may be oriented along the *HORIZONTAL* or *VERTICAL* axes. This does not affect its docking behavior. The *Orientation* property, which is a bound integer, controls this behavior; the default orientation is *HORIZONTAL*. When the orientation is set or changes, the *JToolBar* assigns a horizontal or vertical *BoxLayout* to its *Layout* property. This layout is switched when an *Orientation* property change is detected.

The *Floatable* property is a bound *boolean* property. If it is set to *true*, a user can drag the toolbar from its docking position to a new place on the desktop. Setting it to *false* disables this capability. *JToolBar* listens for changes to this property and automatically docks the toolbar if *Floatable* is set to *false* and the toolbar is already undocked. Toolbars are *Floatable* by default.

JToolBar does not inherit from *AbstractButton* in the way that menu containers do, but it must provide some of the properties that buttons support. The *Margin* property, which is bound and has the value of an *Insets* object, controls the distance between the border of the toolbar and its child components. Its default value is *null,* which is reflected as a zero *Insets*. The *boolean BorderPainted* property, also bound, controls whether the toolbar's border is painted. Its default value is *true* because the drag thumb of the toolbar is implemented as a *Border* delegate.

Observations About JToolBar

JToolBar is not a particularly robust component; it has several problems related to both docking/floating and layout. It does not add much value, and it appears that its Basic and Java/Metal UI code seems to have been put together without the same care as the vast majority of JFC code. Unless the floating capability is an absolute necessity, it is recommended that a *JPanel* or related container be used instead.

Another problem that is encountered is related to the way that the rollover capabilities are implemented in the Java/Metal UI. The net effect is that the button margins are made to disappear, making them look somewhat peculiar. To alleviate these symptoms, the following code can be used to replace the default UI delegate with its basic version:

```
UIManager.put("ToolBarUI," "javax.swing.plaf.basic.BasicToolBarUI");
```

By including this line, the functionality of the toolbar reverts to the basic functionality, but the button margins will be correct. See Figure 6-6.

JProgressBar

This component is used to provide graphical feedback during a lengthy operation. It is similar in many respects to the *JScrollBar* and *JSlider* components, especially because it uses *BoundedRangeModel* as its data and

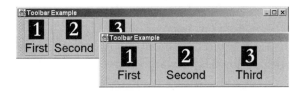

Figure 6-6. *Correcting JToolBar margins*

state model. Unlike its relatives, however, *JProgressBar* is a display-only control and is not capable of accepting user input.

Progress Bar Properties

JProgressBar supports *Minimum*, *Maximum*, and *Value* properties. The implementation of these properties is delegated to the instance of *BoundedRangeModel* associated with the instance of *JProgressBar*. The component depends on the model's implementation to enforce the relationships among these properties. The *Extent* property is not supported. None of these properties is bound in the *JProgressBar* itself, with the exception of an accessibility property change fired when *setValue()* is called. Changes in these values are detected by listening to the model with a *ChangeListener*.

The *Orientation* property can have the integer value *HORIZONTAL* or *VERTICAL*, which will cause the component to be laid out in the specified direction. An exception is thrown if an invalid value is supplied to the mutator method or the constructors that support the orientation parameter. The default orientation is *HORIZONTAL*. *Orientation* is not bound; *revalidate()* is explicitly called when the property's mutator is invoked.

JProgressBar supports an optional *String* property, which causes the value of this property to be rendered as part of the progress representation. This property is bound and has a default value of *null*. Whether this string is hidden or displayed is controlled by a bound *boolean* property *StringPainted*; this property defaults to a value of *false*.

If the value of *StringPainted* is *true* and no *String* value has been set, a string containing the completion percentage, based on the values in the model, is created and displayed. A *public* method *getPercentComplete()* is used to provide this value as a *double*.

JProgressBar also supports the *boolean BorderPainted* property, similar to menus and buttons; its default value is *true*.

JSlider

The *JSlider* component is very closely related to the *JScrollBar* component, but is designed to be a standalone component, not to manage a scroll pane. The *JSlider* uses the *BoundedRangeModel* interface to describe its data and state model and supports a superset of *JScrollBar* properties. Unlike the scroll bar, the *extent* property is managed by methods *getExtent()* and *setExtent()*. Also, there is no notion of visible amount for the *JSlider* component because it is not controlling a *Scrollable* component.

The slider component consists of several parts, which are shown in Figure 6-7.

The slider itself behaves much like the thumb of a scroll bar. It provides the draggable area of the component. The slider is the only portion of the *JSlider* component that must be painted; all others can be optionally hidden.

The slider track is similar to the scroll bar track. It marks the area in which the slider can be moved and also provides an additional area that accepts mouse clicks. Also like the scroll bar, clicking in the track causes the range model to be changed by the block amount. A *boolean* property *PaintTrack* controls whether the track is painted; it is set to *true* by default. Whether the track is painted does *not* affect its mouse click-handling

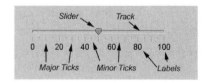

Figure 6-7. *JSlider example*

behavior. Technically, the entire area of the control is considered to be the track, except for the area covered by the slider itself. This means that click behavior is the same on the track bar itself, the ticks and labels, and all other areas bounded by the component.

Ticks and Label Support

Two levels of ticks are provided, known as major and minor ticks. The ticks represent the increments of the slider range, and can serve as restriction on possible values when the snap feature is employed. Both major and minor tick amounts are expressed as delta values, so it is not possible to have ticks that are unevenly distributed in the range. It is amusing to consider modifying *JSlider* to provide logarithmic or other scales of ticks.

Optionally, a set of labels can be associated with a slider. These labels are used to identify values in the range. Labels are defined in an object that implements the *java.util.Dictionary* interface, using an *Integer* key and an *Object*, interpreted with the *toString()* method, as the label's value.

Orientation and Range Inversion

Like the scroll bar, the *JSlider* component provides both a horizontal and a vertical orientation. The orientation can be set in the constructor or with the *setOrientation()* method and can be accessed using *getOrientation()*. The value of orientation can be either *SwingConstants.HORIZONTAL* or *Swing Constants.VERTICAL*. For the vertical orientation, ticks are displayed to the right of the slider and labels to the right of the ticks. Horizontal sliders display ticks below the slider and labels below the ticks. An *IllegalArgument Exception* is thrown if an unacceptable value is used for this property.

Another useful feature of *JSlider* that scroll bars do not provide is the capability to invert the interpretation of the range. The *Inverted* property is a bound *boolean* property that controls this capability. Its default value is *false*. See Figure 6-8.

Labels and Label Tables

The *JSlider* component provides the capability to map labels to specific values in the slider range. This is done by associating a label table with the

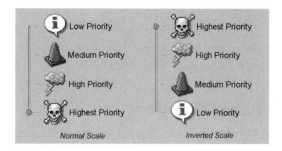

Figure 6-8. *Inverting a JSlider*

slider component. A label table is required to be of type *java.util.Dictionary*, which encapsulates key/value pair mappings. The *LableTable* property of *JSlider*, which is bound, manages the reference to this dictionary.

The *Dictionary* object is populated either manually or automatically using an *Integer* object key and a *Component* value. The *Integer* key is initialized with the value that the particular label might represent; the value is populated with a reference to a component, usually (but not necessarily) a *JLabel*.

A bound *boolean* property is provided named *PaintLabels* that controls whether the labels are displayed. The visibility of labels is taken into account when the preferred size of the *JSlider* is calculated by the UI delegate. The accessor method for this property is named *getPaintLabels()*.

Automatically Generating Labels

JSlider provides two versions of the method *createStandardLabels()*, which generates a *Hashtable* object containing generated keys and *JLabel* values. The first method takes a single integer parameter that represents the interval at which labels should be created. It generates labels starting at the current minimum value for the range model and ending at the maximum value, with one label for each increment that falls into the range. Another version is available that takes an increment as well as a starting point for label generation if it is desirable not to begin creating labels for the beginning of the range.

Automatic Update of Labels

If labels are manually created, the programmer is responsible for ensuring that the labels are consistent with changes to the minimum and maximum of the range. Labels created automatically have a special version of *Hashtable* that encapsulates a property change listener. This listener detects changes in the minimum and maximum values and regenerate labels as needed.

Tick Mark Support

The *JSlider* component provides major and minor tick marks that help the user in making range selection; these ticks can also be used to force the selection of discrete values within a range. Tick spacing is controlled by two properties, *MajorTickSpacing* and *MinorTickSpacing*, both of which are bound integer properties. The spacing range is not enforced, so it is possible to set the major range to be less than the minor range if that is desired. The default value for both properties is zero.

A special feature of the *setMajorTickSpacing()* method is that it automatically generates a label table using *createStandardLabels()* if a label table is not currently assigned and the *PaintLabels* property has the value *true*. The labels provided will map to the values of the major ticks.

A bound *boolean* property *PaintTicks* is provided to control the visibility of the major and minor ticks; its default value is *false*. Its accessor method has the nonstandard name *getPaintTicks()*.

Tick and Value Snapping

Two additional bound *boolean* properties control the behavior of the slider. Depending on how the slider is configured, the value that a slider encapsulates can be forced to a discrete set of values using one of these two snap properties.

The *SnapToValue* property is *true* by default. It causes the position of the slider to always rest on a discrete value that the slider represents. This is useful in the case where few choices exist within a large range. The accessor method is *getSnapToValue()*.

The *SnapToTicks* property overrides the behavior of *SnapToValue*. It forces the value of the slider to be one defined by a major or minor tick position. This means that when this property is *true,* the value of the slider will always be a multiple of the smallest tick increment. The default value of this property is *false* and its accessor is named *getSnapToTicks().*

JToolTip

ToolTips are small text windows that appear over a component when a user keeps the mouse in a position for a length of time or performs an action that requests one (see Figure 6-9). The *JToolTip* class is an encapsulation of a *JComponent* for this purpose.

The implementation of *JToolTip* and its UI delegates is relatively straightforward. The mechanism that supports this functionality can be found in the *JComponent* and *ToolTipManager* classes.

The *JToolTip* class is an extension of *JComponent* and supports two additional properties. The *Component* property contains a reference to the component for which the ToolTip was created; it is not bound. The *TipText* contains the *String* that is displayed in the ToolTip.

ToolTipManager

This class is a singleton class: one instance of this class is shared by all components running in the same application context. Its role is to store a registry of components with ToolTips and display them when mouse, keyboard, or other activity requests it. The single instance of *ToolTipManager* is accessed by the static *sharedInstance()* method.

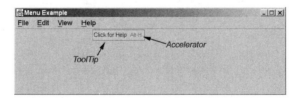

Figure 6-9. *JToolTip with accelerator*

Registering a ToolTip

JComponent contains a method *setToolTipText(String ToolTipText)* that is used to associate ToolTips with a component. The *ToolTipText* property is supported by all extensions of *JComponent*; it is an unbound property with a *String* value. The ToolTip string is stored in the client properties directory of the target component. The method *setToolTipText()* stores the new value of the client property and calls the registration methods of the *ToolTipManager* instance. The *registerComponent()* method of *ToolTipManager* is called, with the target component as a parameter. Prior to this registration, any pre-existing ToolTip is unregistered using the *unregisterComponent()* method. The accessor, *getToolTipText()*, returns the *String* stored in the client properties, presumably a performance measure.

Some components automatically register themselves with the *ToolTipManager* when they are instantiated, namely, *JTabbedPane*, *JTable*, and *JTableHeader*. *JTree*, suprisingly, does not register itself even though it has built-in ToolTip support. Use the following code to register *JTree* instances with the *ToolTipManager*:

```
JTree tree = new JTree(. . .);
ToolTipManager.sharedInstance().registerComponent(tree);
```

ToolTip Support in JComponent

The method *createToolTip()* in *JComponent* is used by the *ToolTipManager* to instantiate an instance of *JToolTip*. It is designed to be overridden in extensions of *JComponent* if an alternative to *JToolTip* is to be used. The default version creates an instance of *JToolTip* and invokes *setComponent*, passing the reference to itself. Currently, no JFC component overrides this method, so no caching of ToolTip objects is done. A more efficient implementation could be used if ToolTip performance becomes an issue.

JComponent provides an alternative version to *getToolTipText* that is used by complex components such as *JTabbedPane*, *JTable*, *JTableHeader*, and *JTree*, as well as a component of the color chooser dialog box. This enables different ToolTips to be displayed depending on the position of the mouse within the bounds of the component. In the case of *JTable*, the ToolTip for a particular cell is dictated by its renderer component. The mouse coordinates are used to determine which cell is under the mouse or is currently selected and returns the correct value. An additional overridable method *getToolTipLocation()* is provided that takes a *MouseEvent* as a parameter. Its purpose is to enable components to convert to alternate coordinate systems; it extracts the mouse location from the event object and returns a *Point* object containing the converted values. The default implementation returns *null*; no JFC components provide any alternative implementations.

ToolTipManager Properties

The singleton instance of *ToolTipManager* provides several properties to globally control the behavior of ToolTips in an application context. The *Enabled* property, which is *boolean*, controls whether the manager shows any ToolTips when requested. The *setEnabled()* method closes any currently active ToolTip if the parameter is *false*.

ToolTip Weights

The *LightWeightPopupEnabled* property is analogous to that of *JPopupMenu*. Much like a popup menu, ToolTips come in light-, medium-, and heavyweight versions, all of which are encapsulated as inner classes of *ToolTipManager*. If an application mixes light- and heavyweight components, this property can be set to *false*, thus forcing an AWT component to be used to render the ToolTip. The default value for this property is *true*, because it is best to create a lightweight ToolTip wherever possible. The value of this property is only relevant when the bounds of the ToolTip are completely within its root pane container.

Lightweight ToolTips are created as instances of *JPanel* and, therefore, must exist completely within a root pane container. When they are made visible, they are placed in the layered pane in the *JLayeredPane.POPUP_LAYER* layer, coexisting with popup menus and the other components displayed in this layer. Being in the *POPUP_LAYER* guarantees that a lightweight ToolTip will always appear above all of the components in the content pane, the default layer of the layered pane, and in the *PALETTE_LAYER* of the layered pane where floating toolbars and menus appear.

Mediumweight ToolTips derive from *java.awt.Panel*. Because they are heavyweight they are guaranteed to be visible above any lightweight components in the same container. They are also added to the layered pane container at the *POPUP_LAYER* level.

Mediumweight ToolTips cannot exist outside the bounds of their top-level window. To accommodate this case a heavyweight version is also provided. This ToolTip inherits from *java.awt.Window* and can thus be completely standalone, because it encapsulates a native peer window with its own real estate. The decision to use a medium- or heavyweight window is based on a containment check of the ToolTip bounds against the top-level container and is not directly controllable.

ToolTip Delay Properties

Three instances of the class *javax.swing.Timer* are instantiated when the *static* singleton instance of *ToolTipManager* is created. Each timer represents a delay property that is globally controlled in the static instance of *ToolTipManager*. The interaction among these timers is driven by the mouse event listener code in *ToolTipManager*.

The *Timer* class supports a *Repeats* property that, when set to *false*, makes it a one-shot timer that fires only once, after an initial delay. The three timers used by *ToolTipManager* all have their *Repeats* property set to *false*.

The *InitialDelay*, *DismissDelay*, and *ReshowDelay* properties of the *ToolTipManager* are all unbound integer properties representing a number of milliseconds. *InitialDelay* controls the amount of time the mouse must rest within the bounds of a component before the ToolTip is displayed; the default value is 750 milliseconds. Setting this to a smaller value makes ToolTips appear more quickly; higher values requires a longer time in the control before the ToolTip becomes visible.

ToolTips are not meant to be permanently visible. The *DismissDelay* property controls how long the ToolTip remains visible; the default value is 4,000 milliseconds. Lastly, the *ReshowDelay* property controls a timer that prevents destruction of the ToolTip until the mouse has been outside the component for the specified length of time. This feature prevents constant creation and destruction of ToolTip instances when the mouse moves rapidly between components. The default value for this property is 500 milliseconds.

The source code for *ToolTipManager* gives the parameter name *microSeconds* for the timer property mutators. This is erroneous because the timer resolution is in milliseconds.

Keystroke Activation

ToolTipManager provides alternate methods for displaying ToolTips using the keyboard or an accessibility-compatible device. The key combination <Ctrl>+<F1> toggles the appearance of ToolTips on any component that is registered for them. The <Esc> key is also registered, but only hides a visible ToolTip. When the <Ctrl>+<F1> keystroke is used to activate a ToolTip, the timers are stopped, thus suspending the ToolTip in the visible state. The ToolTip is also closed when focus is lost on a component whether activated by mouse or keyboard activity.

The Timer Class

The *javax.swing.Timer* class is provided by JFC to enable the capability to trigger a recurring or single action after a specified delay. Timers are created by a separate thread of execution managed by the package-private class *javax.swing.TimerQueue*. Its job is to coordinated the timed execution of all of the *Timer* instances in an application context. *TimerQueue* provides a shared instance of itself to the *Timer* class.

Constructing a Timer

Timer supports only one constructor, which takes an integer delay value (in milliseconds) and a reference to an object that implements *ActionListener*. The semantics of this constructor is that the timer invokes the *actionPerfomed()* method of all interested listeners each time the delay time expires. The listener parameter cannot be *null*.

The *Timer* supports an initial delay property that represents the delay time before the first action event is fired. The initial value of this property is set in the constructor to be the same as the delay value parameter.

The *Timer* object also supports addition and removal of *ActionListener* instances after it is created. The methods *addActionListener()* and *removeActionListener()* manage the timer's internal listener list and enable any external listener to receive action events from an accessible *Timer*.

Controlling a Timer

When a *Timer* object is created, it is initially quiescent. To enqueue the initial timer request, the *start()* method must be invoked. This period lets an implementor add additional listeners or otherwise adjust the properties of the timer before the timer begins to fire action events. The *boolean* method *isRunning()* is used to determine if a timer is currently active. The *stop()* method stops the execution of the timer by dequeuing it and discarding all pending requests.

In addition, a *restart()* method is provided that is a convenience method for a *stop()* followed by a *start()*. This also has the effect of dequeuing all timer requests, but also resets the timer back to its initial delay period.

Timer Properties

Several properties are provided by *Timer* to control characteristics of its execution. All of them are not bound. The *Delay* property represents the recurring delay in milliseconds. Because it must be specified in the only constructor, there is no default value. The *InitialDelay* property controls the number of milliseconds between the invocation of the *start()* method and the firing of the first action event. It has a default value that matches whatever initial value was specified for *Delay*. Either of the mutator methods for these properties throws a *RuntimeException* if the specified delay is a negative value.

The *Repeats* property is a *boolean* that controls whether the timer is recurring or a one-shot. The default value of this property is *true*, meaning that after the *InitialDelay* period, action events will continue to be generated. If the value is set to *false*, the action is only generated once, after the expiration of *InitialDelay*. The *Delay* property is not used in nonrepeating timers.

The *boolean* property *Coalesce* is a resource management enhancement. If its value is true, which it is by default, the *EventQueue* object joins all expirations for a particular timer into a single *ActionEvent*. If the value of this flag is set to *false*, an *ActionEvent* is generated for each event that expires.

Lastly, *Timer* provides some debugging support. A static property called *LogTimers* is provided that has the default value of *false*. If this property is set to *true*, a message is sent to the console each time a timer request is enqueued.

Chooser Dialog Boxes

JFC provides two classes that support the creation of useful dialog boxes that are robust and highly configurable. *JFileChooser* supports the selection of an element of a file system for use in a file read or write operation. *JColorChooser* provides a convenient user interface that enables users to pick a color from a set of selection palettes.

File Chooser

The *JFileChooser* component provides a platform-independent mechanism to select filenames from a hierarchical file system. The component enables specification of filename filters, which can restrict the files and directories that are visible in the selection window. See Figure 6-10.

File chooser components are all managed by their UI delegate classes. The appearance and behavior of these components are not specified in either the abstract or basic UI classes, so look-and-feels are free to implement whatever is suitable for the purpose.

Creating and Displaying a JFileChooser

No *static* methods exist to create a file chooser dialog box. Instead, the programmer instantiates one with one of the supplied constructors and calls one of the show methods to generate and display the dialog box.

The constructor parameters are used to initialize the part of the file system that the chooser is operating on. Using the parameterless constructor initializes the dialog box to point at the user's home directory, that is, the value of the system property *user.home*. The one-parameter versions of the constructor support a *java.io.File* object as a parameter, a *String* parameter containing the path name, or a reference to a *FileSystemView* object; supplying *null* for any of these methods causes operations to occur on the home directory.

The *FileSystemView* class is a wrapper for a platform-independent representation of a file system, and it exists in lieu of similar support that now exists in the JDK 1.2 version of the *java.io* package. *FileSystemView* is an *abstract* class that provides package-level extensions that represent the Microsoft Windows and UNIX platforms, as well as a generic object that can serve in the case that neither of these are suitable. In spite of its name, it is not a view in the MVC sense.

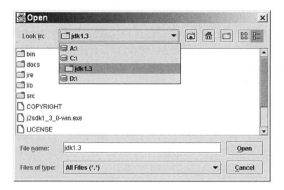

Figure 6-10. *JFileChooser example*

The decision of which *FileSystemView* to use is done by examining the implementation of *separatorChar* in the *java.io.File* class. The *os.name* system property might be a more reliable way of determining the operating system.

Opening a File Chooser

File choosers are opened using the *showDialog()* method. This method takes two parameters, a parent component and an integer specifying in which mode to operate the dialog box. Two additional methods are supplied, *showOpenDialog()* and *showSaveDialog()*, which take only a parent component parameter; the operating mode value is supplied internally. The mode values are recognized by the UI delegate, and the subcomponents initialized accordingly, with values from the look-and-feel defaults.

Three modes are supported. The Open mode, *JFileChooser.OPEN_DIALOG,* is used to select a file or directory for input in a program. Its job is to provide a list of existing files and directories for selection, and supports multiple selection of elements within a directory. The Save mode, *JFileChooser.SAVE_DIALOG,* is used to select a file or directory to serve as output. Only single selection is permitted; when a directory is specified for a save operation, the user can provide part or all of the target filename. A third mode is provided, *JFileChooser.CUSTOM_DIALOG,* that enables the user to specify the values of component properties.

Modes are specified and accessed after instantiation by the *DialogType* property, which is a bound integer. It is set automatically if the load or save version of the open method is used. If an invalid value is used in a call to *setDialogType()*, an *IllegalArgumentException* is thrown.

Retrieving the Selection

Because file choosers are implemented as modal dialog boxes, any call to the show methods block the invoking thread until the dialog box is closed. All three show methods return an integer that represents the reason the dialog box was dismissed; this integer has the value *CANCEL_OPTION* if the dialog box was canceled or *APPROVE_OPTION* if the selection was accepted.

The selection is managed by a bound property that manages a single *java.io.File* object called *SelectedFile*. The mutator for this property, *setSelectedFile()*, can be used to initialize the dialog box with a file path and name before display. If the parameter contains a reference to a file in another directory, the file chooser changes its current directory accordingly. The accessor, *getSelectedFile()*, is used to return the *File* object that represents the selection. The selection value is not considered valid if the return value from the show method is not *APPROVE_OPTION*.

A related property is the *CurrentDirectory*, which is also a bound property that encapsulates a *java.io.File* object. It controls only the directory that is being operated on and does not affect the selection state.

File Filtering

JFileChooser provides two types of file filters: the property method *setFileFilter* enables specification of a *FileFilter* object that eliminates files from the view. The value of this filter is retrievable using the *getFileFilter()* method.

The abstract class *FileFilter* specifes two methods: the first is the *accept()* method, which takes a *File* object as a parameter. This method returns *true* for files that are accepted by the filter; these will be displayed by the chooser dialog box. Returning *false* causes the *File* not to be displayed. The other method, *getDescription()*, returns a string description of the characteristics of the filter.

The following example constructs a file filter object that enables only JPG and GIF files to be selected. Notice that the value is returned as *true* for all directory entries. If *false* were returned, the user would not be able to change directories.

```
JFileChooser chooser = new JFileChooser();

chooser.setFileFilter(new FileFilter() {
      public boolean accept(File file) {
            if (file.isDirectory())
                  return true;
            String fileName = file.getName();
            if (fileName.endsWith(."jpg") || fileName.endsWith(."gif"))
                  return true;
            return false;
      }
      public String getDescription() {
            return ("graphics files (.jpg, *.gif)");
      }
});
chooser.showDialog(. . .);
```

This component-level filter has a default value that causes no filtering to occur. This filter is constructed by the method *getAcceptAllFileFilter()*, which delegates to the UI to generate an appropriate filter.

Another filter mechanism is the chooseable filters that are specified in a combo box. This enables a user to select from a list of defined file types based on their name, file extension, or any other file property. These filters are displayed in the order that they are entered. A user can select from this list of filters to dynamically change the files that are displayed.

The method *addChooseableFileFilter()* takes a parameter of a *FileFilter* instance. It adds the filter to the internal collection and fires a property change event. The *removeChooseableFileFilter()* method is used to remove a filter from the collection. The collection can be indirectly accessed by a method *getChooseableFileFilters()*, which takes no parameters and returns an array of *FileFilter* objects. The *resetChooseableFileFilters()* method depopulates the chooseable filter collection and re-inserts the accept all file filter.

Other JFileChooser Properties and Methods

The file chooser component provides several additional configuration methods that control its selection characteristics.

Selection Mode

The *FileSelectionMode* property is a bound integer that controls what may be selected in a file chooser; the three acceptable values are *FILES_ONLY*, *DIRECTORIES_ONLY,* and *FILE_AND_DIRECTORIES*, each static integers defined by *JFileChooser*. This selection mode does not affect what files are displayed, only those that can be selected.

Subcomponent Configuration

The title of the *JFileChooser* dialog box and the characteristics of the approve button are dictated by the mode in which the chooser was opened. The UI delegate is responsible for interpreting the mode and setting the text, ToolTip, and mnemonic for the approve button. The cancel button, on the other hand, is always set up as cancel regardless of the mode.

To alter the approve button characteristics, several property implementations are provided, each of which is bound. The *ApproveButtonText* is usually set to Open when the chooser is in *OPEN_DIALOG* mode and Save when in *SAVE_DIALOG* mode. The mnemonic and ToolTip for the button are changed using the *ApproveButtonMnemonic* and *ApproveButtonToolTipText* properties, which are of integer and string type, respectively.

The other characteristic of file choosers that can be changed is the *DialogTitle* property, which controls the contents of the dialog box's title bar. This *String* property is also bound.

Adding Additional Components

The *Accessory* property facilitates the addition of an arbitrary *JComponent* that can be used as a preview area or as a place for additional navigational controls. The UI delegate for *JFileChooser* is responsible for adding the component to a suitable container.

The UI delegate is responsible for providing a container that accommodates the accessory component. It is notified of changes to the *Accessory* property through bound property change notification.

Other than containment, the component does not communicate with the *Accessory* component directly. The *Accessory* is responsible for listening for changes to the file chooser and modifying itself as needed. *JFileChooser* does not provide *ChangeEvent* notification; the property change events are a reasonable alternative and let listeners ignore property types that do not affect the *Accessory* component's state.

Miscellaneous Navigation Methods

The *ensureFileIsVisible()* method is invoked by the code for *setSelectedFile()*. Its purpose is to delegate to the UI a request that the file specified by its single *java.io.File* parameter is the one currently visible in the chooser window. This method is a no-op implementation in the *BasicFileChooserUI* class, so this process is expected to be look-and-feel-specific. In the case of the Java look-and-feel, the *MetalFileChooserUI* class implements the selected file in a *JList*; thus, a call to *ensureIndexIsVisible()* is used to produce the desired effect. The *ensureFileIsVisible()* is *public* and can be called to set the currently visible file without altering the selection.

The convenience method *changeToParentDirectory()* is a wrapper for the *setCurrentDirectory()* and *getCurrentDirectory()* methods. It is used by the UI delegate as the target for the up arrow button that moves the selection one level up the directory hierarchy.

The method *rescanCurrentDirectory()* is also *public*; it causes any cached information about the current directory to be discarded and re-read. It, too, has a no-op implementation in the base UI delegate class and depends on a look-and-feel-specific implementation to operate.

Multiple Selection

Although it is not supported in the current look-and-feel versions, the methods are provided for multiple file selection. The *MultiSelection Enabled boolean* property determines whether multiple selection is permitted. The *getSelectedFiles()* and *setSelectedFiles()* methods comprise a bound property that manages an array of *java.io.File* objects.

Color Chooser

The *JColorChooser* class is supported by a UI delegate and a set of associated classes in the *javax.swing.colorchooser* package. It encapsulates a dialog box class that provides multiple mechanisms for color selection (see Figure 6-11).

The mechanisms used for color selection are programmable; they all encapsulate selection of a single color using a state model that supports listening for change events.

As with similar state model classes, a *SelectionModel* property is supported that provides access and modification of the model object concealed in the color chooser. This property is bound to enable model listeners to switch their interest to a new model when it is specified in a *setSelectionModel()* call.

The color value itself is accessed by the *getColor()* method and modified by the *setColor()* method. Both of these methods delegate to the selection model to perform their storage operations using objects of type *java.awt.Color*. Another two versions of *setColor()* are provided: one that takes three integer parameters as the red, green, and blue components of the *Color* object, and one that takes a single integer that is converted to an RGB color value by bit arithmetic.

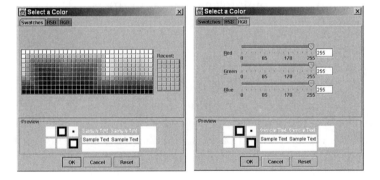

Figure 6-11. *JColorChooser example*

Color Chooser Model

The *ColorChooserModel* is similar to the *SingleSelectionModel* used by menus and tabbed panes. Unlike *SingleSelectionModel*, which encapsulates an *Object* type, *ColorChooserModel* only operates on items of type *Color*. Also unlike *SingleSelectionModel*, no notion of an unselected state exists; in other words, some color is always selected. Thus, no equivalent exists to the *SingleSelectionModel* implementation of *clearSelection()*.

The default implementation of this model is *DefaultColorSelection Model*, which is suitable for most purposes. It provides a protected method *fireStateChanged()* that propagates a *ChangeEvent* object to interested listeners. The methods *addChangeListener()* and *removeChangeListener()* are provided for accessing the listener list. The subcomponents of *JColorChooser* always add themselves as listeners to the current model.

Color Chooser Components

The color chooser pane is comprised of two subcomponents, an upper panel that encloses a *JTabbedPane* and a lower panel that provides a preview of the selected color.

The internal layout of the color chooser is a *BorderLayout*, which assembles the preview window in the *SOUTH* position and the tabbed pane in the *CENTER* position.

The Preview Panel

The preview panel is situated underneath the tabbed pane; its gives a visual indication of what the selected color will look like either in the current color scheme or against system colors. The panel indirectly listens to the *ColorSelectionModel* through an inner class of the UI delegate. The default implementation is *DefaultPreviewPanel*, which provides colored squares and text to indicate the selected colors.

Color Chooser Panels

The tabbed pane is populated with a set of panels, each of which provides it own interpretation of how color selection is made. The standard three panels are:

- *DefaultSwatchChooserPanel*—A swatch panel that provides selection from a set of hardcoded color values. These values represent the most commonly used colors organized by hue.

- *DefaultHSBChooserPanel*—An HSB panel that enables selection by Hue/Saturation/Brightness parameters. This panel displays a slice of a color phase space that is three-dimensional. This panel uses a very interesting class, *SyntheticImage*, to programmatically develop the selection display as parameters change. An algorithm to convert the HSB values to RGB is internally provided.

- *DefaultRGBChooserPanel*—Enables selection by three *JSlider* components that manage individual red, green, and blue values used as input for a *Color* object.

Each of these classes extends *AbstractColorChooserPanel*, which is itself an extension of *JPanel*. This panel is available for further extension if a different color selection process is required, such as CMYK or process color matching.

Selecting Chooser Panels and Previews

The UI delegate for the color chooser, *BasicColorChooserUI*, determines the components that are displayed. It uses a helper class, *ColorChooserComponent Factory,* to create instances of the color selection tabs and the preview panel.

Two *protected* methods in the UI specify how these are created. The method *createDefaultChoosers()* returns an array of type *AbstractColorChooser Panel*. The default behavior of this method is to invoke the static *getDefault ChooserPanels()* method of *ColorChooserComponentFactory*, which instantiates the three standard chooser panels and adds them to the tabbed pane.

The *installPreviewPanel()* is the analogous method that creates an instance of the preview component and adds it to the *JColorChooser*. It invokes the static method *getPreviewPanel()* of *ColorChooserComponent Factory*, which in turn creates an instance of *DefaultPreviewPanel*.

To change this behavior, two options exist: override the *protected* methods in *BasicColorChooserUI*, or use the property interface of *JColor Chooser* to modify its subcomponents after it is instantiated.

Initializing a Color Chooser

The color chooser implementation provides flexibility by offering three modes of operation. The first mode is implemented in a static method *showDialog()*. This method creates and displays a modal color chooser dialog box, providing the selected color as its return value. It takes three parameters: a parent component, a title string, and an initial *Color* value. The parent component reference may be *null*; this causes the dialog box code to use a dummy frame parent. The initial color value may also be *null*, in which case *Color.white* is used as the initial color.

Creating a Color Chooser Dialog Box

The second mode provides more control over the operation of the dialog box by providing access to the *createDialog()* method, which returns an instance of a color chooser dialog box to the caller. The management of the appearance and resources of the dialog box is not automatic, and it is the responsibility of the caller to make the dialog box visible, collect the selected color, and dispose of the dialog box's resources.

The benefit of this mechanism is it enables specification of the color chooser pane that is displayed in the dialog box; this enables any subclass of *JColorChooser* to be used in a dialog box. The first two parameters are the same as *showDialog()*: a parent component and a title string. The third parameter is a *boolean* that controls the initial modality of the dialog box, that is, whether the invoking thread blocks when the dialog box is displayed. The fourth parameter is a reference to a *JColorChooser* object, which enables implementation of subclasses of this object.

The last two parameters are of type *ActionListener*; they are invoked when the OK and Cancel buttons are clicked on the chooser dialog box. This provides control over navigational behavior. These listeners can be used to restrict color selections by examining the chosen color, determining if it is acceptable, and, if necessary, keeping the dialog box active until a different selection is made. This behavior is not possible with the *showDialog()* version because the navigation is encapsulated in the static method.

Standalone Color Chooser Pane

The *JColorChooser* is a legitimate *JComponent* and can be instantiated and used as any other lightweight component. This enables applications to leverage these capabilities in any conceivable way and provides the fullest control over color selection behavior. Its UI delegate performs the usual tasks of installing look-and-feel-specific defaults and registering listeners.

The *BasicColorChooserUI* does not manage the component's minimum, maximum, and preferred sizes, so caution must be taken when using these components with complex layouts. Not providing implementations of the accessor methods for the size properties causes the size to be determined by the enclosing container's layout.

JColorChooser Properties

In addition to the *Color* and *Model* properties, *JColorChooser* has a number of other properties. Bound properties are provided that enable dynamic update of the preview panels and the contents of the tabbed pane. The *getPreview Panel()* method returns a reference to the current instance of the preview panel; *setPreviewPanel()* fires a *PropertyChangeEvent* when a new panel is assigned.

To access the contents of the tabbed pane two approaches are supported. *ChooserPanels* is an array property that represents the current set of tabs. To retrieve the current instances of chooser panels, use the *getChooser Panels()* method that returns an array of *AbstractColorChooserPanel* objects. The *setChooserPanels()* method takes an array of *AbstractColorChooserPanel* objects as a parameter and replaces all of the tabs in the panel with the newly specified set.

For individual access to the tabs, the methods *addChooserPanel()* and *removeChooserPanel()* are provided, which both take a reference to an *AbstractColorChooserPanel*. The *addChooserPanel()* method builds a new array of panel objects with the newly specified one appended. The *removeChooserPanel()* method throws an *IllegalArgumentException* if the specified panel is not in the current set.

JOptionPane

The *JOptionPane* class serves as a factory for producing simple interactive dialog boxes. Serving as an alternative to handcrafting *JDialog* classes, *JOptionPane* provides the capability to generate a dialog box with only a few lines of code, and supports both heavyweight (*JDialog*) and lightweight (*JInternal Frame*) versions. It is also the JFC class with the most misleading name.

The dialog boxes produced by *JOptionPane* are mostly meant for informational messages and prompting responses from users. It is similar to many graphical API facilities that provide message boxes that can be altered parametrically. An additional benefit of using *JOptionPane* is that it enables the prevailing look-and-feel to determine the format and behavior of these generated dialog boxes, thus providing better platform-emulation capabilities. Also, the methods for assigning and retrieving dialog box information are standardized, as are the mechanisms for adding additional components to the dialog boxes.

The default *JOptionPane* contains a message, an icon, and a set of buttons that are configurable by the invoker. The icon and properties of the default components are configurable, but their default behavior is dictated by the UI delegate, *BasicOptionPaneUI*, and the look-and-feel-specific UI classes.

JOptionPane Types

The *JOptionPane* class supports several types of commonly used dialogs: message dialog boxes, confirmation dialog boxes, and input dialog boxes. Each of these is created using either a *static* method, which encapsulates the entire display process, or by creating an instance of *JOptionPane* and directing it to create a suitable dialog box or internal frame.

Message Dialogs

Message dialogs are used strictly to provide information to a user. Only a single OK button is provided to enable the user to close the window. See Figure 6-12.

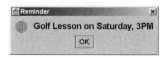

Figure 6-12. *JOptionPane: message dialog*

Confirmation Dialog Boxes

These dialog boxes are used to elicit a simple response from a user. The dialog box is configurable to display a combination of response buttons: Yes/No, Yes/No/Cancel, and OK/Cancel. Other combinations are possible using more configurable versions of the dialog box. See Figure 6-13.

Input Dialog Boxes

JOptionPane can elicit text or selection input as well (see Figure 6-14). If a list of values is provided to the dialog box, it creates a *JTextField*, *JComboBox*, or *JList* depending on the number of selection items provided.

A problem does exist when using input dialog boxes with combo boxes: the *JComboBox* created by the *JOptionPane* is lightweight and is clipped by the bounds of the *JOptionPane* dialog box. To alleviate this problem, use the *createDialog()* method to create the dialog box, find the combo box child component, and change its *LightweightPopupEnabled* property to *false*.

Generic Option Dialog Box

If more flexibility is desired, *JOptionPane* has a mode that enables practically any aspect of the dialog box to be modified. All other versions of the *JOptionPane* dialog boxes discussed previously will eventually create one of these generic dialog boxes (see Figure 6-15).

To add even greater flexibility, *JOptionPane* provides duplicates of all of its supported components that are implemented as *JInternalFrame* objects.

There are some caveats to using the internal versions of *JOptionPane*. First, the dialog box created is not actually a dialog and does not behave

Figure 6-13. *JOptionPane: confirmation dialog*

Figure 6-14. *JOptionPane: input dialog*

modally, that is, it does not block input to the other components in the application. Second, the internal version must be parented by a *JDesktopPane*; it will not allow itself to be created in any other container.

Creating a JOptionPane

JOptionPane supports two different mechanisms to create target dialog boxes; one is through the use of *static* methods, the other by direct instantiation.

Static Creation

JOptionPane supports many *static* methods that encapsulate the display of the dialog box as well as the retrieval of user input.

The *showMessageDialog()* and *showInternalMessageDialog()* methods return *void* because their purpose is to display a message to a user and wait for acknowledgement without reporting any values. There are three versions of this call in each of these two methods.

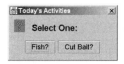

Figure 6-15. *Customizing JOptionPane*

The methods *showConfirmDialog()* and *showInternalConfirmDialog()* provide a dialog box that enables the user to select from a set of predefined buttons. The option type must be one of *YES_NO_OPTION* or *YES_NO_CANCEL_OPTION*. For these confirmation dialogs, the return type is an integer that will contain a defined value that maps to one of the standard buttons: *YES_OPTION*, *NO_OPTION*, *CANCEL_OPTION*, and *OK_OPTION*. Another value provided is *CLOSED_OPTION*, which means the dialog box was closed for some other reason than the selection of one of the buttons.

To create an input version, use the static methods *showInputDialog()* or *showInternalInputDialog()*. These methods return the *String* value that the user entered into its text field component; this value may be *null* if the dialog box was closed without any input.

Creating a generic option dialog box statically is done with *showOptionDialog()* and *showInternalOptionDialog()*. These methods enable the specification of an array of selectable options and return the index of the option that was selected.

Using the createDialog() Technique

JOptionPane also provides a constructor that enables instantiation of an object for later modification. When a *JOptionPane* is instantiated, it configures itself according to the parameters passed in its constructor; these parameters dictate the type of dialog box created. These parameters enable specification of initial values for *JOptionPane* properties.

The method *createDialog()* and its analogous version, *createInternal Frame()*, can be used to create a *JDialog* or *JInternalFrame* instance that can be manipulated using traditional techniques. These methods both require the specification of the parent component that will be the owner of the new window.

JOptionPane Properties

JOptionPane supports a set of bound properties that can be used in the *createDialog()* technique to configure the dialog box and retrieve response values.

The *MessageType* property is used by the UI delegate to determine which icon to display. The value is an integer and must be one of

ERROR_MESSAGE, *INFORMATION_MESSAGE*, *WARNING_MESSAGE*, *QUESTION_MESSAGE,* or *PLAIN_MESSAGE*; otherwise a *RuntimeException* is generated. The value is mapped to an icon in the UI defaults table, which is specified when the look-and-feel is initialized. Although the delegate provides a default icon, the icon can be altered by using the *setIcon()* method and passing a reference to an alternate icon. The *getIcon()* method returns the current icon reference.

The *Message* property is a *String* that makes up the prompt message that is displayed in the dialog box. The methods *getMessage()* and *setMessage()* can be used to access and modify this value.

The *getValue()* method returns an *Object* and is the primary method used to determine the action that the user performed. In the case of confirmation dialog boxes, the return value will be of type *Integer*, containing one of the predefined option values. The *setValue()* method initializes the selection. For dialog boxes that provide multiple options, the *setOptions()* and *getOptions()* methods give access to the array of objects that are presented to the user for selection. In this case, the *getValue()* call returns an *Integer* object containing the index value into the object array. The methods *setInitialValue()* and *getInitialValue()* control which object is selected when the dialog box appears. The *OptionType* property configures the standard button arrangement and can have the value *DEFAULT_OPTION*, *YES_NO_OPTION*, *YES_NO_CANCEL_OPTION,* or *OK_CANCEL_OPTION*. The interpretation of *DEFAULT_OPTION* is left up to the UI delegate.

For text input, the *setInputValue()* method is used to initialize a value in the text field when the dialog box is first displayed. For dialog boxes that provide selection values, the *setSelectionValues()* and *setInitialSelection Value()* methods are used to initialize selection items.

*Life is a copiously branching bush, continually pruned by the grim
reaper of extinction, not a ladder of predictable progress.*
—Stephen Jay Gould, *Wonderful Life*

Chapter 7

The JTree
Component

The *JTree* component is designed to display hierarchical data. Unlike its
cousin the *JList* control, *JTree* uses a one-to-many paradigm to organize
information. This method was popularized with the advent of the
Chicago interface that became the Windows 95 desktop.

The *JTree* component consists of a series of nodes, each of which
represents a single object in the hierarchy. The level of a node in the
hierarchy is indicated by indentation, so child nodes are always visually
set apart from their parent node. The component can provide additional visual information to highlight the data relationships.

To enable navigation through the tree hierarchy, *JTree* provides a
mechanism where child nodes can be interactively or programmatically
expanded and collapsed. To support this feature, nodes are organized
into branch nodes and leaf nodes. Branch nodes are defined as a node
that *may* have child nodes underneath. Leaf nodes are not permitted to

have children. In the default depiction of the tree, branch nodes are represented by folder icons and leaf nodes by document icons. This, as well as many of the other behaviors of the tree control, is capable of being customized using specialized data model and cell renderers. Figure 7-1 shows a typical *JTree* component.

A model interface is used to represent the data managed by the control. This interface, *TreeModel*, allows for a recursive descent down the hierarchy of the tree. The object that implements *TreeModel* reports the number of child nodes at each level and provides access to references to those children.

Each tree has one node that is designated as the root node; all other nodes in the tree fall beneath it in the hierarchy. The root node can be either hidden or visible if the root is not visible, the immediate children of the root node are depicted as occupying the lowest level of the hierarchy. If the root is visible, it will be the only one occupying the lowest level of the hierarchy.

The *JTree* control also manages the state of branch nodes with regard to whether they are expanded or collapsed. A node is collapsed when its children are not visible and expanded when its children appear. The expansion state for a particular branch node is toggled either programmatically or through the interaction of the user. A special area in the tree known as the expansion handle provides a target for users to click as well as visual feedback of the expansion state. Several events are provided to enable interested listeners to detect when a branch is about

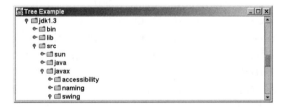

Figure 7-1. *JTree example*

to expand or when a branch has actually expanded. These events are covered in a later section of this chapter.

JTree inherits functionality from *JComponent* that enables it to be inserted into a lightweight container. It also implements the *Scrollable* interface that enables it to interact with *JScrollPane*.

Creating a JTree

The *JTree* component creates a default data model if one is not supplied. Although a parameterized constructor exists that takes a *TreeModel*, creating a tree without a data model is allowed. *JTree* supports several different parameterized constructors that create default data models. The parameter to the constructor can be:

- **An array of *java.lang.Object*—**Causes a model to be generated with a nondisplayed root node. Each member of the array is added as a child of this root node.

- **An instance of *Vector*—**Generates a default model with a nondisplayed root node. Each element of the vector is added as a child of this root node.

- **An instance of *Hashtable*—**Causes a default model to be generated with a nondisplayed root node. Each entry of the hash table is added as a child of this root node.

- **An instance of *TreeNode*—**Causes a model to be generated with a specified node as the root node. The *TreeNode* interface is covered in detail later in this chapter.

Once an instance of the JTree exists, the *getModel()* method can be used to get access to the default model. The behavior of the default model is covered later in this chapter.

The TreeModel Interface

The *TreeModel* interface represents the data model for the *JTree* control. It defines methods that a tree control can use to determine its contents.

- ***public Object getRoot()*—**This method returns an instance of an object that serves as the root for this tree. Although the method returns a reference to a *java.lang.Object*, the expectation of the *JTree* component is an object that implements the *TreeNode* interface. The *JTree* control uses the reference returned by this method as the starting point for discovering the remainder of the nodes in the tree. This method may return a *null*, which signifies that the model contains no elements.

- *public int getChildCount(Object parent)*—Starting with the root node, the control calls this method for every node it discovers. The return value for this method represents the number of child nodes that exist under a particular node. If the return value is zero (or less), this means that no subordinate nodes exist for the specified parent node.

- *public Object getChild(Object parent, int index)*—This method is used to return a reference to the specified child object for the designated parent. The tree control calls this method recursively to access all of the nodes in the tree. The value of the *index* parameter will never be more than the value reported for *getChildCount()*.

- *public int getIndexOfChild(Object parent, Object child)*—This method is complementary to *getChild()*. The purpose is to return an index value for a particular child of a specified object. If the object is not a child of the parent object, the value (–1) is returned.

- *public boolean isLeaf(Object node)*—The model uses this method to determine if a particular node is a leaf or branch. If the return value is *true*, the object is not checked for children and is marked with a document icon. Note that this is a different case than a return value of zero for *getChildCount()*. In that case, it means that the node is a branch, but happens to have no children. If a node is determined to be a leaf, then *getChildCount()* is never actually called.

- *public void valueForPathChanged(TreePath path, Object newValue)*—The *JTree* component enables values to be edited directly in the tree. When the editing cycle is complete, this method is called to notify the data model that a change has occurred. If the tree model is guaranteed never to change, this method can be a *null* implementation (no code in the method body). Editing tree nodes is covered in detail later in this chapter.

- *void addTreeModelListener(TreeModelListener l), void remove TreeModelListener(TreeModelListener l)*—These methods are used to add and remove listeners that are interested in when the tree model changes. If the tree model is guaranteed never to change, these methods can also be *null* implementations.

There is an implementation of this interface in the class *DefaultTreeModel*. This class provides a canonical implementation of tree content. It relies on the delegation of model processing to individual objects that implement the *TreeNode* interface.

The DefaultTreeModel Class

When a *JTree* component is instantiated, the default behavior is to create a default data model. This model will be an instance of *DefaultTreeModel* and handles most tree behavior. It is suitable for most implementations.

The key to the *DefaultTreeModel* class is the behavior of the node objects that it encapsulates. These nodes are expected to be an implementation of the *TreeNode* interface, which describes the relationship between an individual node, its parent, and its children.

The TreeNode Interface

If the *TreeModel* interface can be thought of as an object that represents all of the data managed by a tree, then the *TreeNode* interface provides information about each individual node.

- *int getChildCount()*—Provides the number of children of this node. The behavior is the same for return values of zero—this designates a branch node that has no children.

- *TreeNode getChildAt(int childIndex)*—Returns a reference to a *TreeNode* object for the specified child. The index should never exceed the value returned by the *getChildCount()* call.

- *int getIndex(TreeNode node)*—This is a complementary method to *getChild()* that returns the index of a child node. If the specified node is not a child, the value (–1) should be returned.

- *TreeNode getParent()*—In order for the selection mechanism to properly identify a particular node in the tree hierarchy, it is necessary for a node to have an awareness of which node is its parent. This method returns a reference to that parent node. Note that this enforces the one-to-many nature of the tree data because each node can have one and only one parent.

- *boolean getAllowsChildren()*—This method returns *true* if the node is a branch and permits children. This is useful for setting up branch nodes that are meant to contain inaccessible child data, such as a file directory for which a user has no access permission.

- *boolean isLeaf()*—Returns *true* if the node is a leaf node.

- *java.util.Enumeration children()*—This method returns an object that implements the *Enumeration* interface. It is a convenient way of iterating through the children of a node. If a node uses a *java.util.Vector* object to store its children, this method can be delegated to the *children()* method of *Vector*. The *ConstantNode* example code shows how simple this implementation can be.

It should be well noted that several similarities exist between the *TreeNode* and *TreeModel* interfaces. It is compelling to think of *TreeNode* as the model for a single node because *TreeModel* is the object that represents the entire hierarchy.

This interface is technically not required because the methods in *TreeModel* operate not on *TreeNode* entities but on *java.lang.Object*. However, to maintain consistency and to ensure future compatibility, it is worthwhile to consider using objects that implement *TreeNode*. It is also much easier to take advantage of delegation because the methods map quite neatly. The example of the constant tree model later in this chapter shows how this relationship can be exploited.

The MutableTreeNode Interface

This interface is an extension of the *TreeNode* interface and provides additional methods for mutable nodes. Mutable nodes are expected to change in value and have a variable number of child nodes.

- *void insert(MutableTreeNode child, int index)*—Inserts a new child at the specified index. This causes a shift in the indices of all children with this index or higher.

- *void remove(int index)*—Removes the child at the specified index. This brings about a downward index shift in all indices higher than the one specified.

- *void remove(MutableTreeNode node)*—Identical to the preceding method, except the object reference is specified instead of the index. A corresponding shift in indices also occurs.

- *void setParent(MutableTreeNode newParent)*—Changes the parent of the node to be the specified node.

- *void removeFromParent()*—Causes the node to be removed from its parent. This has the effect of orphaning the node until *setParent()* is called to reassign it to another node.

- *void setUserObject(Object object)*—Updates the data object that this node represents.

Oddly, no *getUserObject()* is defined in this interface. There is an implementation of *MutableTreeNode* that is used by the default tree model. This class, *DefaultMutableTreeNode*, uses a *java.util.Vector* object to store its child nodes. This class is designed to be a general-purpose tree node and is suitable for most implementations. Its behavior centers on the encapsulation of a user object that represents tree data.

In the default case, the value displayed in the tree will be the return value of the *toString()* implementation for the user object. If no *toString()* method is declared, the node displays the object's hash code; this is the default behavior for *java.lang.Object*.

DefaultTreeModel and *DefaultMutableTreeNode* are covered in depth in the JTree Editing section of this chapter.

ConstantTreeNode and DefaultConstantTreeNode

Frequently, there is a need for a nonmutable tree with nonmutable nodes. As an alternative to the *MutableTreeNode* interface, the *ConstantTreeNode* interface and default object can be used. The interface is simple:

```
package com.ketherware.tree;

import javax.swing.TreeNode;

interface ConstantTreeNode extends TreeNode {
}
```

The purpose of this additional interface is simply to mark a node as being immutable; the *instanceof* operator can be used to discern mutable nodes in a heterogeneous tree. Other than that, the interesting part is the implementation of this interface, the *DefaultConstantTreeNode* object.

```
package com.ketherware. tree;

import javax.swing.*;
import javax.swing.tree.*;
import java.util.Vector;
import java.util.Enumeration;

class DefaultConstantTreeNode implements ConstantNode, Cloneable,
            Serializable {
    // Vector containing references to child nodes
    protected Vector children;

    // true if this node allows children
    protected boolean allowsChildren;

    // data for this node
    protected Object data;

    // true if leaf node
    protected boolean isLeaf;

    // parent node
```

```
protected transient TreeNode parent;

// Default constructor
public DefaultConstantTreeNode() {
    // Create empty node
    this(null, null);
}

// Parameterized constructor
public DefaultConstantTreeNode(Object data,
        TreeNode parent) {
    // Create node that allows children
    this(data, parent, true);
}

// Parameterized constructor
public DefaultConstantTreeNode(Object data,
        TreeNode parent, boolean allowsChildren) {
    this(data, parent, allowsChildren, false);
}

// Parameterized constructor
public DefaultConstantTreeNode(Object data,
        TreeNode parent, boolean allowsChildren
        boolean isLeaf) {
    // Store instance data
    this.data = data;
    this.parent = parent;
    this.allowsChildren = allowsChildren;
    this.isLeaf = isLeaf;

    // Create a vector
    children = new Vector();
}

// Append a child node
public void addChild(Object child) {
```

```java
      // delegate to vector
      children.addElement(child);
   }

   // from TreeNode interface
   public TreeNode getChildAt(int index) {
      // delegate to vector
      return children.elementAt(index);
   }

   // from TreeNode interface
   public int getChildCount() {
      // delegate to vector
      return children.size();
   }

   // from TreeNode interface
   public TreeNode getParent() {
      return this.parent;
   }

   // from TreeNode interface
   public int getIndex(TreeNode node) {
      // delegate to vector
      return children.indexOf(node);
   }

   // from TreeNode interface
   public boolean getallowsChildren() {
      return this.allowsChildren;
   }

   // from TreeNode interface
   public boolean isLeaf() {
      return this.isLeaf;
   }
```

```
// from TreeNode interface
public Enumeration children() {
   // no sense reinventing the wheel
   if (children.isEmpty())
      return
         DefaultMutableTreeNode.EMPTY_ENUMERATION;
   // delegate to vector
   return children.elements();
}
// Some methods omitted . . .
}
```

DefaultConstantTreeModel

If an immutable tree node is desirable, then it should be encapsulated in a suitable tree model. The code for *DefaultConstantTreeModel* is also an example of how delegation to *TreeNode* objects can be used to provide the necessary functionality for the model to operate.

```
package com.ketherware. tree;

import javax.swing.*;
import javax.swing.tree.*;
import java.util.Vector;
import java.util.Enumeration;

class DefaultConstantTreeModel implements ConstantTreeModel {
   protected ConstantTreeNode root;
   public DefaultConstantTreeModel() {
      this(null);
   }
   public DefaultConstantTreeModel(ConstantTreeNode root) {
      this.root = root;
   }
   public Object getRoot() {
      return root;
   }
   public Object getChild(Object parent, int index) {
```

```
    // delegate to tree node
    return ((TreeNode) parent).getChild(index);
}
public int getChildCount(Object parent) {
    // delegate to tree node
    return ((TreeNode) parent).getChildCount();
}
public boolean isLeaf(Object node) {
    // delegate to tree node
    return ((TreeNode) node).isLeaf();
}
public int getIndexOfChild(Object parent, Object child) {
    // delegate to tree node
    return ((TreeNode) parent).getIndexOfChild(child);
}
// Append a child node
public void addChild(ConstantTreeNode parent,
        Object child) {
    // delegate to tree node
    return ((ConstantTreeNode) parent).addChild(child);
}
// null implementation - changes not supported
public void valueForPathChanged(TreePath path,
        Object newValue) {
}
// null implementation
public void addTreeModelListener(TreeModelListener l) {
}
// null implementation - laziness triumphant!
public void removeTreeModelListener(TreeModelListener l) {
}
}
```

Implementing a Constant Model

Constant tree models are most useful for display-only trees where the primary purpose is to present data in a hierarchical format without giving editing capabilities. An example of this type of model is used in the Mirror example program.

The Mirror Utility and Reflection

This utility uses the class reflection capabilities introduced in JDK 1.1 to give a hierarchical view of the composition of a class. Reflection is implemented by *java.lang.Class* and by several other classes in the *java.lang.reflect* package. The fundamental use of reflection is to be able to identify all of the constructors, data elements, methods, and inner classes of a particular object or class. This is an enabling feature for JavaBean-oriented development environments because it allows for dynamic instantiation of objects as well as invocation of methods.

A reference to a *Class* object can be acquired in a few different ways:

- The ultimate base class, *java.lang.Object*, supports the *getClass()* method. This returns a *Class* object for any nonprimitive type. Note that *getClass()* is *final*; this prevents overriding this method and returning a bogus instance of the *Class* object.

- A public static method of *Class* called *forName()* allows for creation of a *Class* instance based on a fully qualified class name string. This method throws a *ClassNotFoundException* if the string does not represent a class accessible to the virtual machine. The class must have a constructor that takes no arguments to support this feature. If the class does not have a *no arg* constructor then an *IllegalAccessException* is thrown.

- The *Class* methods return class components that are represented as objects in the *java.lang.reflect* package such as *Constructor, Method,* and *Field.* These objects encapsulate *Class* objects to represent return and parameter types.

Other features such as class loaders, object streams, and data transfer also manipulate class objects. All of these methods can provide an entry into the reflection API.

Once a reference to a *Class* has been acquired, the various methods it supports can be used to retrieve class information. *Class* provides information that is declared in the specified class, as well as all applicable information inherited from classes that have been extended. In this example, only those elements declared will be listed.

The MirrorTreeModel and Supporting Classes

This constant tree model class displays constructors, methods, and fields for a specified *Class* object.

```
package com.ketherware. tree;

import javax.swing.*;
import javax.swing.tree.*;
import java.lang.reflect.*;

public class MirrorTreeModel extends DefaultConstantTreeModel {
    protected Class mirrorClass;
    protected GroupNode constructorsNode;
    protected GroupNode fieldsNode;
    protected GroupNode methodsNode;

    //  static constructor takes class name string as parm
    public static MirrorTreeModel createModel(String name) {
        MirrorTreeModel model = null;
        try {
            model = new MirrorTreeModel(name);
        }
        catch (ClassNotFoundException ex) {
            System.out.println("Invalid class name");
        }
        return model;
    }

    // internal constructor
    protected MirrorTreeModel(String text)
            throws ClassNotFoundException,
            IllegalArgumentException {
        mirrorClass = Class.forName(text);
        String modifiers =
            getModifierText(mirrorClass.getModifiers());
```

```
   if (mirrorClass.isInterface())
      root = new
             DefaultConstantTreeNode(
             modifiers + text);
   else {
      root = new
             DefaultConstantTreeNode(
             modifiers + " class " + text);
      // interfaces don't have constructors
      addConstructors();
   }
   addFields();
   addMethods();
}

// return modifier text for value
public static String getModifierText(int modValue) {
   String modString = "";
   if (Modifier.isAbstract(modValue))
          modString += "abstract ";
   if (Modifier.isFinal(modValue))
          modString += "final ";
   if (Modifier.isInterface(modValue))
          modString += "interface ";
   if (Modifier.isNative(modValue))
          modString += "native ";
   if (Modifier.isPrivate(modValue))
          modString += "private ";
   if (Modifier.isProtected(modValue))
          modString += "protected ";
   if (Modifier.isPublic(modValue))
          modString += "public ";
   if (Modifier.isStatic(modValue))
          modString += "static ";
   if (Modifier.isSynchronized(modValue))
          modString += "synchronized ";
   if (Modifier.isTransient(modValue))
```

```
            modString += "transient ";
    if (Modifier.isVolatile(modValue))
            modString += "volatile ";
    return modString;
}


protected void addConstructors() {
    // Create the constructor node, add to the root node.
    constructorsNode = new
        GroupNode("Constructors", this.root);
    this.root.add(constructorsNode);

    // Iterate through the declared constructors and
    // add them as children
    Constructor[] constructors = mirrorClass.
        getDeclaredConstructors();
    for (int z=0; z < constructors.length; z++) {
        constructorsNode.addChild(
            new ConstructorNode(constructors[z]));
    }
}


protected void addFields() {
    // Create the fields node, add to the root node.
    fieldsNode = new
        GroupNode("Fields", this.root);
    this.root.add(fieldsNode);

    // Iterate through the declared fields and
    // add them as children
    Field[] fields = mirrorClass.
        getDeclaredFields();
    for (int z=0; z < fields.length; z++) {
        fieldsNode.addChild(
            new FieldNode(fields[z]));
    }
}
```

```
protected void addMethods() {
   // Create the methods node, add to the root node.
   methodsNode = new
       GroupNode("Methods", this.root);
   this.root.add(methodsNode);

   // Iterate through the declared methods and
   // add them as children
   Method[] methods = mirrorClass.
       getDeclaredMethods();
   for (int z=0; z < methods.length; z++) {
     methodsNode.addChild(
         new MethodNode(methods[z]));
   }
 }
}
```

These classes are all extensions of *DefaultConstantTreeNode*. They serve as the various components on the tree. The *GroupNode* class just serves as a branch node in the hierarchy.

```
package com.ketherware. tree;

import javax.swing.*;
import javax.swing.tree.*;
import java.lang.reflect.*;

public class GroupNode extends DefaultConstantTreeNode {
   public GroupNode(String caption, TreeNode parent) {
      // Create node that allows children and is
      // not a leaf
      super(caption, parent, true, false);
   }
}
```

MemberNode is an abstract class that serves as a base class for constructor, method, and field nodes. It contains the methods used to list the parameters of a constructor or method and a static method to strip the package names from identifiers.

```
package com.ketherware. tree;

import javax.swing.*;
import javax.swing.tree.*;
import java.lang.reflect.*;

public abstract class MemberNode extends DefaultConstantTreeNode {
   protected String text;
   public String toString() {
      return text;
   }
   protected String addParameters(Constructor constructor) {
      return addParameters(
            constructor.getParameterTypes());
   }
   protected String addParameters(Method method) {
      return addParameters(
            method.getParameterTypes());
   }
   private String addParameters(Class[] parms) {
   }
   protected String stripPackage(String className) {
   }
}
```

To perform the special processing that is required for constructors, methods, and fields, three classes are derived from *MemberNode*. All of them will be configured to be leaf nodes.

```
package com.ketherware. tree;

import javax.swing.*;
import javax.swing.tree.*;
import java.lang.reflect.*;

public class ConstructorNode extends MemberNode {
   public ConstructorNode(Constructor constructor,
            TreeNode parent) {
```

```
        // Create node that does not allow children        //
and is a leaf
        super(constructor, parent, false, true);

        // Build the text string for the constructor
        int mods = constructor.getModifiers();
        text = MirrorTreeModel.getModifierText(mods);
        text += " " + stripPackage(
                constructor.getName());
        text += addParameters(constructor);
    }
}
```

The *MethodNode* class also needs to add the return value. This is added after the modifiers.

```
    package com.ketherware. tree;

    import javax.swing.*;
    import javax.swing.tree.*;
    import java.lang.reflect.*;

    public class MethodNode extends MemberNode {
        public MethodNode(Method method,
                TreeNode parent) {
            // Create node that does not allow children     // and is a leaf
            super(method, parent, false, true);

            // Build the text string for the method
            int mods = method.getModifiers();
            text = MirrorTreeModel.getModifierText(mods);
            text += " " + stripPackage(
                    method.getReturnType().getName());
            text += " " + stripPackage(
                    method.getName());
            text += addParameters(method);
        }
    }
```

Last, the *FieldNode*, which has no parameter string.

```
package com.ketherware. tree;

import javax.swing.*;
import javax.swing.tree.*;
import java.lang.reflect.*;

public class FieldNode extends MemberNode {
   public FieldNode(Field field,
           TreeNode parent) {
      // Create node that does not allow children
      // and is a leaf
      super(field, parent, false, true);

      // Build the text string for the field
      int mods = field.getModifiers();
      text = MirrorTreeModel.getModifierText(mods);
      text += " " + stripPackage(
              field.getType());
   }
}
```

Tree Selection

The *JTree* component has a state model that supports selection of nodes in the tree. The interface that supports this model is *TreeSelectionModel*. Unlike the *JList* control, there is a hierarchical relationship among tree data. Because of this, it is not feasible to identify a particular node simply by reference. Instead the *TreePath* class is used to identify nodes. So, instead of managing selections by index, *TreeSelectionModel* uses single or multiple instances of *TreePath* and offers several methods to map these values to the visible row of the tree. Before covering the selection model in detail, it is important to understand the *TreePath* class.

The TreePath Class

TreePath encapsulates an array of objects, which are usually *TreeNode* instances. This array would contain an element for each level of indentation in the hierarchy. The path is formed by instances of the target node and each of its parent nodes all the way back to the root node. *TreePath* is usually expressed as a path from the root to the target node, so the target node always appears last (see Figure 7-2).

TreePath provides constructors that build a path from an array of *Objects*, a single *Object,* or a pair of *TreeNode* elements. Here are some of the other methods that are provided:

- *public Object[] getPath()*—Returns an array of *Objects* that represents all of the elements in the path.

- *public int getPathCount()*—Returns the number of elements in the path.

- *public Object getLastPathComponent()*—Returns the last element in the path, which is usually the target node. This one method tends to get used quite often.

- *public Object getPathComponent(int element)*—Provides access to each element in the path. This method throws an *IllegalArgumentException* if the element index is not valid.

- *public boolean equals(Object o)*—Enables a comparison between two *TreePaths.*

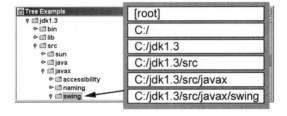

Figure 7-2. *Example of TreePath.*

The TreeSelectionModel Interface

This is the most complex state model in the JFC architecture since it must support a wide array of selection functionality. The following methods are defined in this interface:

- ***void setSelectionMode(int mode)***—This property alters the current selection node. It is similar to the modes supported for the list selection models, except it deals with paths instead of indices. The following modes are supported by the default model:

  - ***SINGLE_TREE_SELECTION***—Enables selection of a single tree path.

  - ***CONTIGUOUS_TREE_SELECTION***—Enables selection of multiple tree paths that must all have the same ancestors. This is the equivalent of selecting multiple files within a directory, but not across different directories.

  - ***DISCONTIGUOUS_TREE_SELECTION***—Enables selections of any number of paths.

- ***int getSelectionMode()***—Returns the current selection mode.

- ***int getSelectionCount()***—Returns the number of paths that are selected.

- ***TreePath getSelectionPath()***—If the mode is *SINGLE_TREE_SELECTION*, returns the selected path or *null*. Otherwise, returns the first path in the selection set.

- ***TreePath[] getSelectionPaths()***—Returns all of the paths in the selection.

- ***int[] getSelectionRows()***—Returns all of the currently selected rows. Keep in mind that is represents rows in the tree and not visible rows in the scroll pane.

- ***void setSelectionPath(TreePath path)***—Sets the currently selected path in any mode.

- ***void setSelectionPaths(TreePath[] paths)***—Enables a user to specify an array of paths to be selected. If the mode is *SINGLE_TREE_SELECTION*, only the first path in the array is used.

- *void addSelectionPath(TreePath path)*—If the mode is *SINGLE_TREE_SELECTION*, the specified path becomes the selected path. Otherwise, the path is added to the list of currently selected paths.

- *void addSelectionPaths(TreePath[] paths)*—For the multiple selection modes, the paths are added to the list of currently selected paths. If the mode is *SINGLE_TREE_SELECTION*, the first path in the array becomes the selected path.

- *TreePath getLeadSelectionPath()*—Returns the last path that was added, regardless of mode.

- *int getLeadSelectionRow()*—Returns the row of the last component of the last tree path selected.

- *int getMaxSelectionRow(), int getMinSelectionRow()*—Returns the highest and lowest selected rows. If the mode is *SINGLE_TREE_SELECTION*, the selected row is returned. If no rows are selected, (–1) is returned.

- *void clearSelection()*—Sets the selection set to empty.

- *boolean isSelectionEmpty()*—This method returns *true* if the selection set is currently empty.

- *void removeSelectionPath(TreePath path)*—Removes the specified path from the selection set.

- *void removeSelectionPaths(TreePath[] paths)*—Removes the specified set of paths from the selection set. If the mode is *SINGLE_TREE_SELECTION*, only the first path in the array is used.

- *boolean isPathSelected(TreePath path)*—This methods returns *true* if the specified path is in the current selection set.

- *RowMapper getRowMapper()*—Returns the *RowMapper* instance that is able to map a path to a row. The *RowMapper* class supports one method, *getRowsForPaths()*, which takes an array of *TreePath* objects as a parameter and returns an array of rows to which the paths map. Paths that are not valid are mapped to the value (–1).

- *void setRowMapper(RowMapper newMapper)*—This method allows the assignment of an alternative object that provides the *RowMapper* functionality.

- *void resetRowSelection()*—This method is designed to cause the *RowMapper* to discard any cached information about row mappings for selected paths and recalculate its information. This method is called automatically in the default selection model when the following methods are called: *setRowMapper()*, *setSelectionPaths()*, *addSelectionPaths()*, *removeSelectionPaths()*, or *clearSelection()*.

- *boolean isRowSelected(int row)*—This method returns *true* if the specified row is currently selected.

- *void addPropertyChangeListener(PropertyChangeListener listener)*—Allows assignment of a property change listener on the *SelectionMode* property. This listener will not be notified of property changes to the tree control itself.

- *void removePropertyChangeListener(PropertyChangeListener listener)*—Removes the *SelectionMode* property change listener.

- *void addTreeSelectionListener(TreeSelectionListener listener)*—This is the method used to associate a tree selection listener with a particular selection model. The *TreeSelectionListener* interface is discussed in detail in the following section.

- *void removeTreeSelectionListener(TreeSelectionListener listener)*—Removes a listener from the selection listener list.

A class called *DefaultTreeSelectionModel* implements this interface. Chances are that the default model is sufficient for most needs, although it is conceivable to create a selection model filter similar to the one discussed in the chapter on *JList*.

Tree Selection Listeners and Events

Similar to the *JList* component, changes in selection are detected by listeners to the selection model. To access the selection model for a tree, use the *getSelectionModel()* method and add an object that implements the *TreeSelectionListener* interface as an external, inner, or anonymous class.

TreeSelectionListener requires implementation of a single method, *valueChanged()*. This method has a single parameter of type *TreeSelectionEvent*. This event object supports the following methods:

- *TreePath[] getPaths()*—Returns an array of all the paths that have been added or removed from the selection. If the selection mode is *SINGLE_TREE_SELECTION*, this method returns an array of one element.

- *TreePath getPath()*—Returns the first path in the list of path changes.

- *TreePath getNewLeadSelectionPath()*—Returns the new current lead path, which is the last selection to be added to the selection list. If the selection mode is *SINGLE_TREE_SELECTION*, this value is identical to that returned by *getPath()*.

- *TreePath getOldLeadSelectionPath()*—Returns the path that was previously the lead path.

- *boolean isAddedPath(TreePath path)*—This method is used to determine whether a particular path returned from *getPaths()* was added or deleted from the selection list. If this method returns *true,* the path was added.

- *boolean isAddedPath()*—This method operates similarly to the preceding method, except that it operates only on the first element in the path list.

- *Object cloneWithSource(Object newSource)*—This method creates a new *TreeSelectionEvent* based on the instance being used. This is apparently a workaround for a problem with Internet Explorer.

The Phile example provides an implementation of a tree selection listener and several other essential points discussed in this chapter.

Editing in JTree

JTree supports a hook that enables a user to change the value of a node directly in the tree. The *TreeCellEditor* property of *JTree* enables a component to be displayed when a value needs to be changed. This component is acquired in a similar fashion to cell renderers, except the component being edited is designed to handle the actual changes to its properties.

An editing session is begun when one of the following occurs: a triple mouse click, or a double mouse click with a delay of 1,200 milliseconds. These conditions cause the beginning of an editing session. When this session begins, the node is replaced by another component, such as *JTextField*, that enables changes to be made. The value in the text field is prefilled with the current value of the node. Trees that have their *Editable* property set to *false* will not invoke property editing. Editing can be accepted, usually by hitting the <Return> key, or canceled by use of the <Esc> key. Actual behavior is look-and-feel-specific.

Example: The Phile Utility

The *Phile* utility was born from an old experiment that was created for an evaluation of the Swing components. It is a simplified version of the Windows 95 Explorer, which was a replacement for the old File Manager. Although not as robust as the real thing, *Phile* does touch on some interesting points about how trees can be used.

How Phile Works

The utility uses a single split pane frame with a tree of directories on the left and a tree of files on the right. *Phile* enables a user to expand and collapse the file directories on the left, which updates the list of files in that directory on the right. Three node types are declared: one called *DirectoryTreeNode,* which serves as a branch node in both trees, and *FileTreeNode,* which represents a leaf node in the right-hand tree.

The third class, *DummyTreeNode,* has a special purpose. There is a useful premise that a program should never show its user more than he or she needs to know. Operating under this assumption, *Phile* does not iterate through the entire tree of directories each time it is invoked. Instead, each directory node is initialized as containing a single dummy node. When the directory node is expanded, only then are the contents of the directory examined. If the directory is empty, the dummy node is retained, but marked as having been traversed. This prevents the program from treating the node as a leaf (as a childless node would be treated by the default model) and eliminates redundant checking of empty directories.

Phile Source Code—DirectoryTreeModel

```java
package com.ketherware.phile;

import javax.swing.*;
import javax.swing.tree.*;
import javax.swing.event.*;
import java.io.File;

// Tree model for directory (left) side
public class DirectoryTreeModel extends DefaultTreeModel {

    // Constructor - create a root node
    public DirectoryTreeModel() {
        super(new DirectoryTreeNode("root"));
        initialize();
    }

    // Model intialization
    protected void initialize() {

        // Get a reference to the root node and get
        // the list of root devices
        DirectoryTreeNode rootNode = (DirectoryTreeNode) getRoot();
        File[] roots = File.listRoots();

        // If no root devices found, we are on UNIX or something
        if (roots == null)
        {
            // Get the list of files in the root
            File rootDirectory = new File(File.separator);
            roots = rootDirectory.listFiles();
            DirectoryTreeNode rootDirNode =
                    new DirectoryTreeNode(rootDirectory);
            rootNode.add(rootDirNode);
            rootNode = rootDirNode;
        }
```

```java
        // Add the child nodes to the root
        addChildren(rootNode, roots);
    }

    // Called by tree control when a node is
    // expanded that contains a dummy node
    public void handleNodeExpand(DirectoryTreeNode expandingNode,
                DummyTreeNode dummyNode, TreeExpansionEvent event)
                throws ExpandVetoException
    {
        // If the node has been traversed, that means it is
        // an empty directory (branch with no children)
        // so the expansion is vetoed
        if (dummyNode.getHasBeenTraversed())
            throw new ExpandVetoException(event);

        // If it has not been previously traversed, it
        // has been now, so set the traversal flag. Add
        // children as required
        dummyNode.setHasBeenTraversed(true);
        File file = (File) expandingNode.getUserObject();
        addChildren(expandingNode, file.listFiles());

        // if the dummy node has not been removed, then no
        // children were added and the expansion is vetoed
        if (dummyNode.getParent() != null)
            throw new ExpandVetoException(event);
    }

    // Add child directories to a node
    protected void addChildren(DirectoryTreeNode node, File[] children) {
        // Assume no children have been added
        boolean childAdded = false;

        // if there are no children, bail out
        if (children == null)
            return;
```

```
            // Iterate through the children
            for (int k=0; k < children.length; k++) {
                // This is a hack to prevent spinning the floppy
                // drive on Windows 32 systems
                if (children[k].getPath().startsWith("A:"))
                    continue;
                // If it is not a directory, skip it
                if (!children[k].isDirectory())
                    continue;

                // create a new child node and set the flag
                // to true
                node.add(new DirectoryTreeNode(children[k]));
                childAdded = true;
            }

            // If a child was added, we need to remove the dummy node.
            // This will cause the dummy node's parent to become <null>.
            // Thus, if no children were added, the dummy node is NOT
            // removed and the node will remain a branch and display as
            // a folder.
            if (childAdded) {
                if (node.getChildAt(0) instanceof DummyTreeNode)
                    node.remove(0);
            }
        }
    }
```

DirectoryTreeNode

```
package com.ketherware. phile;

import javax.swing.tree.*;
import java.io.File;

// This represents a node in the directory tree
public class DirectoryTreeNode extends DefaultMutableTreeNode {
```

```
// This constructor encapsulates a File object
public DirectoryTreeNode(File file) {
    super(file, true);
    add(new DummyTreeNode());
}
// Constructor used for creating a root. Root nodes
// will not have a file associated with them and will
// never be made visible.
public DirectoryTreeNode(String filename) {
    super(filename, true);
}

// Extract the directory name for display
public String toString()
{
    if (getUserObject() instanceof String)
        return (String) getUserObject();
    File file = (File) getUserObject();

    String path = file.getPath();
    if (path.endsWith("\\"))
        return path;
    else
        return file.getName();
}
}
```

FileTreeModel

```
package com.ketherware. phile;

import java.awt.*;
import java.io.File;
import java.awt.event.*;
import javax.swing.*;
import javax.swing.event.*;
import javax.swing.tree.*;
```

```java
// Tree data model for right-hand side of splitter
public class FileTreeModel extends DefaultTreeModel {
    // array of file contained by directory
    protected File[] files;
    protected static final String fileSeparator =
                System.getProperty("file.separator");

    // Constructor, accepts array of file objects
    public FileTreeModel(File[] files) {
        // Create a new root for this model
        super(new DefaultMutableTreeNode("root"));
        DefaultMutableTreeNode rootNode =
                (DefaultMutableTreeNode) getRoot();

        // if there are no files in this directory, do not
        // add any nodes
        this.files = files;
        if (files == null)
            return;

        // Add the directories first
        for (int j=0; j < files.length; j++)
        {
            if (files[j].isDirectory())
                rootNode.add(new FileTreeNode(files[j]));
        }

        // Then add the files
        for (int j=0; j < files.length; j++)
        {
            if (!files[j].isDirectory())
                rootNode.add(new FileTreeNode(files[j]));
        }
    }

    // This is an override of the default model behavior
    public void valueForPathChanged(TreePath path, Object newValue)
```

```
        {
            // Isolate the node that changed
            DefaultMutableTreeNode node = (DefaultMutableTreeNode)
                        path.getLastPathComponent();

            // Get the file object encapsulated by the node
            File file = (File) node.getUserObject();
            String dir = file.getPath();
            int lastSep = dir.lastIndexOf(fileSeparator);
            dir = (lastSep != -1) ? dir.substring(0, lastSep + 1) : dir;

            // Change the filename by replacing the node
            File newFile = new File(dir + newValue.toString());
            file.renameTo(newFile);
            super.valueForPathChanged(path, newFile);
        }

        // inner class representing node in file model
        protected class FileTreeNode extends DefaultMutableTreeNode {
            // If the file is a directory, add a dummy node to make it
            // a branch node. This will cause a folder icon to be used
            public FileTreeNode(File file) {
                super(file, true);
                if (file.isDirectory())
                    this.add(new DummyTreeNode());
            }

            // Display only the filename portion
            public String toString() {
                File file = (File) getUserObject();
                return file.getName();
            }
        }
    }
}
```

DummyTreeModel

```java
package com.ketherware. phile;

import javax.swing.tree.*;

// The dummy node is used to force a directory to appear to
// be a branch even if it has no actual children
public class DummyTreeNode extends DefaultMutableTreeNode {
    // This flag is for performance purposes and
    // prevents empty directories from being re-loaded
    protected boolean hasBeenTraversed;

    // Create a node with the traversal flag reset
    public DummyTreeNode() {
        super("*");
        this.hasBeenTraversed = false;
    }

    // Retrieve the traversal flag
    public boolean getHasBeenTraversed() {
        return this.hasBeenTraversed;
    }

    // Update the traversal flag
    public void setHasBeenTraversed(boolean hasBeenTraversed) {
        this.hasBeenTraversed = hasBeenTraversed;
    }
}
```

PhileFrame

```java
package com.ketherware. phile;

import java.awt.*;
import java.io.File;
import java.awt.event.*;
```

```java
import javax.swing.*;
import javax.swing.event.*;
import javax.swing.tree.*;

// Application frame
public class PhileFrame extends JFrame implements
TreeWillExpandListener {
    protected JSplitPane splitter;
    protected JScrollPane leftScroll;
    protected JScrollPane rightScroll;
    protected JTree dirTree;
    protected JTree fileTree;

    // Frame constructor
    public PhileFrame() {
        setLocation(100, 100);
        setSize(600, 600);
        setTitle("Phile Utility");
        initialize();
    }

    // Create child components
    private void initialize() {
        // Create the tree and list controls, insert them into
        // scroll panes
        dirTree = new JTree(new DirectoryTreeModel());
        leftScroll = new JScrollPane(dirTree);
        leftScroll.setPreferredSize(new Dimension(300, 300));
        fileTree = new JTree();
        rightScroll = new JScrollPane(fileTree);

        // Create the left tree that will contain directories
        dirTree.addTreeWillExpandListener(this);
        dirTree.setRootVisible(false);
        dirTree.setShowsRootHandles(true);
        dirTree.setEditable(true);
```

```java
        // Create the right tree that will contain files
        fileTree.addTreeWillExpandListener(this);
        fileTree.setRootVisible(false);
        fileTree.setShowsRootHandles(false);
        fileTree.setEditable(true);

        // Add the splitter pane
        splitter = new JSplitPane(JSplitPane.HORIZONTAL_SPLIT,
                leftScroll, rightScroll);
        this.getContentPane().add(splitter);

        // Set the tree selection model to only allow single selection.
        // Add a listener, expand and select the first node
        TreeSelectionModel selectionModel = dirTree.getSelectionModel();
        selectionModel.setSelectionMode(

DefaultTreeSelectionModel.SINGLE_TREE_SELECTION);
        selectionModel.addTreeSelectionListener(
                    new PhileTreeSelectionListener(fileTree));
        dirTree.expandRow(0);
        dirTree.setSelectionRow(0);

        // Catch the frame when it closes and end the process
        this.addWindowListener(new WindowAdapter() {
            public void windowClosing(WindowEvent event) {
                System.exit(0);
            }
        });
    }

    // required by interface TreeWillExpandListener
    public void treeWillExpand(TreeExpansionEvent event)
                    throws ExpandVetoException        {
        if (event.getSource() == fileTree)
            throw new ExpandVetoException(event);

        // Get the node that is being expanded
```

```
            DirectoryTreeNode expandingNode = (DirectoryTreeNode)
                        event.getPath().getLastPathComponent();
            DummyTreeNode childNode = null;

            // See if there is a dummy node there
            if (expandingNode.getChildCount() == 1) {
                try {
                    childNode = (DummyTreeNode)
                            expandingNode.getChildAt(0);
                }
                catch (ClassCastException ex) {
                    return;
                }

                DirectoryTreeModel model = (DirectoryTreeModel)
                        dirTree.getModel();
                model.handleNodeExpand(expandingNode, childNode, event);
            }
        }

        // required by interface TreeWillExpandListener
        public void treeWillCollapse(TreeExpansionEvent event)
        {
            // don't care about this event
        }

        public static void main(String[] args) throws java.io.IOException {
            new PhileFrame().show();
        }


        // Provides handling of selection of directory
        protected class DirectoryTreeSelectionListener
                            implements TreeSelectionListener
        {
            // Copy of tree control instance
            private JTree fileTree;
```

```
    // Constructor - save instance of tree control
    public DirectoryTreeSelectionListener(JTree fileTree)
    {
        this.fileTree = fileTree;
    }

    // Invoked when selection changes
    public void valueChanged(TreeSelectionEvent event)
    {
        // Isolate the node that was selected
        DirectoryTreeNode selectedNode = (DirectoryTreeNode)
                event.getPath().getLastPathComponent();
        File file = (File) selectedNode.getUserObject();

        // Build a new model on the right panel that contains
        // the files in the selected directory
        fileTree.setModel(new FileTreeModel(file.listFiles()));
    }
  }
}
```

Exercises

1. Add code to the Mirror utility to toggle the display of inherited methods and fields. Hint: Use a tree model filter or a set of two constant classes that can be toggled with a check box, menu item, or toggle button.

2. Add another level of hierarchy underneath constructors and methods that shows the exceptions they might throw.

3. Add code to display inner classes. Use the same structure as the top-level class to display inner methods and fields. Note: This functionality is only available with JDK 1.2 (Java 2).

4. Add the capability to drill-down to any specified class in the tree and create a Mirror model for that class. Hint: Create a new constant model and update the *Model* property of the frame's tree control.

You do not need to leave your room. Remain sitting at your table and listen. Do not even listen, simply wait, be quiet still and solitary. The world will freely offer itself to you to be unmasked, it has no choice, it will roll in ecstasy at your feet.

—Franz Kafka

Chapter 8

The JTable Component

The *JTable* component is designed to display tabular data in row and column format. It is designed to contain a two-dimensional array of arbitrarily typed data elements known as cells'. These cells can be displayed using default and custom renderers and can be modified in-place by cell editors; both of these mechanisms are similar to those implemented in the *JTree* component. In some respects, *JTable* is simpler than *JTree* because its data is not hierarchical. Unlike *JTree*, *JTable* provides reordering and regrouping of its data by column; these features are implemented by several tightly integrated model and component classes.

JTable implements the *Scrollable* interface and uses certain features of *JScrollPane* and *JViewport* to perform many of its functions, including providing a place for the table headers to be drawn. These column headers, encapsulated in the companion class *JTableHeader*, can be dynamically reordered and resized using mouse drag operations. See Figure 8-1.

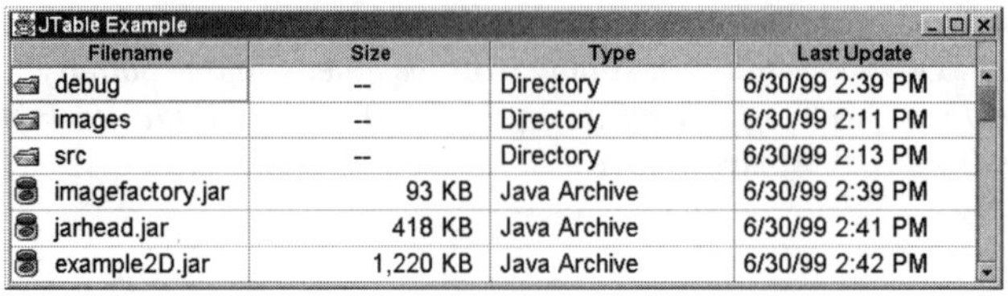

Figure 8-1. *JTable example*

JTable is similar to many familiar implementations of grid and spreadsheet components and application, but does not perform many of the sophisticated operations found in many desktop software packages such as formulas, variables, and macros. Nonetheless, it is a very powerful and flexible component, primarily due to its lightweight implementation and the advantages achieved with Model/View/Controller architecture.

JTable uses several models to encapsulate data, state, and configuration information. A data model based on the *TableModel* interface represents contents of the cells that are described by row and column position, as well as information on the number of rows and columns found in the table. The cells themselves are represented by a generic *Object* type, giving an implementor great versatility in how data is interpreted and displayed.

Another model, the *TableColumnModel*, manages the position and width of the columns as well as providing a mechanism for associating columns with a particular class of object data. The column model is one of the important elements in the *JTable* because it is the place where customizable data renderers and editors are associated with table columns.

TableColumnModel is a collection of *TableColumn* objects, each of which contains the information about a particular column in a table. Along with its *Width* property and resizability control, columns can be configured to have preferred, minimum, and maximum extents.

All of the classes that support *JTable* have complex but well-defined relationships. The communication among these objects is supported mostly by listeners for *JTable*-specific events. Although each of these classes is covered in detail in this chapter, Figure 8-2 shows this relationship.

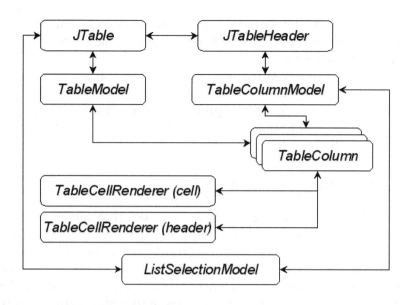

Figure 8-2. *JTable supporting classes*

The *JTable* method *resizeAndRepaint()* is a catch-all procedure for forcing the *JTable* to be redrawn. It is invoked by model and property change listeners when a need for redrawing is established; its standard behavior is to call the *revalidate()* and *repaint()* methods.

Scrolling Support

JTable provides an implementation of the *Scrollable* interface that enables it to interact with its *JScrollPane* parent. *JTable* provides an additional method, *setPreferredScrollableViewportSize()*, that enables explicit assignment of the preferred viewport size. This method is used by *JTable* to control the horizontal scrolling characteristics depending on whether automatic column sizing is enabled. This property is not bound, so if a change is made to this value, the container parent of *JTable* must be revalidated.

If automatic sizing is enabled, the *getScrollableTracksViewportWidth()* method, which is specified by the *Scrollable* interface, will return *true*. This informs the scroll pane that the table will consume exactly whatever width is available in the scroll pane. The method *getScrollableTracksViewportHeight()* is hard-coded to return *false*.

Because of the way *JScrollPane* operates, *JTable* cannot provide column headers without being parented by one. The reason for this is that the *JTableHeader* component that provides headers is not a child of the *JTable*, but is assigned to the auxiliary horizontal viewport of *JScrollPane*, and is thus a sibling of the *JTable* itself.

The TableModel Interface

The cells in a *JTable* are described by a model that implements the *TableModel* interface. In addition to the cell values themselves, this interface characterizes the number of rows and columns in the table as well as indicating whether an individual cell is editable. *TableModel* provides methods to inform *JTable* of the names of the columns as well as the class of data that each column contains. This class information is used to associate data renderers and editors with each column. *JTable* provides a set of default renderers and editors for commonly used data classes.

Row and Column Information

One of the principal characteristics of table data is its shape, that is, the number of rows and columns it contains. The methods *getRowCount()* and *getColumnCount()* both return an integer; these represent the number of cells in the vertical and horizontal directions. Either or both of these values can be zero, which denotes an empty table.

For each column, two additional pieces of information are available: The *getColumnName()* method returns a *String* that represents the initial value for the column header. The method *getColumnClass()* returns an object of type *Class*, which represents the type of the object that is expected to appear in a particular column. Both of these methods take an integer parameter that denotes the zero-based index of the column. The value of this parameter must be within the bounds described by the results of *getColumnCount()*.

Cell Information

The methods *getValueAt()* and *setValueAt()* are used to access and modify the contents of each cell in the table. Cells are identified by their row and column coordinates; these parameters are passed to both methods. The *getValueAt()* method returns an *Object* type, which is also the third parameter of *setValueAt()*. By returning a generic type, the nature of data stored in the table is not limited. Information on type can be retrieved by examining the column information with *getColumnClass()*.

The method *isCellEditable()* returns a *boolean* value, which determines whether a particular cell can have its value dynamically changed by an editor component. The parameters of this method are a row and column pair. A model may implement a mechanism whereby a cell may change in its capability to be edited, so it is always invoked prior to an edit request.

Listening for TableModel Changes

All table model implementations must support the capability to listen for events that are fired when table characteristics or cell data changes. Changes to a table model are signified by reception of a *TableModelEvent* object. Objects that wish to listen for this event can use the *addTableModelListener()* and *removeTableModelListener()* methods to register interest in table model changes. These methods both take a reference to a *TableModelListener* as a parameter. Objects that implement *TableModelListener* must supply a single method, *tableChanged()*, that contains a parameter of type *TableModelEvent*.

TableModelEvent describes the changes that may occur to a table model and is oriented toward describing changes to multiple rows. The methods *getFirstRow()* and *getLastRow()* provide an inclusive range of rows that change. When a single row changes, these values will be the same. A special value *HEADER_ROW* is available to inform a listener that the table headers have changed. Table headers are covered later in this chapter.

The *getColumn()* method is used to determine which column of a table changed. This method may return the special value *ALL_COLUMNS*, which means that the change refers to entire rows of cells. Using the combination of row and column information isolates a single cell, a block of cells, or the entire table. Lastly, the *getType()* method returns one of the values INSERT, UPDATE, or DELETE depending on whether rows were inserted, changed, or removed.

According to its designers, the *TableModelEvent* class is deliberately generic to encourage subclassing its capabilities and to enable more specialized interpretations of its information. It is suggested in the internal documentation that additional special values, preprocessing, or other capabilities could be added.

Delegate Methods of JTable

JTable provides some methods that delegate to the instance of *TableModel* that is the value of its *Model* property. These are *getRowCount()*, *getColumnCount()*, *getColumnName()*, *getColumnClass()*, *getValueAt()*, and *setValueAt()*. These methods provide access to this information without creating an additional indirection to the model instance.

AbstractTableModel

Two base classes are provided that implement the *TableModel* interface. *AbstractTableModel* provides a thin layer of event support, implementing the management of *TableModelListener* objects and the firing of *TableModelEvents*. Default values are provided for column names, classes, and editablility.

Implementors of this class must provide versions of *getRowCount()*, *getColumnCount()*, and *getValueAt()*. A no-op version of *setValueAt()* is provided, which essentially makes *AbstractTableModel* immutable by default. Column names are generated automatically by cycling through the alphabet and assigning each column a capital letter. The default behavior of *getColumnClass()* is to return the value *Object.class*; the *isCellEditable()* method returns *false* by default.

Another method, *findColumn()*, is not required by the *TableModel* interface, nor is it used by *JTable*. Its default implementation returns the column number that maps to a particular column name. Remember that column names do not have to be unique, as is evidenced by the default column naming behavior. Thus, the *findColumn()* method as implemented by *AbstractTableModel* only returns the first matching occurrence in the case of duplicate column names.

Table Event Generation

AbstractTableModel provides a set of methods to fire *TableModelEvent* objects, as well as a mechanism to manage listeners. The method *fireTableChanged()* is ultimately called by the other default methods.

The *fireTableChanged()* method takes a single parameter of type *TableModelEvent*. Its function is to iterate through the list of registered *TableModelListener* objects and invoke the *tableChanged()* method using the event as a parameter.

The methods *fireTableDataChanged()* and *fireTableStructureChanged()* are intended to let listeners determine whether a table event is a data change, meaning only a repaint may be required, or a structure change, meaning that columns and rows have been added, moved, or deleted. The default implementation of *fireTableDataChanged()* simply invokes *fireTableChanged()* with a default *TableModelEvent*; this uses the values zero for the start row, *Integer.MAX_VALUE* for the end row, and the value *ALL_COLUMNS* for the column number. This event is the most generic, representing a change to every row and column in the table. The *fireTableStructureChanged()* method uses a different default event that targets only the header values, specifying a column value of *TableModelEvent.HEADER_ROW*.

Three methods are provided that can be used to notify listeners of row-oriented changes to data. Each of the methods *fireTableRowsInserted()*, *fireTableRowsUpdated()*, and *fireTableRowsDeleted()* invokes *fireTableChanged()* with a *TableModelEvent* that represents a single row; the first and last row values are both set to the specified row, and the value *ALL_COLUMNS* is used for the column identifier. The event type flag is set to INSERT, UPDATE, or DELETE depending on the method called.

In addition, a method *fireTableCellUpdated()* is provided. This method fires a *TableModelEvent* that targets a single cell and uses the UPDATE type. Both row values are set to the specified row; the column value is also used to refer to a specific cell.

DefaultTableModel

DefaultTableModel is a canonical, generic, concrete implementation of *AbstractTableModel*. It provides additional methods to add, insert, move, and delete table information on a row or column basis, and provides a simple collection using nested *Vector* objects.

DefaultTableModel considers all cells it contains to be editable, because it always returns *true* for its implementation of *isCellEditable()*. Subclasses of *DefaultTableModel* that wish to control editing on a row, column, or cell-oriented basis must implement a mechanism to track which cells are editable.

Initializing a DefaultTableModel

The *DefaultTableModel* implementation is used by *JTable* when a table model is not specified in the *JTable* constructor. *JTable* invokes the *createDefaultDataModel()* to create an instance of *DefaultTableModel* if one is needed.

Apart from the default constructor, which creates an empty model (one with zero rows and zero columns), five additional constructors are provided. The first version takes two integer parameters and creates a model of the specified shape containing *null* values; it causes default column names to be generated. Another version takes a *Vector* of column names and an integer representing a row count. Its behavior is similar to the previously discussed constructor, except that it derives the column count from the size of the *Vector* and specifies values for column headers. Another similar version takes an array of *Object* and a row count, the array providing column names instead of a *Vector*. In both cases, the table data is initialized to *null* values.

Two constructors are provided that enable complete initialization of the table data as well as the column names. These constructors use the *setDataVector()* and *getDataVector()* methods of *DefaultTableModel*. The first parameter of *setDataVector* represents the "*Vector* of *Vectors*" that contains the table data; this *Vector* object is expected to contain *Vector* objects that delineate data elements on a row-oriented basis. The *setDataVector* implementation fires the necessary events to alert the *JTable* that a new set of data is available. It also reconstructs and resizes table columns and headers as needed using the second parameter, which is a *Vector of column names*. The constructor that uses this method also provides two *Vector* arguments that map directly to the arguments of *setDataVector()*. The alternate constructor takes a two-dimensional array of *Object* data as its first parameter and a one-dimension array as its second. The first argument is converted to a *Vector* by a *protected static* method *convertToVector()*, which takes an array of *Object* as a parameter and returns a *Vector* representation of those elements. The second argument is the set of column headers; these are also converted to *Vector* representations using the *convertToVector()* mechanism.

Manipulating Rows

In addition to the *getRowCount()* method, which is required by the *TableModel* interface, *DefaultTableModel* provides several procedures that enable manipulation of table rows.

The four methods that are provided are *addRow()*, *insertRow()*, *moveRow()*, and *removeRow()*; these methods map directly to the operations supported by the *TableModelEvent*. All of these methods operate only on complete rows of data.

The *addRow()* method has two versions: the first takes a *Vector* of data elements and the second an array of *Object* elements. Both of these methods append the specified row data onto the end of the model. As with all of the alternative methods that take an array instead of a *Vector*, *addRow()* calls the *convertToVector()* static method and passes the result to the *Vector* version of the method.

The method *insertRow()* is similar to *addRow()*: It provides a *Vector* and an array version, except it provides an additional parameter that specifies the row index to insert the new data, effectively incrementing all row indices of higher elements. If an index is supplied that is greater than the size of the model, the data vector is expanded to accommodate the new index; intervening rows created will contain *null* values. The index is specified as the first parameter in the *insertRow()* method.

The *moveRow()* method enables the altering of single or multiple row indices. It takes three integer parameters: The first two parameters represent the inclusive start and end indices of the block of rows to be moved, and the third dictates the intended new position of the rows. Unlike *insertRows()*, *moveRow()* does not increase the size of the model to accommodate requests, and an *ArrayIndexOutOfBoundsException* is thrown if the range is invalid or the target row exceeds the current row count. This method could be renamed *moveRows()* because it provides multiple-row capability; perhaps another version of *moveRow()* that takes two parameters, the source and destination indices of a single row, should be considered.

To delete individual rows from the model, the *removeRow()* method is used. The single parameter is the index of the row to be deleted. If the row index is not valid, an *ArrayIndexOutOfBoundsException* is thrown by the *Vector* implementation.

The *setNumRows()* method is used to perform a wholesale change to the number of rows in the model. It takes an integer parameter that represents the desired number of rows. If the specified number matches the existing row count, this method is a no-op. Otherwise it removes existing rows and adds empty rows to the model to accommodate the request. Using this method with a parameter of zero is a convenient way to remove all of the rows in the model without a loop construct.

Manipulating Columns

DefaultTableModel provides methods to add new columns to its internal collections and to alter the identifiers. Three versions of the *addColumn()* method are implemented: The first takes a single *Object* parameter that becomes the identifier of the new column. When this version is used, an empty entry is appended to all of the *Vector* collections that are managed by the model. Two additional versions take either a *Vector* of column data or a one-dimensional array of type *Object*. *DefaultTableModel* takes as many values as it can from the supplied sets, while the remainder is initialized to *null*. The *convertToVector()* method is used to convert the array version's data to a *Vector* representation.

Although mentioned in the internal documentation, there is no implementation of *removeColumn()* in the *DefaultTableModel* class. The column model provides all of these column manipulation routines.

DefaultTableModel provides an additional two convenience methods that are used to initialize column headers. The two versions of *setColumnIdentifiers()* take a *Vector* and an array of *Object* and replaces the existing header identifiers with the specified values.

Firing Events

Some additional support is available for generating table events. The *newDataAvailable()* and *rowsRemoved()* methods are used internally by *DefaultTableModel* and simply invoke *fireTableChanged()* with the *TableModelEvent* object that is passed. The other event method, *newRowsAdded()*, is more interesting. It behavior, apart from its eventual invocation of *fireTableChanged()*, is to ensure that *Vector* collections added as row data have the correct number of column entries. The *setSize()* method of *Vector* is used to accomplish this task; it truncates entries beyond that specified by *getColumnCount()* and adds *null* values if not enough data elements exist in the supplied collection.

Creating a Custom Table Model

It is not necessary to use the JFC-provided implementations of table models, and in many cases, significant performance improvements and substantial reduction in memory overhead can be achieved by refining the stock models.

Immutable Table Model

In some cases, a table needs to be displayed that does not allow its values to be altered. In this situation, the additional resources incurred by the base models may not be needed. The following code provides an example of such a table, which is used to provide information about primitive data types:

```java
/**  DataTypesFrame.java
*/
package com.ketherware.samples.datatypes;

import java.awt.*;
import java.awt.event.*;
import javax.swing.*;
import javax.swing.table.*;
import javax.swing.event.*;

public class DataTypesFrame extends JFrame {
    public DataTypesFrame() {
        setTitle("Java Data Types");
        JTable table = new JTable(new DataTypesTableModel());
        this.getContentPane().add(new JScrollPane(table),
BorderLayout.CENTER);
```

```
            table.setPreferredScrollableViewportSize(new Dimension(400, 150));
            this.addWindowListener(new WindowAdapter() {
                public void windowClosing(WindowEvent event) {
                    System.exit(0);
                }
            });
            this.pack();
        }

        public static void main(String[] args) {
            new DataTypesFrame().show();
        }
    }
```

The remainder of this source file contains a class that implements an immutable table model. The data that is contained in the table is defined by the Java language specification and, being unlikely to change, is ideal for this type of model.

```
/**   DataTypesFrame.java (continued)
*/

class DataTypesTableModel implements TableModel {
    static final String[] headers = {
        "Type", "Contains", "Default", "Size", "Min Val", "Max Val"
    };

    static final String[] typeValues = {
        "boolean", "char", "byte", "short",
        "int", "long", "float", "double"
    };

    static final String[] containsValues = {
        "true/false", "Unicode character", "signed integer", "signed integer",
        "signed integer", "signed integer", "IEEE-754", "IEEE-754"
    };

    static final String[] defaultValues = {
```

```java
        "false", "\\u0000", "0", "0",
        "0", "0", "0.0", "0.0"
};

static final String[] sizeValues = {
    "1 bit", "16 bits", "8 bits", "16 bits",
    "32 bits", "64 bits", "32 bits", "64 bits"
};

static final String[] minValues = {
    "n/a", "\\u0000", "-128", "-32768",
    "-2147483648", "-9223372036854775808",
    "+-1.4023...E-45", "+-4.9406...E-324"
};

static final String[] maxValues = {
    "n/a", "\\uFFFF", "127", "32767",
    "2147483647", "9223372036854775807",
    "+-3.4028...E+38", "+-1.7976...E+308"
};

public int getRowCount() {
    return typeValues.length;
}

public int getColumnCount() {
    return headers.length;
}

public Class getColumnClass(int column) {
    return String.class;
}

public String getColumnName(int column) {
    return headers[column];
}
```

```java
public Object getValueAt(int row, int col) {
    switch (col) {
        case 0:
        return typeValues[row];

        case 1:
        return containsValues[row];

        case 2:
        return defaultValues[row];

        case 3:
        return sizeValues[row];

        case 4:
        return minValues[row];

        case 5:
        return maxValues[row];
    }
    return null;
}

public boolean isCellEditable(int row, int col) {
    return false;
}

public void setValueAt(Object value, int row, int col) {
    // no-op
}

public void addTableModelListener(TableModelListener listener) {
    // no-op
}

public void removeTableModelListener(TableModelListener listener) {
    // no-op
}
}
```

Note that no implementation of the event firing methods is present in *AbstractTableModel* and *DefaultTableModel*; the listener management methods are also implemented as no-ops. This is only feasible because, in this type of model, the data just appears without ever being added. The code produces the output shown in Figure 8-3.

Deriving from Model Implementations

In most cases, table models can be created directly from either the *AbstractTableModel* or *DefaultTableModel* classes. *AbstractTableModel* is a leaner implementation than *DefaultTableModel*; it provides the listener management capabilities but does not actually afford any mechanism to store table data. However, this is not always a disadvantage, because with little effort a table model can be wrapped around an existing collection of data. This is important to remember because the *DefaultTableModel* implementation requires the addition of data in array or vector format only, and ultimately ends up copying data into its internal storage scheme.

The example code in this section is from a utility called *JarHead* that provides read-only access to the entries in a JAR (Java archive) file. By using a *JTabbedPane* component, the interface can be implemented to enable a user to switch between a view of the JAR elements and a listing of the contents of the JAR manifest. This manifest contains additional information about archive entries such as a JavaBean indicator flag, version information, CRC, and other values.

To demonstrate the difference in techniques between using *AbstractTableModel* and *DefaultTableModel*, the example code uses the

Type	Contains	Default	Size	Min Val	Max Val
boolean	true/false	false	1 bit	N/A	N/A
char	Unicode character	\u0000	16 bits	\u0000	\uFFFF
byte	signed integer	0	8 bits	-128	127
short	signed integer	0	16 bits	-32768	32767

Figure 8-3. *Immutable table model*

two different techniques to implement the two table models used in the application. First, the *JarHead* class itself:

```java
package com.ketherware.samples.jarhead;

import java.awt.*;
import java.awt.event.*;
import java.io.File;
import java.util.*;
import java.util.jar.*;
import javax.swing.*;
import javax.swing.table.*;
import javax.swing.filechooser.*;

public class JarHead extends JFrame {
    // Table component containing JAR entries
    protected JTable jarTable;
    // Table component containing JAR manifest
    protected JTable manifestTable;
    // Encapsulation of JAR file (new for JDK 1.2)
    protected JarFile jarFile;

    // Constructor — perform frame initialization
    public JarHead() {
        // Set size and location
        this.setSize(500, 200);
        this.setLocation(120, 120);

        // Add a listener to detect when the frame
        // opens and closes
        this.addWindowListener(new WindowAdapter() {
            public void windowOpened(WindowEvent event) {
                // Invoke an 'open' when the window opens
                openAction();
            }

            public void windowClosing(WindowEvent event) {
                exitAction();
```

```java
      }
   });

   // Set the initial title, create menu and frame contents
   this.setTitle("JarHead Utility — [Select a File]");
   this.setJMenuBar(createMenuBar());
   this.getContentPane().add(createTabs());
}

// Create the application menu bar
protected JMenuBar createMenuBar() {
   // Create menu bar instance and add a menu component
   JMenuBar menuBar = new JMenuBar();
   JMenu fileMenu = new JMenu("File");
   fileMenu.setMnemonic('F');
   menuBar.add(fileMenu);

   // Add the 'open' menu item and create a listener
   JMenuItem openMenuItem = new JMenuItem("Open...");
   openMenuItem.setMnemonic('o');
   fileMenu.add(openMenuItem);
   openMenuItem.addActionListener(new ActionListener() {
      public void actionPerformed(ActionEvent event) {
         openAction();
      }
   });

   // Add the 'exit' menu item and create a listener
   JMenuItem exitMenuItem = new JMenuItem("Exit");
   exitMenuItem.setMnemonic('x');
   fileMenu.add(new JSeparator());
   fileMenu.add(exitMenuItem);
   exitMenuItem.addActionListener(new ActionListener() {
      public void actionPerformed(ActionEvent event) {
         exitAction();
      }
   });
```

```
        return menuBar;
    }

    // Create the content of the frame inside a tabbed pane
    protected JTabbedPane createTabs() {
        // Create the tabbed pane and the two tables. Wrap
        // the tables in scroll panes before adding so headers
        // will be visible
        JTabbedPane tabs = new JTabbedPane();
        jarTable = new JTable();
        tabs.add("Entries", new JScrollPane(jarTable));
        manifestTable = new JTable();
        tabs.add("Manifest", new JScrollPane(manifestTable));
        return tabs;
    }

    // Invoked by menu or at application start-up
    protected void openAction() {
        // Retrieve a file object using a JFC file chooser
        File file = chooseJarFile();
        if (file == null)
            return;

        // Using the file reference, create the JAR file wrapper
        // object and use it to populate the two tables
        try {
            jarFile = new JarFile(file);
            JarHeadEntryModel model = new JarHeadEntryModel(jarFile);
            jarTable.setModel(model);
            manifestTable.setModel(new JarHeadManifestModel(
                            model.getManifest())));
        } catch (Exception ex) {
            ex.printStackTrace();
            return;
        }

        // Reset the title to contain the path for the opened JAR
```

```
        this.setTitle("JarHead Utility — [" + file.getPath() + "]");
}

// Invoked by menu or application close request
protected void exitAction() {
    System.exit(0);
}

// Internal method that wraps a JFileChooser object to allow
// selection of the JAR file to display
protected File chooseJarFile() {
    // Create a file chooser and create a filter that
    // allows viewing of JAR files and directory entries only
    JFileChooser chooser = new JFileChooser();
    chooser.setFileFilter(new FileFilter() {
        // Description appears in file chooser dialog
        public String getDescription() {
            return "(*.jar) Java Archive (JAR) Files";
        }

        // Returns 'true' if file is to be displayed
        public boolean accept(File file) {
            // Always display directories
            if (file.isDirectory())
                return true;

            // Examine the filename to see if it has a file
            // extension of '*.jar' (case-insensitive)
            String name = file.getName();
            int period = name.indexOf(".");
            if (period < 0)
                return false;
            String ext = name.substring(period + 1);
            if (ext.equalsIgnoreCase("jar"))
                return true;

            // Do not display anything else
```

```
            return false;
        }
    });

    // Display the modal dialog. If the user cancels, the
    // selected file value will be 'null'
    chooser.showOpenDialog(this);
    this.repaint();
    return chooser.getSelectedFile();
}

// Main method: make some UI changes to make the content a
// little smaller, then create and display the frame
public static void main(String[] args) {
    Font smallFont = new Font("Dialog", Font.BOLD, 11);
    Font cellFont = new Font("Dialog", Font.PLAIN, 9);
    UIManager.put("Table.font", smallFont);
    UIManager.put("TableHeader.font", smallFont);
    UIManager.put("Menu.font", smallFont);
    UIManager.put("MenuItem.font", smallFont);
    UIManager.put("TabbedPane.font", smallFont);
    new JarHead().show();
}
}
```

The table that displays the JAR entry information is called *JarHeadEntryModel*, and it derives from *AbstractTableModel*. Because the model is basically immutable, the listener apparatus is not implemented.

```
package com.ketherware.samples.jarhead;

import java.util.*;
import java.util.jar.*;
import java.io.IOException;
import javax.swing.*;
import javax.swing.table.*;

public class JarHeadEntryModel extends AbstractTableModel {
```

```java
// Reference to JAR file wrapper
protected JarFile jarFile;
// Collection to store JAR entry information
protected ArrayList list = new ArrayList();
// Column name strings
protected static final String[] columnNames = {
    "Name", "Type", "Size", "CompSize"
};

// Constructor — takes a parameter that is a JAR
// file wrapper and adds its contents to the collection
public JarHeadEntryModel(JarFile jarFile) {
    this.jarFile = jarFile;
    Enumeration enum = jarFile.entries();
    while (enum.hasMoreElements()) {
        list.add(enum.nextElement());
    }
}

// Return the number of elements in the collection as the rows
public int getRowCount() {
    return list.size();
}

// Return the number of columns
public int getColumnCount() {
    return columnNames.length;
}

// Return column name
public String getColumnName(int column) {
    return columnNames[column];
}

// Retrieve value from collection
public Object getValueAt(int row, int column)
{
```

```
// Get the JAR entry that corresponds to the row. Use the
// column number to determine which element to display
JarEntry entry = (JarEntry) list.get(row);
switch (column) {
    case 0:
    // 'Name' column
    return entry.getName();

    case 1:
    // 'Type' column - display an indicator if the entry is
    // a directory or if it is compressed.
    if (entry.isDirectory())
        return "[Dir]";
    switch (entry.getMethod()) {
        case JarEntry.STORED:
        return "Stored";
        case JarEntry.DEFLATED:
        return "Deflated";
        default:
        return "???";
    }

    case 2:
    // 'Size' column - does not apply to directories
    if (entry.isDirectory())
        return "—";
    return convertSize(entry.getSize());

    case 3:
    // 'CompSize' column - does not apply to any entries
    // that are not marked as 'DEFLATED'
    if (entry.getMethod() != JarEntry.DEFLATED)
        return "—";
    return convertSize(entry.getCompressedSize());
}
// Should never get here; you may not want to but you must...
return null;
}
```

```java
// Return a string representing a byte count, convert to Kbytes or
// MBytes as required
public String convertSize(long size)
{
    if (size < Math.pow(2, 12))
        return Long.toString(size) + " bytes";
    else if (size < Math.pow(2, 22))
        return Long.toString((long) (size / Math.pow(2, 10))) + " Kbytes";
    else
        return Long.toString((long) (size / Math.pow(2, 20))) + " Mbytes";
}

// Allow the other model to get access to the manifest so
// we don't have to have another reference around
public Manifest getManifest() throws IOException
{
    return jarFile.getManifest();
}
}
```

The third class, *JarHeadManifestModel,* is presented last. It derives from *DefaultTableModel.* The mechanism that creates the rows of the model uses the version of *addRow()* that takes an array of *Object.* When columns and rows are added, the table model events are invoked by code internal to *DefaultTableModel*, although this model is also immutable.

```java
package com.ketherware.samples.jarhead;

import java.util.*;
import java.util.jar.*;
import java.io.IOException;
import javax.swing.*;
import javax.swing.table.*;

public class JarHeadManifestModel extends DefaultTableModel {
    // Constructor — takes a manifest wrapper object as a
    // parameter, creates columns and invokes internal methods
```

```java
   // to add rows
   public JarHeadManifestModel(Manifest manifest) {
      super();
      if (manifest == null)
         return;
      this.addColumn("Entry");
      this.addColumn("Value");

      addMainAttributes(manifest);
      addAttributeEntries(manifest);
   }

   // Add the set of 'main' attributes to the model. These are
   // attributes that apply to the entire archive
   protected void addMainAttributes(Manifest manifest)
   {
      // Only need to process if there are any entries
      Attributes mainAttr = manifest.getMainAttributes();
      if (mainAttr == null || mainAttr.size() == 0)
         return;

      // Iterate through the attribute set and add a row
      // for each 'main' attribute found
      Object[] entry = new Object[2];
      Iterator iter = mainAttr.keySet().iterator();
      while (iter.hasNext()) {
         Object key = iter.next();
         entry[0] = "[Main] " + key.toString();
         entry[1] = mainAttr.get(key);
         this.addRow(entry);
      }
   }

   // Add the individual manifest entries to the model. These
   // are presented as a 'Map of Maps', so we have to do
   // a nested iteration
   protected void addAttributeEntries(Manifest manifest)
```

```
{
    // Get the 'outer' map. This has a key that is the entry
    // name and a value that is a map of all attributes for
    // that particular entry
    Map entryMap = manifest.getEntries();
    if (entryMap == null || entryMap.size() == 0)
        return;

    // Iterate through the outer map
    Object[] entry = new Object[2];
    Iterator iter = entryMap.keySet().iterator();
    while (iter.hasNext()) {
        // Get the entry and add a row for the outer entry
        entry[0] = iter.next();
        Map subMap = (Map) entryMap.get(entry[0]);
        entry[1] = "[" + Integer.toString(subMap.size()) +
                   " entries]";
        this.addRow(entry);

        // Iterate through the inner map
        Iterator subIter = subMap.keySet().iterator();
        while (subIter.hasNext()) {
            // Add a row for the inner entry
            Object key = subIter.next();
            entry[0] = "——— " + key;
            entry[1] = subMap.get(key);
            this.addRow(entry);
        }
    }
}
}
```

A major disadvantage of using *DefaultTableModel* is that because the implementation of event generation and data storage is hidden, there is not much capability for maximizing performance, especially with large tables. Because the *TableModelEvent* firing is done automatically when a row or column is added, or when individual cell data changes, a large number of listener events may be generated. This tends to incrementally affect performance as the number of listeners increases, due to the synchronous manner in which listeners are invoked.

Remember that *DefaultTableModel* is designed for the generic case; if the capability of providing more refined models is available, *AbstractTableModel* or *TableModel* can be used to produce more task-specific model implementations. These classes afford more opportunity for tweaking model operations to suit performance needs.

Other Properties of JTable

With the preliminaries out of the way, it is prudent to address some of the additional properties that *JTable* provides. Many of these properties are data-independent and refer to display and sizing characteristics of the component itself.

Row Size and Spacing

Unlike its cousins the *JList* and *JTree* components, *JTable* does not provide variable height rows. The height of all rows in a *JTable* is controlled by the *RowHeight* property, which is not bound. The specified row height must be greater than zero, and must also include the size of the row spacing. The spacing is controlled by an integer property *RowMargin*, which is also not bound.

A convenience property, *IntercellSpacing*, is provided by *JTable*. It encapsulates its *RowMargin* property along with the *ColumnMargin* property of the column model, representing these values as a single *Dimension* object. This property is not bound either, but the mutator method *getIntercellSpacing()* invokes *resizeAndRepaint()* when it completes the update of the encapsulated properties.

Automated Column Creation

JTable has the capability to initialize the column model from information it gathers from its data model. A *boolean* property *AutoCreateColumns FromModel* controls this behavior. The value of this property is explicitly assigned the value *true* any time a constructor is used that specifies a *null* value for *TableColumnModel*. Otherwise, the column model is expected to be provided.

The column model is initialized by the method *createDefault ColumnsFromModel()*, which accesses methods in the data model to derive column information. The method uses the *getColumnCount(),getColumn Name(),* and *getColumnClass()* methods of *TableModel* to capture default column information.

Automatic Sizing

JTable provides functionality that enables columns to be automatically sized; the integer property *AutoResizeMode* controls this behavior. It accepts the following values defined in Table 8-1.

The *AutoResizeMode* property is not bound; changes to the value cause the *JTable* and *JTableHeader* to be resized and repainted. If an illegal value is supplied to the *setAutoResizeMode()* method, no exception is thrown and a no-op results.

The actual alteration of column width occurs in the *sizeColumnsToFit()* method, which is invoked when the shape of the *JTable* is changed with the *reshape()* method or after a column reordering operation is complete. This method iterates through the column model and adjusts the widths of columns according to the specified resize mode.

Table 8-1. *Header "autosizing" options*

Value	Meaning
AUTO_RESIZE_OFF	Columns are not automatically resized; a horizontal scroll bar is used to view the table if it is larger in width than the viewport.
AUTO_RESIZE_NEXT_COLUMN	Causes the next column after the resize column to expand or shrink.
AUTO_RESIZE_SUBSEQUENT_COLUMNS	Default value—causes all columns after the resize column to be expanded or shrunk.
AUTO_RESIZE_LAST_COLUMN	Causes the last column in the model to be expanded or shrunk to compensate for a column resize.
AUTO_RESIZE_ALL_COLUMNS	Resizes all columns proportionately when a column is expanded or shrunk.

Two versions of *sizeColumnsToFit()* are provided: The first one takes a single *boolean* argument. This flag is set to *true* if the resize operation is to affect only the last column in the table. The other version of this method takes an integer parameter, which represents the column being sized. This method also accepts a special value of negative one (–1), meaning that the columns should be resized without preserving the width of any particular column. This type of invocation is used when the width of the viewport changes or if a column is removed from the column model.

The value of the *AutoResizeMode* property is temporarily changed when the *boolean* parameter version of the *sizeColumnsToFit()* method executes. Based on the value of the parameter, the mode is temporarily set to *AUTO_RESIZE_LAST_COLUMN* if the parameter is *true* and *AUTO_RESIZE_ALL_COLUMNS* otherwise. The method then invokes the other version of *sizeColumnsToFit()* with an argument of negative one (–1), meaning that the adjustment should be performed without regard to a specific column.

Position Information

JTable provides information to its listeners that enables it to map the position of mouse clicks to rows and columns within its bounds. The *rowAtPoint()* method uses the row height and margin to calculate the row where a mouse click occurs. The *columnAtPoint()* method delegates to the column model to retrieve its information.

The *getCellRect()* method provides a *Rectangle* object that represents the bounds of a specified cell. The method takes a row and column parameter along with a *boolean* that is *true* when the *IntercellSpacing* values are to be included in the boundary calculation.

Grid Attributes

JTable provides horizontal and vertical grid lines that can be configured to render in a specific color or be displayed and hidden as desired. Three properties control the grid appearance; none of these are bound, and the *repaint()* method is called in each of the mutator methods. Two *boolean* properties are available, *ShowHorizontalLines* and *ShowVerticalLines,* that control whether the lines are visible. The *GridColor* property manages a *Color* object to control the coloration of grid lines, which controls both horizontal and vertical grid lines. *JTable* does not provide a mechanism to color lines independently, nor does it enable grid line widths to be altered.

ToolTip Support

The ToolTip feature provided by *JComponent* is designed to be revised to fit specific needs; *JTable* is a perfect example of this requirement. The default implementation of *getToolTipText()* generally refers to the entire component. In the case of *JTable*, the ToolTip can be different for each cell in the table. The value of the ToolTip is specified by the implementation of the renderer for a particular table cell. The renderer, which provides a component instance that is used to draw a particular cell, can return a *JComponent* object, thus enabling it to specify individual ToolTips based on cell contents.

The table headers can also specify tooltips that represent column-specific information. This capability is provided by the implementation of the *JTableHeader* component, which is the object that provides column headers for *JTable*.

JTable Column Support

The *JTable* component provides an additional model that manages the configuration of its columns. This model, which is defined by the *TableColumnModel* interface, manages column-specific properties and provides a listener for changes to column information.

The information about a column, which includes width and sizing information as well as references to rendering and editing delegates, is encapsulated in the *TableColumn* class. The *TableColumnModel* implementation is required to return information about the columns it represents as objects of type *TableColumn*.

Column Model Support

JTable supports a bound property *ColumnModel* that contains a reference to a *TableColumnModel* implementation; the methods *setColumnModel()* and *getColumnModel()* manipulate this property. *JTable* also supports a *protected* method *createDefaultColumnModel()* that can be overridden to produce a subclass that uses a particular implementation of *TableColumnModel*. The default behavior of this method is to return an instance of *DefaultTableColumnModel*, which is the canonical implementation of the *TableColumnModel* interface. One of the most flexible capabilities of *JTable* is the capability to provide customized column models, which can greatly enhance the robustness of applications that use the JFC table component.

TableColumn is the target object of the *TableColumnModel*. Although not itself a component, it does support several important properties that are significant in determining the behavior and appearance of cells. This is largely feasible due to the column-oriented manner in which *JTable* is organized.

Unlike its related JFC components that support renderers and editing capabilities, *JTable* alone provides a type-driven mechanism to associate multiple renderers and editors. To accommodate this capability, *JTable* uses the *TableColumn* instances as a repository of class and delegate information. Although this scheme inhibits assignment of delegates to particular cells, the simplicity of associating classes with columns is pragmatic.

JTable Selection Capabilities

JTable provides the capability to select material in the table by row, by column, or by cell. It uses a combination of selection models to accomplish this, but relies on an existing selection model interface, *ListSelectionModel*, to manage its selection state information. Because *ListSelectionModel* already supports single, interval, and multiple selection, it is a matter of adding some additional value-added properties to enable it to be applied to the table paradigm. One of the ways this is accomplished is by using two independent instances of *ListSelectionModel*, one managed by the *JTable* and another by its *TableColumnModel* implementation. It is by combining the information from these two models that the two-dimensional selection behavior is accomplished.

The mechanics of column selection are covered in detail in the section covering the *TableColumnModel* interface and related classes. This section examines the column selection methods that *JTable* provides, although the behavior is actually carried out by the column model delegate.

The *SelectionModel* property is one of the few bound properties that *JTable* supports. It is identical in all respects to the *SelectionModel* property of the *JList*, taking a reference to a *ListSelectionModel* as a parameter. The specified model cannot be *null*.

As with *JList*, the *JTable* implementation of the selection model facilitates the specification of a selection mode to control the user's selection options. The same values can be specified: *SINGLE_SELECTION*, *SINGLE_INTERVAL_SELECTION*, or *MULTIPLE_INTERVAL_SELECTION*. When the mode is set using the *setSelectionMode* property, it is propagated to the selection model that the *JTable* supports for row selection and the column selection model of *TableColumnModel*. In addition, any existing row and column selections are cleared before the properties are updated. The underlying model implementations are responsible for validating and interpreting these mode values, so it is feasible to construct implementations of *ListSelectionModel* or *DefaultListSelectionModel* that accept selection mode values other than those specified.

JTable provides a *protected* method *createDefaultSelectionModel()* that creates a row selection model instance if one is not explicitly provided. Extensions of *JTable* can override this method to provide alternative selection model implementations by default.

JTable has three *boolean* properties that provide additional control over selection characteristics.

Selection Properties

The unbound properties *ColumnSelectionAllowed*, *RowSelectionAllowed*, and *CellSelectionEnabled* manage the behavior of the selection models managed by *JTable* and *TableColumnModel*. *ColumnSelectionAllowed* delegates to *TableColumnModel* to control whether an entire column is selected when a cell within the column is chosen. *RowSelectionAllowed* causes the entire row of cells to be selected when a cell within the row is clicked. These properties are not mutually exclusive. By default, row selection is enabled and column selection disabled.

The *CellSelectionEnabled* property controls the behavior of the *isCellSelected()* method. The method takes a row and column pair as parameters and returns *true* if the specified cell is selected. If the *CellSelectionEnabled* property is set to *true*, then the *isCellSelected()* method returns *true* only if both the specified row and column are selected. If the value is *false*, *isCellSelected()* checks if either the row or the column that the cell is in is selected.

Determining Selection

Several methods are provided that delegate to the row and column selection models for the purpose of reporting the current selection state. The methods *getSelectedRowCount()* and *getSelectedColumnCount()* return the number of rows and columns currently selected. To retrieve selection indices, the *getSelectedRows()* and *getSelectedColumns()* are used; both return an array of integers containing the selected indices or *null* if no selections exist. For single selection applications, the methods *getSelectedColumn()* and *getSelectedRow()* can be used. If these methods are used with a multiple selection mode in effect, the first selected column or row index will be returned.

Three *boolean* methods are provided: *isRowSelected()*, *isColumnSelected()*, and *isCellSelected()*; these return a value of *true* if the specified row, column, or cell is selected. The *isRowSelected()* and *isColumnSelected()* methods take a single integer that specifies a row or column to check; *isCellSelected()* takes a row and column pair. The interpretation of whether a particular cell is selected depends on the value of the *CellSelectionEnabled* property. If this property is *true*, a cell is selected only if both its row and its column are selected. If *false*, a cell is selected if it is inside a selected row or column.

Selecting Rows, Columns, and Cells

JTable is primarily designed to support multiple selection, as is borne out by examination of the convenience methods it supplies to programmatically alter the selection. The methods provided are consistent with those implemented by *ListSelectionModel*, except they are duplicated to accommodate both the row and column selection model delegates.

A total of six methods provide management of selection intervals, each taking a pair of integers that represent the inclusive range of the selection. The *set* methods, *setRowSelectionInterval()* and *setColumn Selection Interval()*, replace the current selection with the specified range. These methods can be used to programmatically select a single row or column by specifying the same index for both parameters. The *add* version of the methods *addRowSelectionInterval()* and *addColumnSelectionInterval()* is used to increase the selection set, and appends the specified interval to the currently selected indices. The *removeRowSelectionInterval()* and *removeColumnSelectionInterval()* methods perform the opposite functionality; that is, they remove the specified internal from the selection set.

In the event that the selection mode is *SINGLE_SELECTION*, the second parameter to all six of these methods is ignored, if *DefaultListSelectionModel* is used.

JTable also provides two methods that operate on both column models: *selectAll()* selects all rows and columns in the table, and *clearSelection()* sets the selection set to empty.

The TableColumnModel Interface

The additional data model that *JTable* supports, *TableColumnModel*, provides access to column-specific information. The *JTable* component UI delegate uses a series of event listeners to coordinate the behavior of the data model, the column model, and the selection models.

Implementations of *TableColumnModel* are used not only to access column information, but to handle the addition, removal, repositioning, and selection of columns. The interface also specifies a mechanism to register for changes in the column model by enabling interested listeners to register as listeners for column model change events.

Accessing Column Information

The *TableColumnModel* implementation must provide information about the number of columns the model represents, and must also enable users to select and find a column in order to extract or modify its properties. The *getColumnCount()* method returns the number of columns that the model is currently supporting. The values that are between zero and the result of *getColumnCount()* less one are the valid indices into the column model. To retrieve a particular *TableColumn* object, the *getColumn()* method is provided. This method takes an integer parameter that represents a column's position in the model. It is important to remember that a position in the model may not necessarily be the same as the view position in the component because columns can be reordered programmatically or by mouse drag operations.

The *getColumnIndex()* method takes an *Object* type as its single parameter and returns an integer value. This method facilitates searching of the current model to see if an existing column has the specified object as its column identifier. If so, the index value is returned; otherwise the method responds with a value of (–1). Another method, *getColumns()*, returns a reference to a *java.util.Enumerator* object; this object can be used to iteratively access the columns in a model in index order.

Manipulating Columns

TableColumnModel provides three methods that can be used to alter the column structure, *addColumn()*, *removeColumn()*, and *moveColumn()*. The add and remove methods each take a single parameter that is a *TableColumn* object. The *removeColumn()* method checks the column object reference against the model for a match; it does not examine any descriptor information. The move version takes two integer parameters representing the original and new column index for a particular move operation.

The *TableColumn* objects, which are managed by the column model, provide a property called *ModelIndex* that ties a particular column in the *TableColumnModel* to a column in the data model. The *moveColumn()* method only changes the location of the column in the column model; the mapping to the data model does not change. Whether a particular column is moveable is controlled by the *JTableHeader* component that exists in the column headers.

JTable provides two public methods that delegate to the column model for mapping column coordinates. The first, *convertColumnIndexToModel()*, uses the value of the *ModelIndex* property of the specified column to derive the associated model index. The second, *convertColumnIndexToView()*, converts a column index to a visible area. This method is used primarily by *JTable's* repaint logic; when it detects a model change, a repaint request is enqueued that is isolated to the columns that have been modified. This mechanism defers the repainting of columns that are not in the visible area of the viewport.

Column Selection Support

Because *JTable* supports selection of its contents by row, column, or cell, an additional selection model is required. *JTable* itself uses the *ListSelectionModel* interface, which makes it inherently row-oriented; by combining this information with an additional column-oriented selection model, the entire gamut of selection capabilities is enabled.

The selection model for *TableColumnModel* is based on the *ListSelectionModel* interface; it is managed by a *SelectionModel* property, which is not bound. The default implementation of *TableColumnModel*, *Default TableColumnModel*, assigns itself as a listener to the new selection model specified by *setSelectionModel()*. Because it is not a bound property, any implementation of *TableColumnModel* that does not inherit from *DefaultTableColumnModel* must perform this activity to propagate model listening capabilities.

As with all implementations of *ListSelectionModel*, the column selection can be configured to enable selection of only a single column, to restrict selection to a set of contiguous columns, or to enable any combination of columns to be individually selected. This can be accomplished by setting the *setSelectionMode()* to *SINGLE_SELECTION*, *SINGLE_INTERVAL_SELECTION*, or *MULTIPLE_INTERVAL_SELECTION,* respectively. Selection of columns can be reset programmatically by invoking *clearSelection()* on the selection model delegate.

TableColumnModel specifies a *boolean* property *ColumnSelectionAllowed* that controls whether column selection is enabled for the entire column model. If it is set to *true*, selection of columns can be achieved by clicking the column headers. *TableColumnModel* requires two methods that return column selection information. The *getSelectedColumnCount()* method returns the number of columns currently selected and the *getSelectedColumns()* method returns an array of integers that contain the indices of all columns that are selected.

Other Column Model Methods

The *ColumnMargin* property, which has a default value of one (1), controls the distance between columns. This cannot be set for individual columns; it applies to the entire set represented by the column model.

The *TableColumnModel* interface requires two additional methods. The *getColumnIndexAtX()* method is used when processing *MouseEvent* instances to translate mouse coordinates to column indices. Second, the *getTotalColumnWidth()* method returns the entire width of the table. This value is used by the table header and scrolling interface to determine the horizontal scrolling characteristics. For example, this value is checked by *JTable* support for the *Scrollable* interface to determine whether to enable the *x*-axis scroll bar; it is also used in some automatic column sizing routines.

TableColumnModelListener

TableColumnModel specifies management of a listener list for changes to the column model. These methods, *addTableColumnModelListener()* and *removeTableColumnModelListener()*, manage objects of type *TableColumn ModelListener*.

This listener supports five methods. Three of these methods are *columnAdded()*, *columnRemoved()*, and *columnMoved()*, each of which supply a *TableColumnModelEvent* object as its parameter. These are meant to be fired when the *addColumn()*, *removeColumn()*, and *moveColumn()* methods are invoked. The *TableColumnModelEvent* class extends *EventObject*, and provides two additional methods, *getFromIndex()* and *getToIndex()*, which specify the column range to which the event pertains.

The *columnMarginChanged()* method is invoked when the value of the *ColumnMargin* property is changed, providing a *ChangeEvent* as a parameter. By default, reception of this method by a *JTable* component causes it to be resized and repainted. Lastly, the *columnSelectionChanged()* method propagates changes to the selection model by specifying a *ListSelectionEvent* parameter. It is an alternative mechanism for detecting column selection changes.

DefaultTableColumnModel

The canonical table column model is *DefaultTableColumnModel*. Apart from providing all of the column management and selection features, this object provides methods to generate events for *TableColumnModelListener* objects that are registered with the model. The *fireColumnAdded()*, *fireColumn Removed()*, and *fireColumnMoved()* methods take a *TableColumnModelEvent* as a parameter. The *fireColumnSelectionChanged()* method takes a *ListSelectionEvent* object; the method *fireColumnMarginChanged()* does not take any parameters because the *ChangeEvent* object provides no extra information.

The TableColumn Class

TableColumn is a concrete class that stores the per-column information in a *JTable*. *TableColumn* elements are managed by a *TableColumnModel*, which provides a mutable collection of columns that map to tabular elements in the data model. *TableColumn* contains many of the important elements used to customize the behavior of cells in the *JTable* component.

TableColumn Properties

Two identifiers are used to refer to *TableColumn* objects. Both are supported as *Object* types. The first of these is the *HeaderValue* property; this is the identifier used to display the column header and is passed to the renderer delegate that is responsible for drawing column headers. Another property, called *Identifier*, is used to search for columns within the column model. If a value is not explicitly assigned to the *Identifier* property, the value of the *HeaderValue* is used. The default behavior of the header component, *JTableHeader*, is to render the value returned by a call to *toString()* on *HeaderValue*, but this behavior can be altered by providing a substitute renderer for the table header.

Width Properties

The *TableColumn* object controls the width of each column in the column model, and a rich set of methods is provided to alter its sizing behavior. There are four width properties, each of integer type: *Width*, *PreferredWidth*, *MaxWidth,* and *MinWidth*.

The *Width* property is the absolute width, that is, the actual width of the column in pixels. This is the only one of the width properties that is bound, because it is the only one that ultimately affects the column's size. *PreferredWidth*, on the other hand, is a suggestion to the *JTable* component as to the desired size of the column. The *sizeColumnsToFit()* method implemented by *JTable* uses preferred widths in determining the desired size of columns. The width is distributed to fit inside the available viewport area. The column model implementation does not use the *PreferredWidth* value in its sizing and caching calculations, only the value of *Width* itself.

The two other integer properties are *MinWidth* and *MaxWidth*, which represent the minimum and maximum allowed sizes that a particular column may have. Although these properties are not bound, changes in them will be reflected in the *Width* property if the current width is not within the interval specified by *MinWidth* and *MaxWidth*. If a change to either of these properties causes the *Width* value to be out of range, it is adjusted using *setWidth()* to ensure it is valid.

No method protects a user from setting the *MaxWidth* value to be less than the *MinWidth*, so caution should be used to avoid this situation as it will lead to unpredictable results. The property mutator code does ensure the values are greater than zero. Although the internal documentation claims the default value for *MaxWidth* is 2,000, the code in *TableColumn* initializes it to the value *Integer.MAX_VALUE*. The initial value for *MinWidth* is hard-coded to 15 pixels. Both of these default values would probably be better suited being managed by *UIDefaults*, which would allow look-and-feel-specific defaults to be established.

The *Resizable* property is *boolean* and controls whether an individual column can be resized by clicking and dragging its vertical borders. The value of *Resizable* is *true* by default, and the property is not bound. There is another method of controlling resizability using the *ResizingAllowed* property in the *JTableHeader* component, which controls whether all of the columns can be resized. Neither the *Resizeable* nor *ResizingAllowed* properties affect the capability to programmatically alter the width of a column; only the capability for mouse drag changes.

The last width-related method that *TableColumn* provides is the *sizeWidthToFit()* method. This operation causes the *Width, MaxWidth,* and *MinWidth* property values to be adjusted to accommodate the width of the column header, taking into account the size of the header value. The necessary size is established by requesting the preferred size of the component used to render the column header. The actual data in the column is not examined, nor is the column's *PreferredSize*. The *sizeWidthToFit()* method is not used internally by *JTable* or its related components.

Renderer and Editor Delegates

The *TableColumn* objects that are associated with a *JTable* provide the capability to map header and cell renderers as well as cell editors to a particular column. This behavior overrides the default renderer behavior of *JTable* that uses a table cell element's class as a mechanism for assigning these delegates. The *HeaderRenderer* and *CellRenderer* properties manages renderer delegates on a per-column basis; the *CellEditor* property accomplishes the same cell editors. Cell renderers and editors are covered in depth later in this chapter. Of these properties, the *HeaderRenderer* and *CellRenderer* properties are bound.

Note that changing the *CellEditor* property will not stop an existing cell editing session and this should be done manually when an editor change takes place in either the *TableColumn* or *JTable*.

TableColumn Event Support

Although *TableColumn* is not a component, it does support property change listener management for its properties. The *DefaultTableColumnModel* adds itself as a property change event listener for all columns that are added to it. The *DefaultTableColumnModel* implementation of *PropertyChangeListener* only performs one function: It invalidates its width cache when it detects a change to the *Width* property of a column it is managing.

Two other public methods are provided, *enableResizedPosting()* and *disableResizedPosting()*, that support an unsynchronized counter that appears to control whether column width changes are continually posted. These methods have been superseded by the *UpdateTableInRealTime* property of the *JTableHeader* component.

JTable Constructors and Initialization

JTable has seven constructors. The default (parameterless) constructor and two other versions all redirect to an ultimate constructor that takes three parameters: a reference to a *TableModel*, a reference to a *TableColumnModel*, and a reference to a *ListSelectionModel*. The default constructor passes *null* values for all three arguments. This causes the methods *createDefaultDataModel()*, *createDefaultColumnModel()*, and *createDefaultSelectionModel()* to be invoked, creating an empty table backed by a *DefaultTableModel*. Two additional versions provide only a *TableModel* parameter, or a *TableModel* and *TableColumnModel*. In these versions, default delegates are created for the unspecified parameters.

Three more constructors are provided. The first takes two integer parameters and propagates these values to the constructor of *DefaultTableModel*; this creates an empty table with the specified shape. The last two constructors use the same construction methods for *DefaultTableModel*; one takes a pair of *Vector* objects and the other a pair of *Object* arrays. Although these match the *DefaultTableModel* constructors, these *JTable* constructors *do not* create a *DefaultTableModel*. For some reason, these two constructors create an anonymous extension of *AbstractTableModel* and use the provided *Vector* and array elements as a data store. Because of this, the parameters are marked as *final*. It seems plausible that the reason this is done is to prevent unnecessary cloning of collection data while constructing a new table model. It is important to remember that *DefaultTableModel* is not always used as the target of *JTable* constructors.

The *addNotify()* method is overridden by *JTable*; it invokes the protected method *configureEnclosingScrollPane()* when it is finished being added to a container. This method is responsible for initializing the column headers and assigning them to the enclosing *JScrollPane*.

Another protected method, *initializeLocalVars()*, initializes many of the properties of *JTable*, and is also instrumental in configuring some of the *JTable* delegate objects that implement cell rendering, editing, ToolTips, auto-scrolling, and table headers. It also initializes the preferred viewport size to be 450 pixels wide and 400 pixels high.

The JTableHeader Component

JTableHeader is an implementation of *JComponent* that serves to provide an area for *JTable* headers to be rendered. It provides control over the resizing and reordering of the columns in the table for which it is associated, and also provides the capability to create the column model for a *JTable* instance. In fact, it could be considered that *TableColumnModel* is really the model for the *JTableHeader* component, much in the way that *TableModel* serves for *JTable*. *JTableHeader* has its own set of defaults that are managed by *UIManager*, and can therefore provide look-and-feel-specific header implementations.

The instance of *JTableHeader* is created by the invocation of the *createDefaultTableHeader()* method of *JTable*; extensions of *JTable* can provide an alternate component to serve as the table header. The default column model is instantiated when the *createDefaultColumnModel()* method of *JTable* is invoked; the default implementation returns an instance of *DefaultTableColumnModel*. This method is invoked when the *JTable* is created without an initial column model. The column model can be specified by one of the two constructors of *JTableHeader*; the default value for the column model property is *null* if one is not specifed, or if the default constructor for *JTableHeader* is used. *JTableHeader* registers as a listener for *TableColumnModelEvent*, enabling it to react to changes in the column model.

After the *JTableHeader* instance is created by *JTable*, it passes a reference to itself as a value for the *Table* property. This property has a value of type *JTable* and is not bound; the initial value is *null*. The value of this property is used by the accessibility support for the *JTable* component and by the UI delegate for the *JTableHeader* component. This connection enables the delegate to access the *JTable* associated with a particular header because the table does not directly parent the header.

JTableHeader Properties

Among the features that *JTableHeader* implements are resizing and reordering of the columns it contains. These capabilities are enabled by coordination between the *JTable* and *JTableHeader* components, as well as additional support code in the table and header UI delegates.

Column Resizing and Reordering

Three *boolean* properties are implemented in *JTableHeader* that control column characteristics for an entire table. The *ReorderingAllowed* property is *true* by default; if it is set to *false*, columns cannot be reordered by mouse dragging. The *ResizingAllowed* property is also *true* by default, and controls whether any of the columns in the table can by dynamically resized. The *UpdateTableInRealTime* property controls whether *TableColumnModelEvent* objects are generated continually as the column width is changed during a drag operation. The value is *true* by default; if it is set to *false*, a single *TableColumnModelEvent* is fired when the drag operation is complete, that is, when the user releases the mouse button.

JTableHeader implements the capability for column resizing and reordering in its UI delegate, *BasicTableHeaderUI*. It communicates important information to the UI through the use of three properties. The *ResizingColumn* property contains a *TableColumn* value during the time that a resize operation is taking place. This information is used by the UI delegate to dynamically change the column's *Width* property during a resize operation.

Two more properties, *DraggedColumn* and *DraggedDistance,* are used by the column reordering mechanism in the UI delegate. The *DraggedColumn* property manages a *TableColumn* value that is used during the drag phase of a column reorder operation. The *DraggedDistance* is an integer property that represents the distance a column has moved during a reorder operation; it is used to calculate the final position of a column when the operation is complete.

Other Features of JTableHeader

JTableHeader provides some additional methods that are analogous to features of *JTable*. The *columnAtPoint()* method is used to translate a mouse click or other screen coordinate to a column index. It is used by the column resizing and reordering code to determine whether to move a column or to change its width when a drag operation occurs. The *getHeaderRect()* method returns a *Rectangle* object that represents the bounds of a header cell.

Lastly, an implementation of *getToolTipText()* is provided that returns different ToolTip values depending on the header column in which the mouse pointer comes to rest. This feature, as well as the final example in this chapter, uses the *columnAtPoint()* method to translate screen coordinates to a column index when the mouse is within the bounds of the *JTableHeader* component.

JTable Rendering and Editing

JTable uses cell renderer components to display cell values and uses cell editor components to edit cell values. The components used to render and edit cell values may be set on a per-column or per-class basis by the data and column models of the *JTable*.

Table Cell Renderer

Components that are used as renderers must implement the *TableCellRenderer* interface. This interface specifies a single method, *getTableCellRendererComponent()*, that passes the renderer component information that the renderer component uses to depict the cell value.

JTable provides the capability to assign cell renderers based on the column in which a particular cell is located or on the class of the cell value. The method *getCellRenderer()* is used by *JTable* to retrieve a component for displaying a table cell. In this method there is logic to first enable the assignment of a renderer by the *TableColumn* implementation found in the column model.

Header Renderers

The *TableColumn* class provides the capability of assigning a renderer for the column header it represents. This renderer has the same semantics as those for cell rendering, except it does not take the column class into account.

Default Renderers

If a renderer is not assigned to a column, a hash table collection of default renderers is available that is indexed by *Class* type. The *Class* value used to assign the renderer is the value returned from the *getColumnClass()* method of the datamodel, not the class of the object returned from *getValueAt*. The standard renderers can be modified using the *setDefaultRenderer()* method of *JTable*, passing it a *Class* instance and a reference to a *TableCellRenderer* delegate. Default renderers are retrieved using the *getDefaultRenderer()* method, which takes a *Class* object as a parameter and returns the stored renderer delegate reference.

The protected method *createDefaultRenderers()* is responsible for creating the standard renderers that *JTable* provides. Each of these renderers is an implementation of the *DefaultTableCellRenderer* class, which is the canonical implementation of *TableCellRenderer* that is look-and-feel aware.

JTable provides renderers for commonly used classes, specifically, the *Number, Date, ImageIcon, Boolean,* and *Object* classes, each assigning a version of *TableCellRenderer*. For each of the default classes but *Boolean*, a version of *DefaultTableCellRenderer* is assigned. In the case of *Object* types, the cell is rendered as a *JLabel* with the caption taking the result of a call to *toString()*. This means that if no custom renderers for objects of a specific type are set, then they will be displayed as *Strings* using a *JLabel* component. *Number* and *Date* objects are also rendered as *JLabel* instances, except their values are calculated by *NumberFormat* and *DateFormat* methods. *ImageIcon* values are displayed as *JLabel* objects, displaying the icon in a *JLabel*.

Assigning Renderers

Default renderers can be replaced by assigning a new renderer to a *Class* using the *setDefaultRenderer()* method. The internal hash table that contains the mappings is keyed by the *Class* instance.

An example for creating a custom renderer is given in the *FileTable* example at the end of the chapter. In this example, a custom renderer is used to interpret the size and modification time of a file and display it in a nonstandard way.

Cell Editing

Cell editing is similar to the rendering process, but provides the additional capability of updating the data model with newly entered values. Instances of cell editors are associated with cells by assigning them to a *TableColumn* instance or by associating a default editor with a *Class* type in the data model. Components that are intended to be used as cell editors must implement the *TableCellEditor* interface, which, in turn, extends the *CellEditor* interface.

The CellEditor Interface

This interface is used by editors for the *JTree* component as well as the *JTable* component. It contains methods that are used by these components and their UI delegates to communicate with the editor implementation.

Two of the methods take an *EventObject* as a parameter and return a *boolean* value. The *isCellEditable()* method is used to determine whether an editing session is capable of being created; it is invoked before the editing session begins. In the case of both *JTree* and *JTable*, additional properties control whether a cell is editable; these are checked before the editor methods are invoked, thus saving the overhead of starting an editing session only to cancel it immediately thereafter. The other method is *shouldSelectCell()*, which returns true if the selection of the table or tree cell should be changed to the cell being edited. This method generally returns *true*.

Once an editing session has begun, a method is invoked to initialize the editor and propagate the current value into the component. These methods are specified by the extensions of *CellEditor* that are specific to the operating component. In the case of tree node editing, the method is *getTreeCellEditorComponent()*; for table cells it is *getTable CellEditorComponent()*. Both of these methods pass a reference to the tree or table, the current value of the cell or node, the selection and focus states, and other component-specific parameters that are used to initialize the editor component.

The editing session can be stopped programmatically or by some other means employed by the UI delegates for the table or tree component. Editing can end when the changes are either accepted or discarded. The *stopCellEditing()* method ends the editing session and causes the value being edited to be updated in the data model. This method returns a *boolean* value of *true* if the editing was successfully stopped. To stop editing without saving changes, the *cancelCellEditing()* method is invoked.

When the editing session is stopped, the component that invokes the editor calls the method *getCellEditorValue()*, which returns an *Object* type that represents the new value of the cell or node. This value is then propagated to the data model for the actual update, which causes appropriate data model events to be fired.

Cell Editor Events

CellEditor implementations employ an event listener that the invoking component can use to detect the results of the editing session. The methods *addCellEditorListener()* and *removeCellEditorListener()* are required by the *CellEditor* interface. Components that use editors add themselves to the listener list for editor changes in order to detect when the editing session has concluded.

Both of these methods take a parameter of type *CellEditorListener*, which is an interface that defines two methods, each having a *ChangeEvent* object as its single parameter. The *editingStopped()* method of *CellEditorListener* is invoked by an editor component when its implementation of *stopCellEditing()* is invoked. This event signals the component that it should invoke *getCellEditorValue()* to retrieve the new element value and propagate the change to the data model. When the *editingCanceled()* method is invoked, this means that the editing session was terminated and the new value should be discarded.

Table Cell Editors

The *TableCellEditor* interface defines a single method, *getTableCellEditor Component()*. This method is invoked by the component when the editor is initialized. When an editing session is required, the method *editCellAt()* is called. This method has two versions, both of which have a row/column index pair to identify a particular cell; the other version has an additional parameter of type *EventObject* that is passed to the *isCellEditable()* and *shouldSelectCell()* methods in order for them to operate. The first version ultimately calls the second with a *null* value for the *EventObject* parameter.

The *isEditing()* method of *JTable* returns *true* if an editing session is currently in progress. This method is used while processing events that may affect the editing session before terminating the editing session. For example, when the *JTable* component loses focus, any editing that is occurring must be terminated. When an editing session is in progress, the *EditingColumn* and *EditingRow* properties identify the cell currently being edited; the *getEditorComponent()* method returns a reference to the component being used for editing while it is in progress.

The method that actually creates the editor component is called *prepareEditor()*. Its job is to retrieve the instance of the cell editor, add it to the component being edited as a child window, set the editor's bounds to match that of the target cell, and invoke the *getTable CellEditorComponent()* method to initialize it with appropriate values. The complement of this method is the *removeEditor()* method, which is invoked when the editing session is complete. Its removes the component from the containing table and repaints the underlying cell with the new or pre-existing value, depending on the result of the editing session.

Default Table Cell Editors

The *DefaultCellEditor* class is a factory for creating standard editor components. It provides several constructors that wrap standard editing components, specifically, *JTextField*, *JCheckBox* and *JComboBox*. These default editors are suitable for use with either *JTree* or *JTable* components because they implement the editor interface defined by both components.

The *JTable* component invokes a method *createDefaultEditors()* that creates instances of *DefaultCellEditor* suitable for modifying cells of type *Object*, *Number*, or *Boolean*. *Object* and *Number* cells are edited with a *JTextField*; *Boolean* values are manipulated with a *JCheckBox*-based editor. In all cases, an editor associated with a *TableColumn* implementation takes precedence over the default editors.

If an editor is not specified in the *TableColumn*, the *Class* type of the cell is used as a key to a hashtable containing editor instances as values.

The *getDefaultEditor()* method takes a *Class* parameter and returns an editor appropriate for that type. The *setDefaultEditor()* method takes a *Class* parameter and a *TableCellEditor* parameter and either adds or replaces the entry in the hashtable for that particular class. The pre-existing editors can be replaced, or any additional classes specified in this manner.

It must again be mentioned that if a default editor is invoked, the *Class* type returned by the *getColumnClass()* method of *TableModel* is used to determine a cell's type, not the actual type of data that the cell contains.

Creating a Custom Editor

Although standard editors are available, it is not uncommon to require an alternate means to perform data entry on a table cell. A classic example is data entry of numeric fields. One approach would involve creating a subclass of *JTextField* that accepted only numeric keystrokes, but another concept involves use of a spinner component that enables a user to click arrow buttons to change a numeric value. This eliminates some data entry problems, but may not be appropriate for changing the value of very large numbers.

The example program is a table containing a set of chapters for an imaginary book, along with some page-count estimates. As is widely known, sometimes predicted page counts can vary from the initial outline of a book, and this grid supports incrementing and decrementing of the page counts using a spinner component as a cell editor. Figure 8-4 shows the editor when it is active on a cell.

Preliminary Page Count		_ □ ×
	Title	Page Count
Chapter 1	The Last Washing	123
Chapter 2	Hoedown in The Crimea	53
Chapter 3	The Zen of Jelly	139
Chapter 4	My Dinner with Bill	227
Chapter 5	My Favorite Wavelengths	▲ 95 ▼
Chapter 6	Newton's Fourth Law	186
Chapter 7	How Not to Be Seen	95
Chapter 8	Lymph and You	226
Chapter 9	The Duct Tape Incident	158
	TOTAL	1,302

Figure 8-4. *Table editor example*

When the editing is complete, and the user clicks another cell or causes focus to be lost on the table, the editing session is ended and the new value is posted to the cell. Notice that the total is also updated by the edit action. See Figure 8-5.

The *TableEditor* example consists of a *JFrame* containing a single *JTable*. The frame and table are initialized in the following code:

```
package com.ketherware.samples.tableeditor;

import java.awt.*;
import java.awt.event.*;
import java.util.Random;
import javax.swing.*;
import javax.swing.table.*;

public class TableEditor extends JFrame {
    // Set up the frame in the constructor
    public TableEditor() {
        this.setLocation(100, 100);
        this.setTitle("Preliminary Page Count");
        JTable table = new JTable(new ChapterTableModel());
        this.getContentPane().add(new JScrollPane(table), BorderLayout.CENTER);

        // Intialize the table and column sizes
```

Preliminary Page Count		_□×
	Title	Page Count
Chapter 1	The Last Washing	123
Chapter 2	Hoedown in The Crimea	53
Chapter 3	The Zen of Jelly	139
Chapter 4	My Dinner with Bill	227
Chapter 5	My Favorite Wavelengths	105
Chapter 6	Newton's Fourth Law	186
Chapter 7	How Not to Be Seen	95
Chapter 8	Lymph and You	226
Chapter 9	The Duct Tape Incident	158
	TOTAL	1,307

Figure 8-5. *Table editing complete*

```
        table.setPreferredScrollableViewportSize(new Dimension (402, 200));
        TableColumnModel columnModel = table.getColumnModel();
        TableColumn column = columnModel.getColumn(0);
        column.setPreferredWidth(100);
        column = columnModel.getColumn(1);
        column.setPreferredWidth(200);
        column = columnModel.getColumn(2);
        column.setPreferredWidth(100);

        // Set up the spinner as an editor for the Integer class
        table.setDefaultEditor(Integer.class, new NumericSpinner(50, 0, 250));
        this.addWindowListener(new WindowAdapter() {
            public void windowClosing(WindowEvent event) {
                System.exit(0);
            }
        });
        this.pack();
    }

    public static void main(String[] args) {
        new TableEditor().show();
    }
}
```

The other class in this module is a simple extension of *AbstractTableModel* that provides the data for the example. Notice that the *setValue()* method is overridden; otherwise editing values would not get propagated back to the data model. Also overridden is the *isCellEditable()* method, to ensure that the page counts—not including the total—are the only editable cells.

```
class ChapterTableModel extends AbstractTableModel {
    private static String[] columnNames = {
        "", "Title", "Page Count"
    };

    private static String[] chapterNames = {
        "The Last Washing", "Hoedown in The Crimea", "The Zen of Jelly",
```

"My Dinner with Bill", "Favorite Wavelengths", "Newton's Fourth Law",
"How Not to Be Seen", "Lymph and You: Perfect Together",
"The Duct Tape Incident", "TOTAL"

```java
};

private Integer[] values;

// Set up some random values for the page counts
ChapterTableModel() {
    Random rand = new Random();
    values = new Integer[chapterNames.length];
    for (int b=0; b < chapterNames.length; b++) {
        values[b] = new Integer(rand.nextInt(200) + 50);
    }
}

// Return number of columns
public int getColumnCount() {
    return columnNames.length;
}

// Return number of rows
public int getRowCount() {
    return chapterNames.length;
}

// Retrieve the model values
public Object getValueAt(int row, int column) {
    // For the 'total' cell, add up all of the page counts
    if (column == 2 && row == getRowCount() - 1) {
        int total = 0;
        for (int b=0; b < values.length - 1; b++)
            total += values[b].intValue();
        return new Integer(total);
    }

    switch (column) {
        // For column zero, just report the chapter number
```

```
        case 0:
        if (row == getRowCount() - 1)
            return "";
        return "Chapter " + Integer.toString(row + 1);

        // Report the chapter name
        case 1:
        return chapterNames[row];

        // Report the numeric value
        case 2:
        return values[row];
    }
    // Should never get here
    return null;
}

public String getColumnName(int column) {
    return columnNames[column];
}

// Update the new editor value into the appropriate cell
public void setValueAt(Object value, int row, int column) {
    values[row] = (Integer) value;
}

// Return class Integer for the last column, String for others
public Class getColumnClass(int column) {
    if (column == 2)
        return Integer.class;
    return String.class;
}

// Only the last column is editable, except for the total
public boolean isCellEditable(int row, int column) {
    return (column == 2 && row < getRowCount() - 1);
}
}
```

The *NumericSpinner* is an editor component that is implemented as a *JPanel* extension. To qualify as a table cell editor, it implements the methods specified by the *TableCellEditor* interface.

The spinner is simply constructed from a *JLabel* and two arrow buttons. The spinner uses *DefaultBoundedRangeModel* as its model delegate and updates its label when the arrow buttons are actuated.

```
package com.ketherware.samples.tableeditor;

import java.awt.*;
import java.awt.event.*;
import java.util.*;
import javax.swing.*;
import javax.swing.table.*;
import javax.swing.event.*;
import javax.swing.plaf.basic.*;

public class NumericSpinner extends JPanel
                          implements TableCellEditor, ChangeListener {
    protected EventListenerList listenerList = new EventListenerList();
    protected ChangeEvent changeEvent = new ChangeEvent(this);
    protected DefaultBoundedRangeModel model;
    protected BasicArrowButton upButton =
                new BasicArrowButton(SwingConstants.NORTH);
    protected BasicArrowButton downButton =
                new BasicArrowButton(SwingConstants.SOUTH);
    protected JLabel text = new JLabel();

    // The constructor initializes the model, creates the
    // sub-components and initializes all listeners
    public NumericSpinner(int value, int min, int max) {
        model = new DefaultBoundedRangeModel(value, 0, min, max);
        setLayout(new BorderLayout());
        add(upButton, BorderLayout.WEST);
        add(downButton, BorderLayout.EAST);

        // Make the label look more like a cell
        text.setForeground(Color.black);
```

```
    text.setHorizontalAlignment(JLabel.CENTER);
    text.setFont(UIManager.getFont("Table.font"));
    add(text);

    // Add the whole container as a listener for model changes
    // and create listeners for the button actions
    model.addChangeListener(this);
    upButton.addActionListener(new ActionListener() {
        public void actionPerformed(ActionEvent event) {
            decrement();
        }
    });
    downButton.addActionListener(new ActionListener() {
        public void actionPerformed(ActionEvent event) {
            increment();
        }
    });
}

// Return the editor component with the value initialized. Since the
// spinner is listening for model changes, we do not have to directly
// update the spinner value
public Component getTableCellEditorComponent(JTable table, Object value,
            boolean isSelected, int row, int column) {
    model.setValue(((Integer) value).intValue());
    return this;
}

// Increment the spinner, beep if at top of range
protected void increment() {
    if (model.getMinimum() == model.getValue()) {
        Toolkit.getDefaultToolkit().beep();
        return;
    }
    model.setValue(model.getValue() - 1);
}
```

```
// Decrement the spinner, beep if at bottom of range
protected void decrement() {
    if (model.getMaximum() == model.getValue()) {
        Toolkit.getDefaultToolkit().beep();
        return;
    }
    model.setValue(model.getValue() + 1);
}


// Implementation of ChangeListener will detect model changes
// and reflect them in the label caption
public void stateChanged(ChangeEvent event) {
    text.setText(Integer.toString(model.getValue()));
}


// Return the new value from the editing session
public Object getCellEditorValue() {
    return new Integer(model.getValue());
}


// Always allow editing
public boolean isCellEditable(EventObject anEvent) {
    return true;
}


// Select the row that contains the cell being edited
public boolean shouldSelectCell(EventObject anEvent) {
    return true;
}


// Callback method to inform the editor that the editing has ended
public boolean stopCellEditing() {
    fireEditingStopped();
    return true;
}


// Callback method to inform the editor that the editing was canceled
public void cancelCellEditing() {
```

```
            fireEditingCanceled();
    }

    // Add an interested listener
    public void addCellEditorListener(CellEditorListener listener) {
        listenerList.add(CellEditorListener.class, listener);
    }

    // Remove an interested listener
    public void removeCellEditorListener(CellEditorListener listener) {
        listenerList.remove(CellEditorListener.class, listener);
    }

    // Notify interested listeners that editing was stopped
    protected void fireEditingStopped() {
        Object[] listeners = listenerList.getListenerList();
        for (int z = listeners.length - 2; z >= 0; z -= 2) {
          if (listeners[z] == CellEditorListener.class) {
             CellEditorListener listener =
                            (CellEditorListener) listeners[z + 1];
             listener.editingStopped(changeEvent);
          }
        }
    }

    // Notify interested listeners that editing was canceled
    protected void fireEditingCanceled() {
        Object[] listeners = listenerList.getListenerList();
        for (int z = listeners.length - 2; z >= 0; z -= 2) {
          if (listeners[z] == CellEditorListener.class) {
             CellEditorListener listener =
                            (CellEditorListener) listeners[z + 1];
             listener.editingCanceled(changeEvent);
          }
        }
    }
}
```

Filtering and Sorting JTable Data

Similar to list and tree data, *TableModel* implementations can also be used with model filtering. As with all model filtering, the notion is the same: to wrap an existing model in a class to alter the way it reports information. This technique is used to implement column-oriented sorting for a directory browser utility.

In this example, several of the useful techniques for customizing *JTable* behavior are used. Apart from model filtering, which provides the sorting capabilities, table cell renderers are used to provide special interpretations of data elements found in the *File* object. For example, a file's size is represented by a *long*; simply depicting this as a *String* is not a particularly good way to represent a file size. To furnish an alternative, a renderer is used to convert the value to kilobytes or megabytes depending on the magnitude of the file's size. Another renderer is available to interpret the file modification date/time differently than by default.

The model filter itself is implemented as an extension of *AbstractTableModel*. In this case, because the actual data is already expected to be located in a collection, no need exists to bring the functionality of *DefaultTableModel* into the picture. *SortingTableModelFilter* provides a constructor that takes a reference to a *TableModel*, using the supplied model as a delegate. The filter mechanism sorts the model's data and inserts a sorted collection of indices into a *Vector* collection. The behavior that the model performs is to provide an alternate version of *getValueAt()* that translates the provided row index into its equivalent sorted index. This simple transformation is all that is required to provide sorted tables.

The additional code that is provided gives some value-added functionality by replacing the default *JTableHeader* implementation with one that is mouse-click aware. A *MouseListener* enables detection of click events within the header area; this information is used to provide a dynamic sort with column selection. Double-clicking the column header regenerates the sorted index array based on the collation of the data in the selected column. An asterisk is also added to the header to denote the current sort column. See Figure 8-6.

The internal mechanism of *JTable* keeps track of column data as it is rearranged. This enables reordering of columns that preserve the selected sort order. Because of the way that *JTableHeader* traps mouse clicks for column dragging, a double-click is used to denote a change to the sort column. See Figure 8-7.

```
package com.ketherware.samples.filetable

import java.util.*;
import javax.swing.table.*;

public class SortingTableModelFilter extends AbstractTableModel {
    // Delegate model (reference to model being filtered)
    protected TableModel model;

    // Collection used to store sorted index information
    protected Vector sortedIndex;

    // Current sort column
    protected int sortColumn;

    // Default sort column
    public static final int DEFAULT_COLUMN = 3;

    // Constructor — takes a model reference as a parameter
    public SortingTableModelFilter(TableModel model) {
        this.model = model;
        sortColumn = DEFAULT_COLUMN;
        resortModel();
    }

    public void setSortColumn(int newColumn) {
```

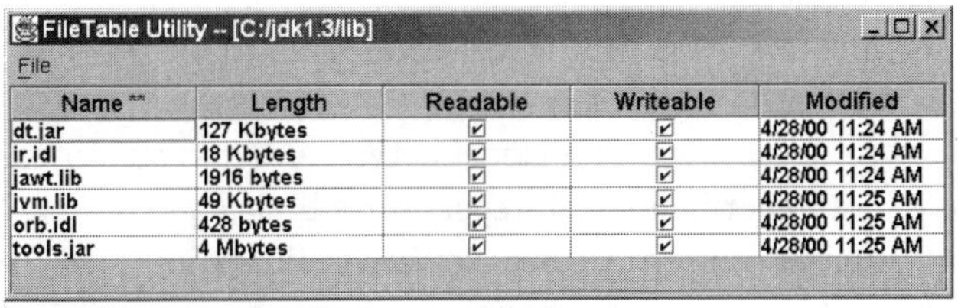

Name	Length	Readable	Writeable	Modified
dt.jar	127 Kbytes	☑	☑	4/28/00 11:24 AM
ir.idl	18 Kbytes	☑	☑	4/28/00 11:24 AM
jawt.lib	1916 bytes	☑	☑	4/28/00 11:24 AM
jvm.lib	49 Kbytes	☑	☑	4/28/00 11:25 AM
orb.idl	428 bytes	☑	☑	4/28/00 11:25 AM
tools.jar	4 Mbytes	☑	☑	4/28/00 11:25 AM

Figure 8-6. *Unsorted table*

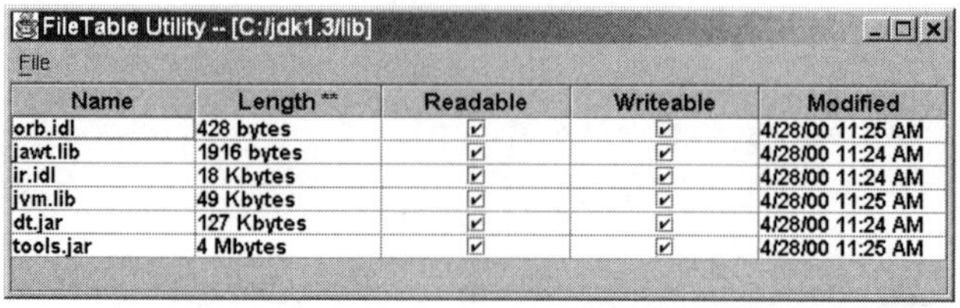

Figure 8-7. *Sorted table*

```
        if (this.sortColumn == newColumn)
            return;
        this.sortColumn = newColumn;
        resortModel();
        fireTableDataChanged();
    }

    public int getSortColumn() {
        return this.sortColumn;
    }

    // Sort the model using an insertion sort
    public synchronized void resortModel() {
        // Discard the old list and create a new one
        // with the proper initial capacity
        sortedIndex = new Vector(model.getRowCount());

    nextElement:
        for (int row = 0; row < model.getRowCount(); row++) {
            for (int j = 0; j < row; j++) {
                Object element = model.getValueAt(row, sortColumn);
                Integer index = (Integer) sortedIndex.get(j);
                Object compare = model.getValueAt(index.intValue(), sortColumn);
                if (compareElements(element, compare) < 0) {
                    sortedIndex.insertElementAt(new Integer(row), j);
                    continue nextElement;
```

```
        }
      }
      sortedIndex.addElement(new Integer(row));
    }
  }

  // Allows sort algorithm to operate on different types
  protected int compareElements(Object element, Object compare) {
    if (element instanceof Long)
      return ((Long) element).compareTo(compare);
    else if (element instanceof Date)
      return ((Date) element).compareTo(compare);
    else
      return element.toString().compareTo(compare.toString());
  }

  // Redirect this required method to use the sorted index array
  public Object getValueAt(int row, int col) {
    Integer index = (Integer) sortedIndex.get(row);
    return model.getValueAt(index.intValue(), col);
  }

  // Delegate to model
  public int getRowCount() {
    return model.getRowCount();
  }

  // Delegate to model
  public int getColumnCount() {
    return model.getColumnCount();
  }

  // Delegate to model
  public String getColumnName(int column) {
    return model.getColumnName(column);
  }
```

```
        // Delegate to model
        public Class getColumnClass(int column) {
            return model.getColumnClass(column);
        }
    }
```

The *FileTableModel* class is an extension of *AbstractTableModel*. Its function is to create a *JTable* representation of the contents of a directory. To accomplish this, a constructor is provided that takes a *File* object reference, which represents the target directory in the file system.

```
package com.ketherware.samples.filetable;

import java.io.*;
import java.util.*;
import java.text.DateFormat;
import javax.swing.*;
import javax.swing.table.*;

public class FileTableModel extends AbstractTableModel {
    // Date format singleton object
    protected static DateFormat format = DateFormat.getInstance();
    // Collection to store directory entry information
    protected ArrayList list = new ArrayList();
    // Column name strings
    protected static final String[] columnNames = {
        "Name", "Length", "Readable", "Writeable", "Modified"
    };

    // Constructor — takes a parameter that is a directory
    // and adds an entry for each file it contains to the collection
    public FileTableModel(File directory) {
        String path = directory.getPath();
        String[] files = directory.list();

        for (int j=0; j < files.length; j++) {
            list.add(new File(path, files[j]));
        }
```

```
    }

    // Return the number of elements in the collection as the rows
    public int getRowCount() {
        return list.size();
    }

    // Return the number of columns
    public int getColumnCount() {
        return columnNames.length;
    }

    // Return column name
    public String getColumnName(int column) {
        return columnNames[column];
    }

    // Return column class
    public Class getColumnClass(int column) {
        if (column == 2 || column == 3)
            return Boolean.class;
        else if (column == 1)
            return Long.class;
        else if (column == 4)
            return Date.class;
        return Object.class;
    }

    // Retrieve value from collection
    public Object getValueAt(int row, int column)
    {
        File file = (File) list.get(row);

        switch (column) {
            case 0:
            // Name column
            if (file.isDirectory())
```

```
            return "[" + file.getName() + "]";
        return file.getName();

        case 1:
        // Length column
        if (file.isDirectory())
            return new Long(-1);
        return new Long(file.length());

        case 2:
        // True if file is readable
        return new Boolean(file.canRead());
        case 3:
        // True if file is writable
        return new Boolean(file.canWrite());

        case 4:
        // Modification timestamp
        return new Date(file.lastModified());
    }
    // Should never get here, hope we don't
    return null;
}

// Return a string representing a byte count, convert to Kbytes or
// MBytes as required
public static String convertDate(Date date)
{
    return format.format(date);
}

// Return a string representing a byte count, convert to Kbytes or
// MBytes as required
public static String convertSize(long size)
{
    if (size < 0)
        return "";
```

```
        if (size < Math.pow(2, 12))
            return Long.toString(size) + " bytes";
        else if (size < Math.pow(2, 22))
            return Long.toString((long) (size / Math.pow(2, 10))) + " Kbytes";
        else
            return Long.toString((long) (size / Math.pow(2, 20))) + " Mbytes";
    }
}
```

The next module contains the *main()* method and is responsible for initializing the application frame. Furthermore, this module contains the renderers that are used to interpret the information retrieved from the *File* objects.

An important part of the initialization is the invocation of the *JFileChooser* dialog box. This is the mechanism used to determine the directory that the application operates upon. A *FileFilter* extension is created as an anonymous class; this is how nondirectory file entries are ignored.

```
package com.ketherware.samples.filetable;

import java.awt.*;
import java.awt.event.*;
import java.io.File;
import java.util.*;
import javax.swing.*;
import javax.swing.table.*;
import javax.swing.filechooser.*;

public class FileTable extends JFrame {
    // Table component containing file entries
    protected JTable fileTable;

    // Constructor — perform frame initialization
    public FileTable() {
        // Set size and location
        this.setSize(500, 200);
        this.setLocation(120, 120);
```

```java
      // Add a listener to detect when the frame
      // opens and closes
      this.addWindowListener(new WindowAdapter() {
         public void windowOpened(WindowEvent event) {
            openAction();
         }

         public void windowClosing(WindowEvent event) {
            exitAction();
         }
      });

      // Set the initial title, create menu and frame contents
      this.setTitle("FileTable Utility — [Select a Directory]");
      this.setJMenuBar(createMenuBar());
      fileTable = new JTable();
      this.getContentPane().add(new JScrollPane(fileTable));

      fileTable.setDefaultRenderer(String.class, new SortingTableCellRenderer());
      fileTable.setDefaultRenderer(Long.class, new SortingTableCellRenderer());
      fileTable.setDefaultRenderer(Date.class, new
SortingTableCellRenderer());
      fileTable.setAutoCreateColumnsFromModel(true);
   }

   // Create the application menu bar
   protected JMenuBar createMenuBar() {
      // Create menu bar instance and add a menu component
      JMenuBar menuBar = new JMenuBar();
      JMenu fileMenu = new JMenu("File");
      fileMenu.setMnemonic('F');
      menuBar.add(fileMenu);

      // Add the 'open' menu item and create a listener
      JMenuItem openMenuItem = new JMenuItem("Open...");
      openMenuItem.setMnemonic('o');
      fileMenu.add(openMenuItem);
```

```java
        openMenuItem.addActionListener(new ActionListener() {
            public void actionPerformed(ActionEvent event) {
                openAction();
            }
        });

        // Add the 'exit' menu item and create a listener
        JMenuItem exitMenuItem = new JMenuItem("Exit");
        exitMenuItem.setMnemonic('x');
        fileMenu.add(new JSeparator());
        fileMenu.add(exitMenuItem);
        exitMenuItem.addActionListener(new ActionListener() {
            public void actionPerformed(ActionEvent event) {
                exitAction();
            }
        });
        return menuBar;
    }

    // Invoked by menu or at application start-up
    protected void openAction() {
        // Retrieve a file object using a JFC file chooser
        File dir = chooseDirectory();
        if (dir == null)
            return;

        // Using the directory reference, create a table model.
        // Reset the title to contain the directory
        FileTableModel model = new FileTableModel(dir);
        fileTable.setModel(new SortingTableModelFilter(model));
        this.setTitle("FileTable Utility — [" + dir.getPath() + "]");
        setupRenderers(fileTable.getColumnModel());
    }

    protected void setupRenderers(TableColumnModel columnModel) {
        // Assign renderers to the table header and cells
        SortingTableHeader header = new SortingTableHeader(columnModel);
```

```
fileTable.setTableHeader(header);
header.setTable(fileTable);

Enumeration enum = columnModel.getColumns();
while (enum.hasMoreElements()) {
    TableColumn column = (TableColumn) enum.nextElement();
    TableCellRenderer oldRenderer =
            column.getHeaderRenderer();
    column.setHeaderRenderer(new SortingTableHeaderRenderer(
            fileTable, oldRenderer));
}
}

// Invoked by menu or application close request
protected void exitAction() {
    System.exit(0);
}

// Internal method that wraps a JFileChooser object to allow
// selection of the directory to display
protected File chooseDirectory() {
    // Create a file chooser and create a filter that
    // allows viewing of only directory entries
    JFileChooser chooser = new JFileChooser();
    chooser.setFileSelectionMode(
            JFileChooser.DIRECTORIES_ONLY);
    chooser.setFileFilter(new FileFilter() {
        // Description appears in file chooser dialog
        public String getDescription() {
            return "Select a directory";
        }

        // Returns 'true' if file is to be displayed
        public boolean accept(File file) {
            // Only display directories
            if (file.isDirectory())
                return true;
```

```
                return false;
            }
        });

        // Display the modal dialog. If the user cancels, the
        // selected file value will be 'null'
        chooser.showOpenDialog(this);
        this.repaint();
        return chooser.getCurrentDirectory();
    }

    // Main method: make some UI changes to make the content a
    // little smaller, then create and display the frame
    public static void main(String[] args) {
        Font headerFont = new Font("Dialog", Font.BOLD, 12);
        Font smallFont = new Font("Dialog", Font.BOLD, 11);
        Font cellFont = new Font("Dialog", Font.PLAIN, 9);
        UIManager.put("Table.font", smallFont);
        UIManager.put("TableHeader.font", headerFont);
        UIManager.put("Menu.font", smallFont);
        UIManager.put("MenuItem.font", smallFont);
        UIManager.put("TabbedPane.font", smallFont);
        new FileTable().show();
    }
}

class SortingTableHeader extends JTableHeader {
    protected int sortColumn = -1;
    SortingTableHeader(TableColumnModel columnModel) {
        super(columnModel);
        this.addMouseListener(new SortingTableHeaderMouseAdapter());
    }

    class SortingTableHeaderMouseAdapter extends MouseAdapter {
        public void mouseClicked(MouseEvent event) {
            if (event.getClickCount() != 2)
                return;
```

```
            int column = columnAtPoint(event.getPoint());
            setSortColumn(column);
        }
    }

    public int getSortColumn() {
        SortingTableModelFilter modelFilter =
            (SortingTableModelFilter) getTable().getModel();
        return modelFilter.getSortColumn();
    }

    protected void setSortColumn(int newColumn) {
        if (this.sortColumn == newColumn)
            return;
        this.sortColumn = newColumn;
        SortingTableModelFilter modelFilter =
            (SortingTableModelFilter) getTable().getModel();
        modelFilter.setSortColumn(newColumn);
    }
}

class SortingTableHeaderRenderer extends DefaultTableCellRenderer {
    TableCellRenderer oldRenderer;
    JTable table;

    SortingTableHeaderRenderer(JTable table, TableCellRenderer oldRenderer) {
        this.table = table;
        this.oldRenderer = oldRenderer;
    }

    public Component getTableCellRendererComponent(JTable table,
                    Object value, boolean isSelected,
                    boolean hasFocus, int row, int column) {
        String newValue = value.toString();

        JTableHeader header = this.table.getTableHeader();
        if (header != null && header instanceof SortingTableHeader) {
```

```
                SortingTableHeader sortingHeader = (SortingTableHeader)
                        this.table.getTableHeader();
                if (sortingHeader.getSortColumn() == column)
                    newValue += " **";
            }
            return oldRenderer.getTableCellRendererComponent(table,
                    newValue, isSelected, hasFocus, row, column);
        }
    }

    class SortingTableCellRenderer extends DefaultTableCellRenderer {
        public Component getTableCellRendererComponent(JTable table,
                        Object value, boolean isSelected,
                        boolean hasFocus, int row, int column) {
            String newValue = value.toString();
            if (value instanceof Date)
                newValue = FileTableModel.convertDate((Date) value);
            else if (value instanceof Long)
                newValue = FileTableModel.convertSize(((Long)
    value).longValue());

            return super.getTableCellRendererComponent(table,
                    newValue, isSelected, hasFocus, row, column);
        }
    }
```

Exercises

1. Implement a version of *JarHead* that presents the manifest information as a *JTree* instead of a *JTable*. Use the main entries collection as a node, and create a node for each set of attribute entries.

2. How would a mutable implementation of *JarHead* be implemented? Create an extended version of *JarHead* that allows for editing of entry names and comments, addition and deletions of entries, or editing of the manifest using a *JTree* or *JTable*.

3. Implement a version of *FileTable* that enables the creation and deletion of files and altering of file attributes (such as readability and writeability).

The opposite of a correct statement is a false statement. But the
opposite of a profound truth may well be another profound truth.
—Niels Bohr

Chapter 9

Pluggable Look-and-Feel

JFC supports the capability to select the overall way an application appears to a user. The pluggable look-and-feel mechanism, or PLAF, supports the capability to produce applications that behave and appear the same on different operating platforms. Two types of PLAFs are available: cross-platform (see Figure 9-1) and platform-emulation. Cross-platform PLAFs are designed to provide a common application style that is implementation- neutral.

Three platform-emulation versions are also available that simulate the X/Motif, Microsoft Windows, and Macintosh interfaces. See Figures 9-2 and 9-3.

It is also possible to develop custom look-and-feel (LAF) implementations, although it is extremely complex and difficult to do. The existing LAF implementations have many intricacies related to performance and graphic enhancement; replacing them is a serious and lengthy undertaking.

Look-and-feel classes are derived from an abstract class *LookAndFeel*. All other LAF classes are derived from *BasicLookAndFeel*, which is an

Figure 9-1. *The Java Look-and-Feel*

abstract extension of *LookAndFeel*. This chapter explores these classes and the facilities that support them.

The Look-and-Feel Philosophy

The concepts behind interface delegation and pluggable look-and-feel are a fundamental part of the JFC architecture. By adopting the doctrine of lightweight components and the Model/View/Controller paradigm (MVC), the framework for dynamic interface configuration is practicable.

The essential capabilities of PLAF reside in the *JComponent* class, the common ancestor of Swing components. Unlike heavyweight components, which depend on peer objects provided by the native operating system, JFC's lightweight components must encapsulate all of the capabilities to render themselves visually. In what is possibly the most brilliant facet of the Swing architecture, this concept is taken a step further: Not only are component painting features encapsulated in objects, these objects can be logically grouped and dynamically assigned to component instances.

Figure 9-2. *The Motif Look-and-Feel*

Figure 9-3. *The Windows Look-and-Feel*

It is likely that anyone with experience developing graphical user interfaces recalls many cases where application-level interface configuration is required. This may involve something as simple as a font or color change or may involve sophisticated support for nested components. In any case, a challenge is immediately apparent: Through what mechanism will interface changes be stored and propagated to application components? Although all graphical operating systems provide some amount of interface configurability, these may vary among operating platforms. Thus, in the spirit of cross-platform compatibility, there is no easy answer, especially in the case of heavyweight components.

Again, the lightweight/MVC architecture provides the necessary framework for such capabilities. Because the component does not really exist so far as the operating system is aware, the programmer has free reign to implement interface configurability. To achieve some standardization, the PLAF model was developed.

Pluggable look-and-feel classes are the mechanism by which interface configurations are encapsulated. PLAFs provide information on several elements related to configuration, the most important being a dictionary of default values that all application code uses to determine how to visually represent components. This dictionary is known as the *UIDefaults* dictionary and is the key to PLAF implementation.

How UIDefaults Are Used

UIDefaults extends *java.util.Dictionary* by way of *java.util.Hashtable*, which makes it a key/value pair manager. When a *UIDefaults* object is accessed, a unique key is provided that maps to a particular value. According to the *java.util.Dictionary* class, any nonprimitive (that is, any type derived from *java.lang.Object*) can be stored as a value using any nonprimitive *Object* type as a key; this enables all sorts of useful information to be stored in *UIDefaults* objects including colors, fonts, borders, strings, and, especially, references to UI delegate objects.

UIDefault Keys

To ease debugging and tracing, *String* objects are conventionally used by JFC components as the keys into the *UIDefaults* table. The target value of the dictionary is referred to as a *UIResource*, which is also the name of a PLAF interface that plays an important role in component property configuration. Some examples of typical *UIDefault* keys are listed in Table 9-1.

Surprisingly, no formal standardized reference exists to the keys used by LAF classes, which must match those used by the Swing components. If a programmer wants to alter the defaults for a particular object, the name may not have a different interpretation in a future release. Fortunately, it appears likely that Sun and other possible implementors of UI delegate classes will use a constant, if not necessarily consistent, set of resource keys.

UIDefault Levels

JFC supports three levels of *UIDefaults*:

- **System Defaults**—These are defaults specified by JFC's internal code. Currently, the system specifies only one default, and it has a key value of *FocusManagerClassName*. The value of this default is a

Table 9-1. *Examples of UIDefault keys*

Key	Meaning
ButtonUI	UI Delegate to paint *JButton* component
TreeUI	UI Delegate to paint *JTree* component
menuText	RGB color value for menu text
Menu.margin	Default insets for lightweight menus
Table.font	Default font for *JTable* cells

string with the class name of the default focus manager, *javax.swing.DefaultFocusManager*. It is specified in the *UIManager* class code in a private method called *initializeSystemDefaults()*. This method is invoked once when the default LAF is initialized.

- **LAF Defaults**—When a look-and-feel is set, one of its primary functions is to modify the *UIDefaults* table to contain the information to support its resources. The abstract look-and-feel, *BasicLookAndFeel*, contains default values for many defaults. When a new look-and-feel is created, the implementation either uses the defaults specified by *BasicLookAndFeel* or supplies its own values.

- **User Defaults**—A JFC application can alter the *UIDefaults* table dynamically. When this occurs, the supplied value overrides the LAF and its system defaults. These changes are not overridden if a new look-and-feel is loaded.

The current *UIDefaults* are accessed by using the *UIManager* class, which also provides a mechanism to listen for new look-and-feel changes. The *UIManager* class is covered in detail in the "UIManager" section later in this chapter.

User Defaults Example

An illustration of the use of *UIDefaults* is the case described earlier. For example, a user-specified requirement might call for application labels to have a red foreground. In the pre-JFC days, you had several options:

1. Create a subclass of *java.awt.Button* that sets the background and foreground properties:

```
public class MyButton extends java.awt.Button {
    public MyButton(String caption)
    {
super(caption);
this.setForeground(java.awt.Color.red);
    }
    . . .
}
```

This approach has some serious disadvantages. First, interactive development environments may not recognize the *MyButton* class as behaving like a *Button*. Second, the color is hardcoded, which means that if the requirement changes, you cannot accommodate the new color without recompiling the code for *MyButton*. Also, any similar changes you make to other components would require an additional subclass.

2. Add code to each label declaration that specifies the property values:

```
. . .
Button okButton = new Button("OK");
okButton.setForeground(java.awt.Color.red);
. . .
```

This solution is also problematic because it involves two additional lines of code for every *Button* required by an application. This would undoubtedly increase the maintenance needs for an application. Not only would it increase the number of maintainable lines of code, but would also require cut-and-paste propagation to other components that need this capability.

JFC and the *UIManager* class offer a much better solution. You need only one line of code to ensure that all instances of *JButton* have a red foreground:

```
. . .
UIManager.put("Button.foreground", Color.red);
. . .
```

Because this is a static method, the code could be inserted into the *main()* method of the application. It will function as long as it appears before the instantiation of any *JButton* control. To make it function *after* buttons are created, add this line of code:

```
. . .
SwingUtilities.updateComponentTreeUI(this);
. . .
```

This method recursively descends down the component tree starting with the component specified in the parameter and updates all of the UI delegates and defaults. You should also use this method when the look-and-feel is changed after components are created to cause the LAF changes to take effect.

A Closer Look at UIDefaults

This class is an extension of *java.util.Hashtable* and is the primary repository for LAF information. As described in the previous section, LAF defaults are managed in a key/value pair arrangement according to the implementation of *java.util.Dictionary*. Code in the *UIDefaults* class handles synchronization of this table to prevent incomplete LAF changes or other side-effects. The current *UIDefaults* are managed by the *UIManager* class. To modify defaults, a reference to the current default table is retrieved by a static method of the *UIManager* class.

Instances of *UIDefaults* can be constructed by a default constructor or by an array of *java.lang.Object* that represent the key/value pairs. Each odd-numbered element represents a key, and its successive element represents the value. A method also exists named *putDefaults()* that also takes an array of key/value pairs and adds them to the existing defaults, if any.

UIDefaults() overrides the *java.util.Hashtable* of *get()* and *put()*. The *get()* method takes a *java.lang.Object* as a parameter and returns the *java.lang.Object* that represents the value for that key. If the key does not exist, *null* is returned. The *put()* method takes two *java.lang.Object* parameters that represent a key/value pair.

Retrieval Methods

To simplify the retrieval of defaults from the table, several additional methods are provided that return specific default types instead of a generic object. Table 9-2 lists these methods.

Each of these methods returns a *null* if the key is not valid or if the value associated with the key cannot be resolved to the specified return value. The *instanceof* operator is used in each of these methods to test if the value is convertible. The exception is the *getInt()* method, which tests whether the value is of type *java.lang.Integer* because primitives cannot be directly stored in a *UIDefaults* table.

Table 9-2. *Retrieval methods in UIDefaults*

public Font getFont(Object key)	*public Color getColor(Object key)*
public Icon getIcon(Object key)	*public Border getBorder(Object key)*
public String getString(Object key)	*public int getInt(Object key)*
public Insets getInsets(Object key)	*public Dimension getDimension(Object key)*
public Font getFont(Object key)	*public Color getColor(Object key)*

The UIResource Interface

In the *javax.swing.plaf* package is an interface with an empty implementation called *UIResource*. This interface serves as a signature for objects created by UI delegates. This enables the *UIManager* and other LAF code to distinguish property values as being subject to update when the look-and-feel is changed.

This marker serves as a mechanism to tell if a property of a *JComponent* has been explicitly set by a programmer. When a *JComponent* is created, its properties are loaded with values specified by the *UIDefaults* for the current LAF. When property values are specified in a look-and-feel, the convention is to use classes that implement the *UIResource* interface.

It is possible, of course, to change the value of these properties after the component is created. If a property's value is explicitly set with a non-*UIResource* value, a new UI delegate will not dynamically change the value when it is associated with the component. For example, in *BasicLookAndFeel*, a standard font is specified for menu objects as a *FontUIResource* object. If an application specifically changes the menu font, it is expected that the font change would need to be permanent even if the look-and-feel were to change. When the LAF is dynamically changed, these values are updated only if the current property is *null* or contains some other object that implements *UIResource*.

Several classes are provided that inherit from commonly used resource classes to provide objects you can use as default values. In most cases, these classes provide only constructors that match the base class, although there are cases where some methods are delegated to encapsulated resource objects. These are some of the *UIResource* classes available for use as default values:

- *ColorUIResource*
- *BorderUIResource*
- *IconUIResource*
- *InsetsUIResource*

It is strongly recommended that *UIResource* versions of property value classes be used only as default values for UI delegates. *UIManager* interprets these values as having been assigned by the LAF and alters them if any dynamic changes to look-and-feel occur.

Retrieving a UI Delegate Class

When a component is created or when a look-and-feel is changed, a new delegate object must be associated with it. Two *UIDefaults* methods, both called *getUIClass()*, are provided to retrieve the appropriate class. Both methods return a *java.lang.Class* object as its result and take a *String* representing the UI class ID as a parameter. The alternate version of this method takes a reference to a *ClassLoader* object to handle difficulties that might arise by attempting to load delegates from a different class loading mechanism, such as might be provided by an integrated development environment.

The *String* ID that is supplied to this method is provided by the JFC component for which the delegate class is being created. The method *getUIClassID()*, provided by *JComponent*, is overridden to return a string that matches the UI class ID for the defaults. If a new *JComponent* subclass is created that is meant to have its own UI delegate, this method must be overridden to return a specific value.

Retrieving a UI Delegate Object

The *getUIClass()* is intended to be used internally by a very significant method provided by *UIDefaults* called *getUI()*. The *getUI()* method is used to return an actual instance of a UI delegate when a JFC component is created or the look-and-feel changes. This method is also intended to be used internally, but can be called to retrieve a delegate object for any existing *JComponent* instance. If the supplied parameter specifies a component that does not have a UI delegate, this method returns a *null*.

Preventing UI Delegate Errors

In certain cases, especially when subclassing *UIDefaults* for auxiliary LAFs, *getUI()* generates errors for missing entries. The method *getUIError()* can be overridden to prevent error messages from being sent to the console and from throwing an *Error* object.

Lazy and Active Values

UIDefaults also provides two public subinterfaces that can be used to create special handling for values stored in the table: *LazyValue* and *ActiveValue*. Both interfaces specify a single method called *createValue()* that takes a *UIDefaults* reference as a parameter and returns a generic *Object*.

LazyValue is used for default values that do not need to be instantiated or initialized until they are actually requested. This feature helps reduce the number of object resources a LAF might need. For example, there is little reason to load an icon for a particular component if it is unused. Value objects that implement *LazyValue* are not initialized until a *get()* is actually performed on the matching key. When the *get()* is performed an actual value is inserted into the defaults table by invoking the *createValue()* method. Because the initial value is an instance of the *LazyValue* interface and the subsequent value is not, a mechanism to perform one-time initialization is enabled.

ActiveValue is used in exactly the same way as *LazyValue*, except instead of doing a one-time invocation of *createValue()*, it is called each time the value is accessed. Thus, a new value can be constructed for the key each time a *get()* is performed. *ActiveValue* is used in only one place in the JFC code, when a *ListCellRenderer* delegate is requested. This enables the *JList* component to revise the renderer obejct that is provided each time one is required.

Listening for Default Value Changes

UIDefaults enables interested listeners to register for changes to *UIDefaults* property changes. A property change event is generated and fired whenever the *put()* method of *UIDefaults* is invoked and the key is an instance of *String*. Unlike many other property changes, the event is fired if *put()* is called even if the value does not actually change.

Individual change events are not generated when the *putDefaults()* method is used to update multiple properties using a key/value array. In this case, a single *PropertyChangeEvent* is fired with a property name of *UIDefaults* and *null* values for the before and after states.

UIManager

The *UIManager* class provides many important static methods that support the UI delegation mechanism of JFC. It provides an important set of features that enable pluggable look-and-feel. Among other resource-saving features, *UIManager* supports deferred initialization of LAF objects until they are explicitly requested.

The LookAndFeel Property

UIManager provides a static-bound property named *LookAndFeel* that represents the currently active LAF. The accessor method, *getLookAndFeel()*, returns a reference of type *LookAndFeel*. Two mutator methods are provided; one version of *setLookAndFeel()* takes a parameter of type *LookAndFeel*, the other takes a *String* class name. Both methods can throw *UnsupportedLookAndFeelException* if the specified LAF class is not supported on the execution platform, as well as class and file loading exceptions. The property change listener is registered with static implementations of *addPropertyChangeListener()* and *removePropertyChangeListener()*. Only one class in the JFC library actually listens for this property change: the default toolbar UI delegate *BasicToolbarUI*.

Default LAF Classes

UIManager provides default LAF class names. The two types of defaults that it supports are the system LAF, which represents the platform-emulation LAF of the current implementation, and the cross-platform LAF, which is hardcoded to the Java (Metal) look-and-feel class. The methods to retrieve these defaults return a *String* type and are named *getSystemLookAndFeelClassName()* and *getCrossPlatformLookAndFeelClassName()*. Because neither of these methods nor the *UIManager* class is final, it is possible to alter these values, although only after the default case has been initialized.

Installed LAF Classes

Another feature that *UIManager* provides is a simple database of the LAF classes known as the installed look-and-feels. This feature provides a convenient list for user-initiated selection of the current look-and-feel.

The installed list is a simple array of objects of type *LookAndFeelInfo*, which contains only the look-and-feel name along with its class name in *String* format. The static method *getInstalledLookAndFeels()* returns this array upon request. The *LookAndFeelInfo* class is a static inner class of *UIManager*. It provides the accessor methods *getName()* and *getClassName()* to return the values of those properties. A parameterized constructor is provided to create new instances of this class to pass as parameters to other methods.

Two methods are supplied for altering the set of installed LAFs. The *installLookAndFeel()* method takes a single instance of *LookAndFeelInfo* and adds it to the static array. Another method, *setInstalledLookAndFeels()*, takes an array of *LookAndFeelInfo* objects and replaces the installed list with this array. The *installLookAndFeel()* method calls *setInstalledLookAndFeels()* internally to make its changes.

In actuality, LAFs are not actually installed when they are added to this list. The actual installation of a look-and-feel occurs when it is made the current LAF by *UIManager*. It would be a very inefficient use of resources to load all of the objects required by a look-and-feel if it is not actually being used. The loading of a look-and-feel is an expensive operation.

Access to UI Defaults

UIManager also provides static methods that provide access to the current set of defaults and the defaults provided by the current look-and-feel. The method *getDefaults()* returns a reference to the current *UIDefaults* object and enables any access or modification operations to be performed. The method *getLookAndFeelDefaults()* returns a *UIDefaults* object that represents the default values for the current LAF, without any alterations that may have been made by assigning a user default.

Several static shortcut methods are provided that delegate to the current set of defaults. Table 9-3 lists those shortcut methods.

Auxiliary Look-and-Feel Support

UIManager has some specific support for Auxiliary LAFs. Auxiliary LAFs are objects that add additional functionality and delegate capability.

It is a common misconception that elements of PLAF classes are mix-and-match. This is not the case, however, because the PLAF code is solely

Table 9-3. *Shortcut methods in UIManager*

Shortcut Method:	Equivalent To:
UIManager.get (…)	*UIManager.getDefaults().get(…)*
UIManager.put (…)	*UIManager.getDefaults().put(…)*
UIManager.getFont(…)	*UIManager.getDefaults().getFont(…)*
UIManager.getColor(…)	*UIManager.getDefaults().getColor(…)*
UIManager.getIcon(…)	*UIManager.getDefaults().getIcon(…)*
UIManager.getBorder(…)	*UIManager.getDefaults().getBorder(…)*
UIManager.getString(…)	*UIManager.getDefaults().getString(…)*
UIManager.getInt(…)	*UIManager.getDefaults().getInt(…)*
UIManager.getInsets(…)	*UIManager.getDefaults().getInsets(…)*
UIManager.getDimension(…)	*UIManager.getDefaults().getDimension(…)*

responsible for ensuring that the correct delegates are present in the *UIManager* tables. The intention of the LAF design is to provide complete flexibility among the various implementations. This is beneficial because it enables the PLAF classes to be completely standalone, but results in the inability to provide LAF functionality that remains in place regardless of the LAF that is operable.

Furthermore, the Swing developers stated that extension from existing PLAF classes is an unsound strategy because it ties the user to a particular LAF selection, which may change radically or not be supported in future JDK releases. This leaves Swing programmers with little choice but to manually modify the *UIDefaults* table to ensure that alternative delegates are used.

The concept of Auxiliary look-and-feel is an attempt to compensate for this restriction, although it turns out to be fundamentally unworkable. The classes that implement this, known as multiplexing look-and-feel (MLAF), are implemented in the *javax.swing.plaf.multi* package.

What MLAF does is enable more than one delegate to be associated with a particular *JComponent*. It accomplishes this by replacing the current LAF with the multiplexing version. The MLAF classes do not contain any actual component code, but provide a *Vector* collection that is iterated through when certain calls are made to the delegate APIs.

When an Auxiliary LAF is installed, the existing delegates are moved to the zero position of the *Vector* objects that are managed by the MLAF delegates. This ensures that a viable delegate method is called before any auxiliary method.

This solution is unworkable because it can only be used to provide UI delegate features other than those already present in the LAF delegate classes. Because the methods on the delegates are always invoked with the regular LAF first, there is no way to avoid or modify the initial behavior. So, the Auxiliary delegates can only draw on top of pre-existing graphics or respond to methods after actions may have already been taken. Including the overhead introduced by the instantiation of dozens of *Vector*s in the delegates helps make this an untenable solution to practical UI customization.

Component UI Delegates

All objects used as a UI delegate must inherit from the abstract class *ComponentUI*. This is the type of object that is returned from calls to the *getUI()* method of *UIDefaults()* to generate these delegate instances. The *ComponentUI* class contains code invoked by the *JComponent* implementation of *paint()* and *update()* along with a static constructor method that returns instances of the delegate class when *getUI()* is invoked. This method, called *createUI()*, must be implemented by every inheritor of the *ComponentUI* class to prevent an exception from being thrown.

The *ComponentUI* version of *update()* is invoked by the *JComponent* version of *paint()* through an intermediate method of *JComponent* called *paintComponent()*. This additional level of abstraction is required to support the use of component borders, which are painted by separate delegate objects. The *update()* method also checks the opacity of the component and fills the background with the appropriate color if *isOpaque()* returns *true*.

Installing and Uninstalling UI Delegates

ComponentUI contains other methods that are designed to be overridden. The methods *installUI()* and *uninstallUI()* both take a *JComponent* argument. The *installUI()* method is invoked when the *setUI()* method of

JComponent is invoked or when a *JComponent* is generated from persistent storage using the *readObject()* method. It is generally the place where component-level defaults are defined, subcomponents are created, listeners are added, and appropriate keyboard actions registered.

The *uninstallUI()* method is invoked on a UI delegate when it is replaced by another delegate, or when certain operations occur in *JComponent* serialization. This method is generally where all of the objects that were created in *installUI()* are uninstalled, all listeners removed, and all keyboard actions reset.

Size-Related Methods

Ordinarily, in heavyweight components, the peer object determines the size of a component. In the lightweight world, there is no peer object to rely on for this information. Also, the size of a component depends on the implementation of the component UI by the current look-and-feel, taking into account differences in margins, fonts, icons, and other factors. Thus, *JComponent* delegates the reporting of component size to the component UI because it is the place where the actual painting of the component will take place. It is, therefore, a conventional task of the delegate to determine the preferred, maximum, and minimum sizes of its target component.

These familiar methods—*getPreferredSize()*, *getMinimumSize()*, and *getMaximumSize()*—are implemented with an additional parameter of a *JComponent* instance. This parameter is needed because UI delegates are often shared across multiple components. Component UI objects must be stateful delegates and access the properties of the component they are operating on when this method is invoked by a layout manager or other interested party.

The default implementation of *getPreferredSize()* in *ComponentUI* returns *null*, which causes the management of preferred size to be relegated to the layout manager or to the *Dimension* value stored in the component. The default implementation of maximum and minimum size methods both invoke *getPreferredSize()* by default.

In the case of preferred, maximum, and minimum sizes, delegation to the *ComponentUI* takes place only if a value for any of the sizes was not explicitly set using the mutator methods of *JComponent*. If a value for these sizes is detected, the value of the size is used. To restore a *JComponent* so that its UI delegate again controls sizing, set the preferred, maximum, or minimum sizes to *null*.

ComponentUI also contains methods used by the Accessibility package to determine the number of accessible children in a particular UI implementation and to return the accessible context for any of these children.

ComponentUI Subclasses

All UI delegates ultimately inherit from *ComponentUI*, but generally inherit from a descendant of *ComponentUI* that is specific to a component. These classes, which, like *ComponentUI*, are located in the *javax.swing.plaf* package, contain the basic component-specific features that UI delegates supply. In almost all cases, these subclasses are also abstract and do not contain any additional methods. For the most part, the essential features of UI delegation are actually implemented in the delegates of the *javax.swing.plaf.basic* package.

The LookAndFeel Class

The abstract class *LookAndFeel* serves as a base class for all PLAF implementations. The *LookAndFeel* class is designed to encapsulate all of the features and information about a particular LAF and is responsible for initializing all of the resources a LAF may require.

Abstract Methods of LookAndFeel

To provide a consistent mechanism to acquire information about a look-and-feel inheritor, several abstract methods are specified. These methods are invoked by *UIManager* code to retrieve information about a LAF before its resources are actually loaded; all methods are in the form of read-only properties. The *getName(), getID(), and getDescription()* methods all return *String* objects that represent various descriptions of the LAF class. The *getName()* method is intended to provide a terse name for a LAF suitable for use in a menu or other selection component. The *getID()* method returns a familiar name that represents the fundamental look-and-feel. It is used to identify subclasses of standard LAFs as being related to their superclasses. Last, the *getDescription()* method returns a more verbose description of a look-and-feel suitable for status bars, tooltips, or as a place for containing copyright or other relevant information.

The *isNativeLookAndFeel()* is a read-only *boolean* property that returns *true* for a LAF that represents the platform emulation for the native operating system. For example, this method returns *true* for the Motif LAF when running on an X/Windows platform. Thus, JFC implementations for different native platforms have this minor distinction in the way they are implemented.

In addition, a method called *isSupportedLookAndFeel()* is specified that returns *true* if the LAF is intended for the current operating platform. This method is used, for example, to prevent the Mac OS emulation LAF from being loaded on other operating platforms, supposedly for copyright infringement concerns.

LookAndFeel Initialization

When a *LookAndFeel* class is created, its primary task is to create the *UIDefaults* table that represents the LAF's resources. When a LAF class is developed, the method *getDefaults()* is overridden to return a *UIDefaults* table with all of the proper keys and values in place. The method is called by the *UIManager* method *setLookAndFeel* when a LAF is about to be made the current one.

The *LookAndFeel* base class specifies two methods that are used when a LAF object is loaded, *initialize()* and *uninitialize()*. The *initialize()* method is used instead of a standard or static constructor to perform any one-time initializations that are required. The reason given in the internal documentation for *LookAndFeel* is that it is not sensible to go through the effort of initializing a LAF and its resources only to find that it is not supported when *isSupportedLookAndFeel()* returns *false*. The *uninitialize()* method is called when a LAF is about to be replaced; it provides an opportunity to free up resources that are no longer needed.

Resource Installation Features

The *LookAndFeel* class provides additional support for initialization of component properties, specifically colors, fonts, and borders.

The static method *installColors()* takes three parameters: a reference to a *JComponent* and two *String* keys, one for the background color and one for the foreground. This method updates only the colors of the component if the existing values are *null* or are an instance of *UIResource*. The *installColorsAndFont()* method takes an additional parameter with the default key for a *java.awt.Font* resource. In both methods, the caller must ensure that the supplied keys are legitimate.

For border resources, the static methods *installBorder()* and *uninstall Border()* are provided. The *installBorder()* method takes a *JComponent* reference and a *String* key to a border *UIResource*. If the value of the border property of the component is *null* or is an instance of *UIResource*, the border property is assigned to the value represented by the supplied key. The converse method, *uninstallBorder()*, assigns *null* to the border property if the current value is an object that implements *UIResource*.

Other LookAndFeel Methods

The *makeIcon()* method is a static convenience method that loads GIF-format files into icons. It is an excellent example of the *LazyValue* interface because the mechanism used is invoked only when the resource is actually retrieved from its *DefaultUI* table. The *createValue()* method uses a privileged thread to synchronously load a buffer of bytes and generate an image using the *ImageIcon* class. The value returned by *makeIcon* is of type *IconUIResource*; this is a subclass of *Icon* that also implements *UIResource*.

Another static method provided by *LookAndFeel* is *makeKeyBindings()*. This method returns an array of key bindings suitable for use with *JTextComponent*, JFC's base class for text-oriented components. The key bindings are built from an array of objects representing a keystroke and action pair. Methods internal to *LookAndFeel* provide the capability of parsing formatted text strings into objects of type *javax.swing.event.KeyStroke*, which represent an encapsulated keyboard operation. The other part of the pair is a *javax.swing.event.Action* object that represents an encapsulation of a component action. These classes, and all other key binding issues, are discussed in detail in the text component chapter.

BasicLookAndFeel

The *BasicLookAndFeel* class is an abstract implementation of the *LookAndFeel* class. Its purpose is to provide the minimal level of UI functionality for all JFC components. The Java (Metal), Motif, Windows, and Mac LAF implementations all inherit from *BasicLookAndFeel*. This relationship enables LAF implementors to create a new UI for a component or enables the default values in *BasicLookAndFeel* to render components.

Basic Defaults

As discussed in the section on the *LookAndFeel* class, the primary purpose of these classes is to provide default UI delegates and other resources to components when they are created or when the LAF is changed. *BasicLookAndFeel* provides access to the basic UI delegates for all JFC components. These basic delegates are generally what a LAF designer will inherit from because the component UI classes in the *java.swing.plaf* package do not have enough drawing capability to satisfy the needs of most JFC components.

The *getDefaults()* method as implemented in *BasicLookAndFeel* creates an empty defaults table and populates it using four protected methods: *initClassDefaults()*, *initSystemColorDefaults()*, *loadSystemColors()*, and *initComponentDefaults()*. Implementors of custom LAFs will probably want to override these methods along with *getDefaults()* to load the defaults specific to the new LAF.

The *initClassDefaults()* method takes a single parameter that is a *UIDefaults* table. Its responsibility is to load the UI delegates for all standard JFC components. By convention, the key value for these delegates is the same as the name of the component UI class. The *Basic* UI delegate classes prefix this name with *Basic*. When these classes are specified, they must provide absolute package names because they are loaded by class name.

Another method that takes a *UIDefaults* parameter is *initSystem ColorDefaults()*. This method is responsible for supplying the initial values for all system colors. Color values are specified using a special string notation, #RRGGBB, where hexadecimal color values replace their corresponding letters. The pound sign prefix enables the use of the *decode()* methods of *java.awt.Color* to convert this value to a *ColorUIResource* when it is stored. The default implementation of *initSystemColorDefaults()* calls *loadSystemColors()* to attempt to initialize application colors to match those of the operating platform.

The *loadSystemColors()* method is used to load native colors by using the constants specified in the *java.awt.SystemColor* object. It uses the reflection API to attempt to match the color default keys to the static members of this class if the current look-and-feel returns *true* for the *isNativeLook AndFeel()* method. Otherwise, it converts the string values of the default colors into *ColorUIResource* objects and adds them to the defaults table.

Last, the *initComponentDefaults()* method creates all resources relevant to the LAF and stores them in the defaults table. This is the place where shared resources such as borders, renderers, and additional colors are created, icon and other bundled resources are specified, and other LAF values such as default margins, insets, and *String* values are determined.

Borders

JFC components support a bound property that facilitates the assignment of a control border. This border is specified as an object that implements the *javax.swing.border.Border* interface. Several predefined borders are provided with the JFC package; each of them has additional properties that control how a border appears. Because borders are common to all JFC components, sizing of components is designed to account for the amount of space a border takes when a component is laid out.

Standard JFC components do not have borders associated with them by default; instead, the active look-and-feel controls the creation of borders when component UIs are initialized. A component's border can also be changed programmatically or set to a *null* value.

Built-in Borders

JFC provides several predefined borders for application use. These borders can also be subclassed as another way to create custom borders.

EmptyBorder

This border option creates a transparent border around a component. Two constructors are available for specifying insets; one version takes a reference to an *Insets* object and the other takes a series of four integer values (top, left, right, and bottom). *EmptyBorder* can be useful as an element of a *CompoundBorder* to provide a fixed separator between a component and its border or the border and its parent container.

LineBorder

This class provides opaque symmetric borders of a specified color. Two constructors are provided; one takes a *Color* object as a single parameter and creates a one-pixel border of the specified color. The alternate version takes a second parameter that enables specification of the border width. Two static convenience methods are also available, *createBlackLineBorder()* and *createGrayLineBorder()*, which create one-pixel borders in those respective colors.

Two additional methods are provided for accessing the values of the color and line thickness properties of a *LineBorder: getLineColor()* and *getThickness(). LineBorder* does not provide a method to alter these properties after the border is created.

BevelBorder, SoftBevelBorder

The bevel borders produce a similar effect: Components that use beveled borders appear to be below or above the surface of its container. Both implementations provide fixed-size two-pixel borders that enable the specification of the two highlight and two shadow colors that furnish the 3-D illusion (see Figure 9-4). The main difference between *BevelBorder* and *SoftBevelBorder* is that *SoftBevelBorder* draws corners that appear more rounded.

Figure 9-4. *BevelBorder example*

EtchedBorder

EtchedBorder has similar 3-D capabilities as the bevel borders, but provides a more subtle effect. This border is used extensively by the Java (Metal) look-and-feel. It creates a border of fixed size (two pixels in all directions) that has the appearance of a bead on the viewing surface or a line cut into the viewing surface (see Figure 9-5). *EtchedBorder* allows for the specification of the direction of the etching, which can have the value *RAISED* or *LOWERED*. Also, the colors used to represent the highlight and shadow colors that make up the border can be designated.

Four constructors are provided by *EtchedBorder*. The default constructor creates a lowered etch using the default etch colors for the look-and-feel. Alternates enable the specification of the direction—lowered or raised—and the colors used to render the etch.

MatteBorder

MatteBorder is a very useful but somewhat unusual class. It inherits from *EmptyBorder;* although this may seem unusual, it has the effect of enabling asymmetrical borders because *EmptyBorder* enables the specification of an *Insets* object (see Figure 9-6). *MatteBorder* also enables the specification of a *Color* or a tiled *Icon* object to serve as the actual matte portion of the border.

TitledBorder

The *TitledBorder* class is actually a type of compound border that combines more than one element into a border type. The *TitledBorder* enables specification of its two components, a border and a title string. *TitledBorder* enables the placement of the title in different positions relative to the border (see Figure 9-7). *TitledBorder* is also unique among the

Figure 9-5. *EtchedBorder example*

Figure 9-6. *MatteBorder example*

standard borders because it provides methods to enable the modification of border properties after it is instantiated.

Table 9-4 shows the variety of properties available with the *TitledBorder* implementation. The properties for title justification and position also have two values that specify the default values: *DEFAULT_JUSTIFICATION* and *DEFAULT_POSITION*.

CompoundBorder

CompoundBorder is not actually a border, but it provides a constructor facilitating the specification of two borders combined into a third border that encapsulates the behavior of both borders (see Figure 9-8). The constructor for *CompoundBorder* uses the first border specified as the outside border and the second as the inside. *CompoundBorder* automatically handles the calculation of the insets of the combination of borders and delegates the painting of each border when it is required. The borders used by *CompoundBorder()* can be accessed by the methods *getOutsideBorder()* and *getInsideBorder()* but cannot be modified after the border is created.

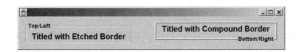

Figure 9-7. *TitledBorder example*

Table 9-4. *TitledBorder options*

Property	Accessor	Mutator	Values
Border	getBorder()	setBorder()	Border object
Title Text	getTitle()	setTitle()	String title
Title Color	getTitleColor()	setTitleColor()	Color object
Title Font	getTitleFont()	setTitleFont()	Font object
Title Justification	getTitleJustification()	setTitleJustification()	CENTER, LEFT (default), RIGHT,
Title Position	getTitlePosition()	setTitlePosition()	TOP (default), ABOVE_TOP, BELOW_TOP, BOTTOM, ABOVE_BOTTOM, BELOW_BOTTOM

It is feasible to create compound borders with more than two borders by combining them two at a time into a *CompoundBorder* and then specifying these as the parameters for a *CompoundBorder*. There is no effective limit on the number of borders that can be combined this way, although it is important to bear in mind that the code joining the borders does incur more overhead than uncombined borders.

By implementing the interfaces or extending the objects provided by JFC, you can create an unlimited number of *Border* objects with practically any appearance. The only limitation on borders is that they must be rectangular; other than that, lack of imagination is the only other limitation.

The Border Interface

The *Border* interface consists of three methods: one paints the content of the border and two describe the amount of space a border requires to paint itself. The first method, *paintBorder()*, draws the border inside the component's graphics context, similar to the *paint()* method of *Component* or *ComponentUI*. The other two methods, *getBorderInsets()* and *isBorderOpaque()*, define the size and transparency of the border area.

The *getBorderInsets()* method returns an *Insets* object. This object, which has four size components, describes the thickness of the top, left, bottom, and right edges of the border. These values will all be equal when the border is symmetrical, but this does not always have to be the case. The insets of the

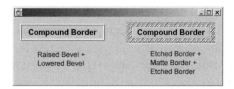

Figure 9-8. *CompoundBorder example*

border can also be *(0, 0, 0, 0)*, which basically means the component does not have a border at all. Whatever the values returned by this method may be, they are all taken into consideration when determining how much space a component requires. The border property is bound so that containers can revalidate their layouts when borders are altered for child components.

The third method is *isBorderOpaque()*, which returns *true* or *false* depending on whether the border paints its background. It is cognate with the *isOpaque()* method of *JComponent*, except it refers to the border alone and not the component. Thus, it is possible to have an opaque component with a transparent border and vice versa.

AbstractBorder

This class is a canonical implementation of the *Border* interface. It is recommended that this class be used for creating a custom border instead of implementing the interface directly because it supports an additional set of methods, one static and one instance implementation, called *getInteriorRectangle()*. These are convenience methods that determine the size a component must be to fit inside a border of a particular size. The instance version of this method delegates to the static version, so the result of either call should be deterministic.

Border Painting

Because the border of a *JComponent* is painted by the border delegate and not the UI object, a separate mechanism is used to actuate the painting of a border. *JComponent* provides a protected method *paintBorder()* that accesses the current border delegate and calls the border's version of *paintBorder()*. If the border is *null,* no action is taken.

The insets of the current border are also used by *JComponent*. The default implementation of *getInsets()* delegates to *getBorderInsets()* of the border object if one is specified, and calls the superclass version if the border is *null*.

Creating a Custom Border

To create a custom border, inherit from *AbstractBorder* and override the three methods of *Border* as required. By default, the *paintBorder()* method is a "no-op," *isBorderOpaque()* returns *false,* and *getBorderInsets()* returns an *Inset* object with zero size in all four directions.

Custom Border Properties

Generally, custom borders will have some properties associated with them. Unlike components, however, no built-in mechanism exists for listening to property changes to a border delegate. Thus, borders are usually constructed with read-only immutable properties. Another reason these properties are not modifiable is that many border objects are designed to be shared, and setting properties across multiple components might not be desirable.

A notable exception to this pattern is *TitledBorder*, which provides mutators for many of its properties. This is probably because *TitledBorder* is not generally shared among components and has much richer configuration capabilities than other standard borders. Another reason is that *TitledBorder* plays a special role in accessibility integration.

Custom Border Example—HandleBorder

The following class code defines an object derived from *AbstractBorder*. Thus, it is suitable to be used as a property value for any *JComponent* inheritor or as a default value in a look-and-feel.

HandleBorder was designed to provide a border with a solid one-pixel line and eight-direction sizing handles, as you might see in a drawing or modeling program (see Figure 9-9). It supports two properties, which are both immutable. The *size* property controls the size of each handle, which is symmetrical around the border. The *position* property controls where the

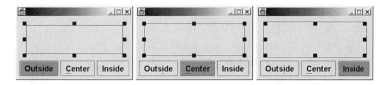

Figure 9-9. *Custom border example (HandleBorder)*

line appears relative to the handles. The line can be aligned with the inside of the handles, the outside of the handles, or made to bisect the handles.

```
package com.ketherware.plaf;

import java.awt.*;
import java.awt.event.*;
import javax.swing.*;
import javax.swing.border.*;

public class HandleBorder extends AbstractBorder {
    // Size gets this value if not specified
    public static final int DEFAULT_SIZE = 5;
    // Size cannot be less than this value
    public static final int MINIMUM_SIZE = 3;
    // Line will bisect handles
    public static final int CENTER_POSITION = 0;
    // Handles will be outside of the line
    public static final int OUTSIDE_POSITION = 1;
    // Handles will be inside the line
    public static final int INSIDE_POSITION = 2;
    // Position gets this value if not specified
    public static final int DEFAULT_POSITION = CENTER_POSITION;

    // Internal property value for size
    protected int size;
    // Internal property value for handle position
```

```
        protected int handlePos;

        // Default constructor - use default size and position
        public HandleBorder() {
            this(DEFAULT_SIZE, DEFAULT_POSITION);
        }

        // Constructor - use default size, specify position
        public HandleBorder(int handlePos) {
            this(DEFAULT_SIZE, handlePos);
        }

        // Constructor - specify size, position
        public HandleBorder(int size, int handlePos) {
            // Ensure size is at least minimum
            if (size < MINIMUM_SIZE)
size = MINIMUM_SIZE;
            this.size = size;

            // Ensure position has a valid value
            if (handlePos != INSIDE_POSITION &&
            handlePos != CENTER_POSITION &&
            handlePos != OUTSIDE_POSITION)
handlePos = DEFAULT_POSITION;
            this.handlePos = handlePos;
        }

        // Retrieve size of border
        public int getSize(){
            return this.size;
        }

        // Retrieve handle position of border
        public int getPosition() {
            return this.handlePos;
        }
```

```
// Return the amount of space the border will take as an Insets object
public Insets getBorderInsets(Component c) {
    return new Insets(this.size, this.size, this.size, this.size);
}

 // Draw the border
public void paintBorder(Component c, Graphics g,
                int x, int y, int width, int height)  {
    // Draw the line according to the specified position
    switch (this.handlePos)
    {
        case CENTER_POSITION:
        g.drawRect(this.size / 2, this.size / 2,
                width - this.size,
                height - this.size);
        break;

        case OUTSIDE_POSITION:
        g.drawRect(0, 0, width - 1, height -1);
        break;

        case INSIDE_POSITION:
        g.drawRect(this.size - 1, this.size - 1,
                width - (this.size * 2 - 1),
                height - (this.size * 2 - 1));
        break;
    }

    // Draw top left, center, right handles
    g.fillRect(0, 0, this.size, this.size);
    g.fillRect((width / 2) - (this.size / 2), 0, this.size, this.size);
    g.fillRect(width - this.size, 0, this.size, this.size);

    // Draw center left, right handles
    g.fillRect(0, (height / 2) - (this.size / 2), this.size, this.size);
    g.fillRect(width - this.size, (height / 2) - (this.size / 2), this.size,
    this.size);
```

```
    // Draw bottom left, center, right handles
    g.fillRect(0, height - this.size, this.size, this.size);
    g.fillRect((width / 2) - (this.size / 2), height - this.size, this.size,
    this.size);
    g.fillRect(width - this.size, height - this.size, this.size, this.size);
}
}
```

The example in Figure 9-9 shows the *HandleBorder* being used in a simple frame. The toggle buttons replace the border of a *JPanel* in the center of the frame depending on the selection state.

Inside this example, the following code appears:

```
...
centerToggle.addActionListener(new ActionListener() {
    public void actionPerformed(ActionEvent event) {
        borderPanel.setBorder(new HandleBorder(
                            HandleBorder.CENTER_POSITION);
    }
});
...
```

Notice that the code sets only the border property. In the default case of *JComponent*, the component is repainted directly in the *setBorder()* call, not in a property change handler. In addition, the component's layout is revalidated if the border's insets change. By performing this check, unnecessary layout operations are eliminated.

In practice, it would probably be wise to implement a factory object that provides shared instances of borders where possible. This is left to the reader as an exercise, as is the implementation of enhancements such as controlling which handles are visible, altering the color of the line or handles, or having control over the width of the line.

Custom Border Example—RegalBorder

This border was developed for a talk on development of UI delegates and is a good example of how to create a custom border.

```
package com.ketherware.plaf;
```

```java
import java.awt..*;
import java.awt.event.*;
import javax.swing.*;
import javax.swing.border.*;
import javax.swing.plaf.basic.*;

public class RegalBorder extends AbstractBorder {
    // border width
    public static final int DEFAULT_SIZE = 5;
    public static final int MINIMUM_SIZE = 3;

    // inlay colors
    public static final int SAPPHIRE_INLAY = 0;
    public static final int EMERALD_INLAY = 1;
    public static final int RUBY_INLAY = 2;
    public static final int DEFAULT_INLAY = SAPPHIRE_INLAY;

    private static Color RUBY = new Color(106, 0, 0);
    private static Color EMERALD = new Color(0, 120, 150);
    private static Color SAPPHIRE = new Color(0, 0, 150);
    private static Color[] colors = { SAPPHIRE, RUBY, EMERALD };

    // border size - since this is symmetric only one value is needed
    protected int size;

    // border type - specifies inlay color
    protected int type;

    // Default constructor - use default size and inlay
    public RegalBorder() {
        this(DEFAULT_SIZE, DEFAULT_INLAY);
    }

    // Constructor - specify size, use default inlay
    public RegalBorder(int size) {
        this(size, DEFAULT_INLAY);
    }
```

```
// Constructor - specify size and  inlay
public RegalBorder(int size, int type) {
    // Make sure size is legit
    if (size < MINIMUM_SIZE)
        size = MINIMUM_SIZE;
    this.size = size;

    // Make sure inlay is legit
    if (type != SAPPHIRE_INLAY &&
                type != EMERALD_INLAY &&
                type != RUBY_INLAY)
        type = DEFAULT_INLAY;
    this.type = type;
}

// size accessor
public int getSize() {
    return this.size;
}

// return insets of border (symmetrical)
public Insets getBorderInsets(Component c) {
    return new Insets(this.size, this.size,
                this.size, this.size);
}

// Called by JComponent to render the border
public void paintBorder(Component c, Graphics g,
                int x, int y,
                int width, int height) {

    // iterate through size of border
    for (int p=0; p < this.size; p++)
    {
        // paint outer bezel
        if (p == 0) {
            RegalGraphicsUtils.drawThinBezel(g, p,
```

```
                        p + y - 2, width - (p * 2 + 1),
                        height - (p * 2) + 1,
                        RegalGraphicsUtils.OUTER);
        }
         // paint inner bezel
        else if (p == this.size - 1)
        {
            RegalGraphicsUtils.drawThinBezel(g, p,
                        p + y - 2, width - (p * 2 + 1),
                        height - (p * 2) + 1,
                        RegalGraphicsUtils.INNER);
        }
         // paint inlay
        else
        {

            g.setColor(colors[this.type]);
            g.drawRect(p, p + y - 2,
                        width - (p * 2 + 1),
                        height - (p * 2) + 1);

        }
    }
  }
}


// A subset of the utils class that is included in the Regal LAF
class RegalGraphicsUtils
{
    public static int OUTER = 0;
    public static int INNER = 1;

    private static Color shadowColor = new Color(180, 180, 0);
    private static Color highColor = new Color(240, 240, 0);

    // Draw a thin (one pixel) bezel on the specified graphics
    // context. Specify position, size and type (inner, outer)
    public static void drawThinBezel(Graphics g, int x, int y,
                int width, int height, int type)
```

```
    {
        // set colors based on type
        if (type == INNER)
            g.setColor(shadowColor);
        else if (type == OUTER)
            g.setColor(highColor);
        else
            return;

        g.drawLine(x, y, x + width, y);
        g.drawLine(x, y, x, y + height);

        // set colors based on type
        if (type == INNER)
            g.setColor(highColor);
        else
            g.setColor(shadowColor);

        g.drawLine(x, y + height, x + width, y + height);
        g.drawLine(x + width, y, x + width, y + height);
    }
}
```

Creating a Custom LAF

One of the intended purposes of the LAF architecture is to be able to create custom UI delegates for components that extend the default Swing components or for new controls that are developed. Because the LAF classes that are provided are tightly encapsulated, a somewhat extreme approach must be used to create components that behave or appear differently.

It is strongly recommended that the LAF implementations not be modified in any way. This is fundamentally to enable the underlying LAF code to be changed by Sun without upsetting the underlying functionality. This, coupled with the evidence of examining the capabilities of Auxiliary LAF, means that the normal method of loading delegates must be skirted.

It is possible, if the reader so desires, to extrapolate the creation of individual UI delegates to develop a new look-and-feel. This is not recommended for some very pragmatic reasons. First, creating a complete LAF implementation is a ponderous amount of work. Second, most commercial development projects will want applications that are consistent and give users a sense of familiarity. In most cases, radically different looks will implement unusual application feedback, which may cause confusion to users. These reasons, coupled with the enormous amount of regression testing that would be required to validate the behavior of a custom LAF, should be enough impetus to dissuade even the most avid programmer to pursue alternatives.

Index